Catherine D. LeTourneau

Allan E. Bellman, Ph.D.

Jill A. Perry, Ph.D.

The Publisher of *Progress in Mathematics*

Program Reviewers

The publisher wishes to thank for their comments and suggestions the following teachers and administrators, who read portions of the series prior to publication.

Marcia J. Phillips
Curriculum Director/Assistant Principal
Happy Valley School-Peoria
Peoria, Arizona

Lynn M. LeTourneau
Principal
Our Lady of Charity
Cicero, Illinois

Esther Park
Teacher, Grade 4
Saint Columbkille Partnership School
Brighton, Massachusetts

Lisa A. Nelson, Ph.D.
Assistant Principal
St. Vincent de Paul School
Omaha, Nebraska

Kimberly N. Stevenson
Principal
Holy Trinity Catholic School
McKees Rocks, Pennsylvania

Elizabeth Snow
Principal
Sacred Heart Cathedral School
Pensacola, Florida

Jane Carrillo
Teacher, Kindergarten
St. Leo School
Versailles, Kentucky

Molly Schwaiger
Academic Director
Partnership Academy
Richfield, Minnesota

Barbara Jones
Mathematics Department Chair
Rumson Country Day School
Rumson, New Jersey

Jodie L. Dawe
Teacher, Grade 3
Christopher Elementary School
Christopher, Illinois

Judy Helton
Teacher, Grade 2
St. Leo School
Versailles, Kentucky

Dr. Jeanne Gearon
Principal
Our Lady of Lourdes Catholic School
Saint Louis, Missouri

Theresa Hurst
Teacher, Grade 2
St. Martin de Porres Marianist School
Uniondale, New York

Chad Riley, Ph.D.
Principal
St. Joseph Catholic School
Arlington, Texas

Cover Series Design: Silver Linings Studios

Photo Credits

Cover: Getty Images/Bettmann: *top*; molotovcoketail: *bottom*.

Interior: Shutterstock.com/Barry Blackburn: 154; Job Narinnate: 140; photastic: 177; Tnymand: 198. United States coin images from the United States Mint.

Illustrators

Joseph Taylor. Shutterstock.com/Agor2012, incredible_movements, miniaria, whanwhan.ai, Zmiter.

Printed in the United States of America.
ISBN: 978-1-4217-9043-5
2 3 4 5 6 7 8 9 10 WEBC 22 21 20 19 18

For additional online resources, go to SadlierConnect.com.

Welcome to Sadlier Math

Dear Third Grader,

Do you know why math is important? Well, we all use math every day. We use it when we:

- read food labels
- read a clock
- plant a garden
- observe weather patterns
- shop
- and much more!

Throughout your books are special signs and symbols. When you see them, be sure to stop and look.

Objective This is what you will be studying in the lesson.

Math Words Look at these words. They are important math vocabulary words for the lesson.

Problem Solving Get ready to apply math in real-world contexts.

Write About It This is a question or topic for you to write about.

PRACTICE These are exercises for you to show what you know.

MORE PRACTICE These are exercises for you to build more understanding.

HOMEWORK These are exercises for you to do at home.

We wrote this book just for you!

The Authors

Contents

Chapters 1–16

Chapter 1 Number Sense

Chapter 2 Addition Within 1000

Chapter 3 Subtraction Within 1000

Chapter 4 Multiplication and Division Concepts

Chapter 5 Multiplication Facts

Chapter 6 More Multiplication Facts

Chapter 7 Division Facts

Chapter 8 More Division Facts

Chapter 9 Fraction Concepts

Chapter 10 Fractions: Comparison and Equivalence

Chapter 11 Measurement

Chapter 12 Data

Chapter 13 Time

Chapter 14 Two-Dimensional Shapes

Chapter 15 Area

Chapter 16 Perimeter

Name ______________________ Date ______________

LESSON 1-1

Read and Write Multidigit Numbers

Jake uses blocks to model a number.

What are three ways Jake can write the number he models?

The blocks are models of hundreds, tens, and ones. Jake models 2 hundreds, 4 tens, and 3 ones.

Jake can write the number in different forms.

The expanded form is 200 + 40 + 3.

The standard form is 243.

The number name is two hundred forty-three.

Study these examples.

h	t	o	Expanded Form	Standard Form	Number Name
7	4	0	700 + 40 + 0	740	seven hundred forty
9	0	5	900 + 0 + 5	905	nine hundred five

MORE PRACTICE

Write the expanded form, standard form, and number name for each number.

	h	t	o	Expanded Form	Standard Form	Number Name
1.	6	5	9			
2.	7	1	5			
3.	3	3	3			
4.	4	0	8			
5.	2	1	0			

6. Explain how to form the greatest possible 3-digit number from the digits 7, 1, and 9.

____

____

HOMEWORK

Write the correct digit in the place value for each number. Then write the expanded form and number name.

1. 325 ______ hundreds ______ tens ______ ones

   Expanded form: ______ + ______ + ______

   Number name: ____________________

2. 640 ______ hundreds ______ tens ______ ones

   Expanded form: ______ + ______ + ______

   Number name: ____________________

3. 803 ______ hundreds ______ tens ______ ones

   Expanded form: ______ + ______ + ______

   Number name: ____________________

Problem Solving

4. Mia uses 3 different base-ten blocks to model a 3-digit number. What is the number?

   ____

5. Six 3-digit numbers contain the digits 4, 6, and 8. What are they?

   ____

   ____

6. David's father is making a payment to WXYZ Electric Company for 2 hundreds 3 tens 5 ones dollars. Write the standard form in the box and the number name on the line.

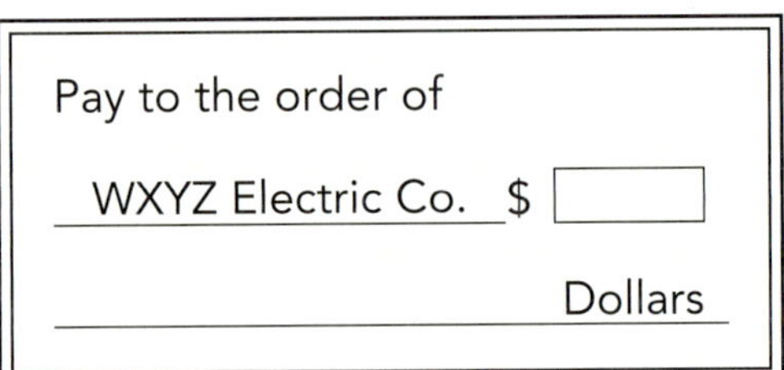

Write About It

7. Ava said, "There are only three hundred 3-digit numbers." Is her statement true or false? Explain your reasoning.

   ____

   ____

   ____

Name ______________________ Date ____________

LESSON 1-2

Understand the Number Line

You can represent numbers on a number line.

A number line is a line used to show the order of numbers and their distances from zero.

- To show 12, draw a number line starting at 0 with 1 as the distance between each tick mark, called the interval.
- Then mark the point numbered 12. The part of the number line from 0 to 12 has a length of 12 units.

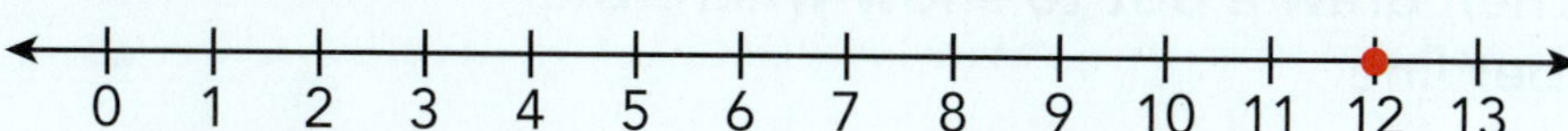

Study these examples.

You can use larger intervals to represent greater numbers. To show 120, draw a number line with 10 as the interval. Then mark the point that represents 120.

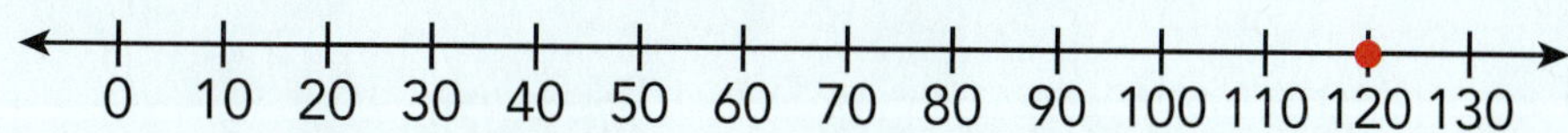

You can use a number line to find sums.

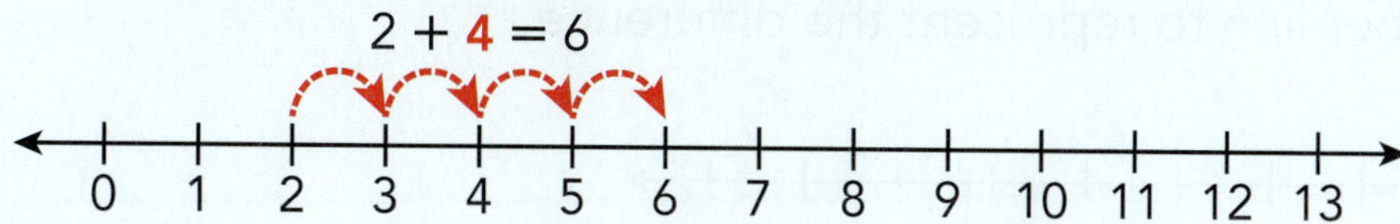

You can also use a number line to find differences.

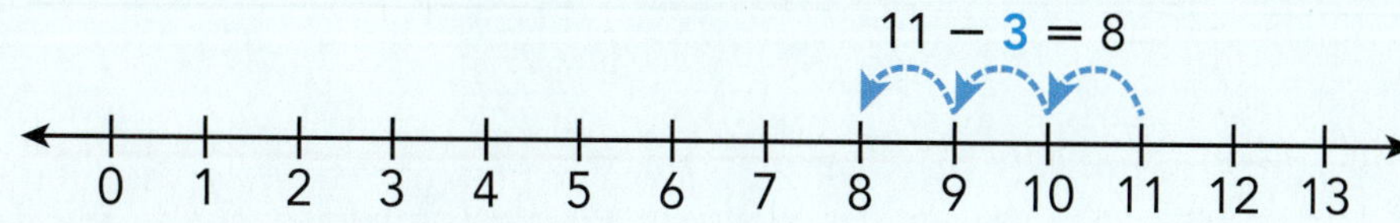

MORE PRACTICE

Plot a point on the number line to represent each number.

1. 46 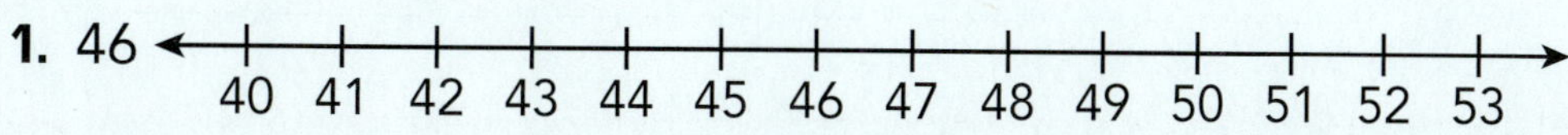

2. 64 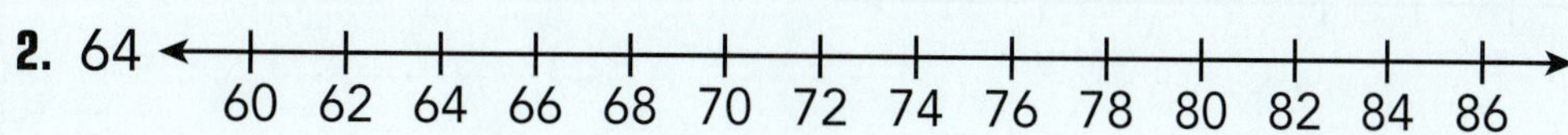

HOMEWORK

Show the sum or difference on the number line. Complete the equation.

1. $3 + 8 =$ ______

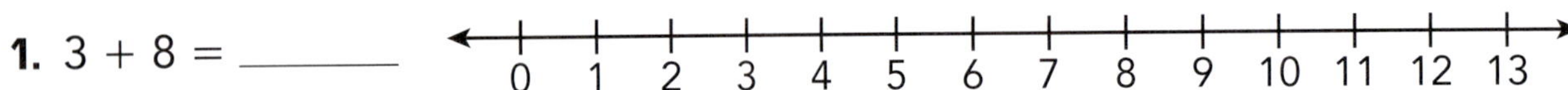

2. $10 - 6 =$ ______

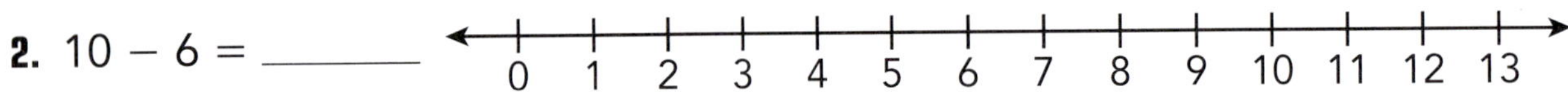

Label the number line. Then draw a dot to show where the number lies on the number line.

3. 245

4. 782

Problem Solving

5. The English alphabet has 26 letters. The Russian alphabet has 32 letters. What is the difference in the number of letters? Use the number line to represent the difference.

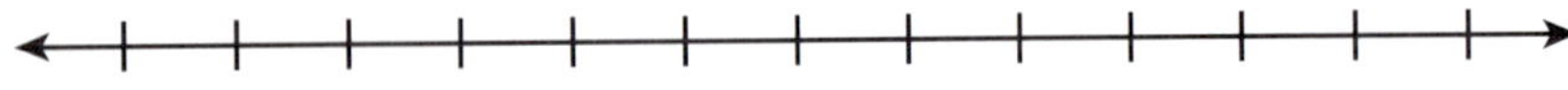

____

Write About It

6. Describe how to draw a number line to show the problem $35 + 40$. Then draw the number line and solve the problem.

____

____

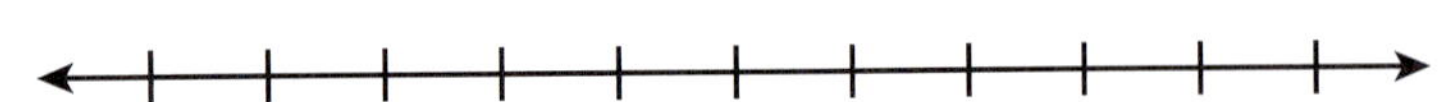

Name ______________________ Date ____________

LESSON 1-3

Compare and Order Numbers

Order 245, 170, and 215 from greatest to least.

♦ Use a number line to compare and order the numbers.

Find 245, 170, and 215 on a number line.

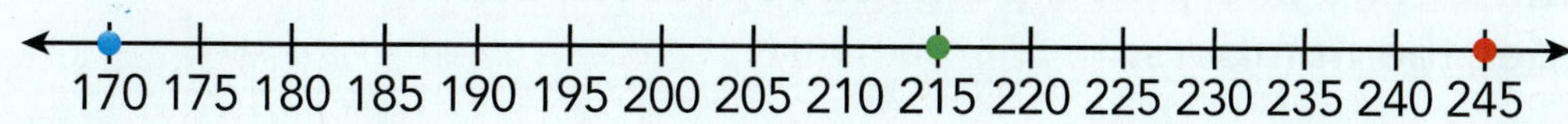

170 is to the left of 215. 170 is less than 215. Write 170 < 215.

245 is to the right of 215. 245 is greater than 215.
Write 245 > 215.

♦ Use the values of the digits to compare and order.

Compare hundreds. → Compare tens.

Compare hundreds.	Compare tens.
245	245
170	215
215	
100 < 200	40 > 10
170 is least.	245 > 215

From greatest to least, the numbers are 245, 215, 170.

MORE PRACTICE

Use the number line for Exercises 1–8.

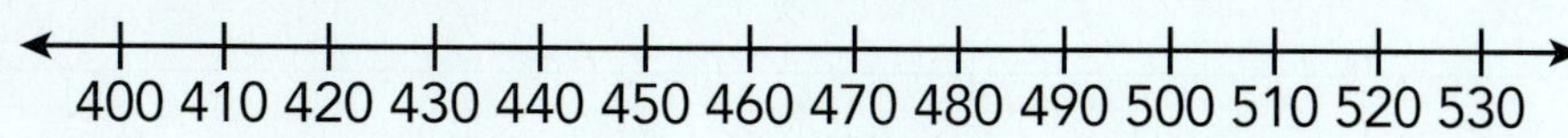

Compare. Write <, =, or >.

1. 407 ______ 412 **2.** 490 ______ 490 **3.** 410 ______ 510

4. 400 ______ 440 **5.** 405 ______ 410 **6.** 480 ______ 408

Write in order from least to greatest.

7. 410, 510, 450 ______________ **8.** 425, 415, 475 ______________

HOMEWORK

Compare. Write <, =, or >.

1. 398 ______ 389
2. 451 ______ 541
3. 712 ______ 72
4. 692 ______ 692
5. 905 ______ 915
6. 891 ______ 981

Complete the number line and plot a point to represent each number. Then order the numbers.

7. 854, 458, 548

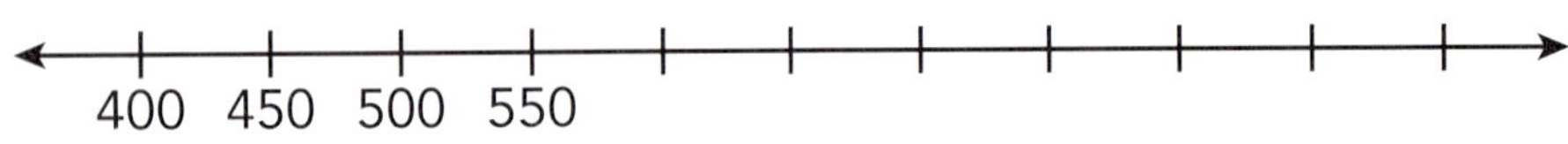

Greatest to least: ______________

Least to greatest: ______________

Problem Solving

The table shows driving distances between Austin, Texas, and other cities in Texas. Use the information in the table for Exercises 8–11.

From Austin to:	Miles
Amarillo	495
Houston	165
Fort Worth	189
El Paso	577
Lubbock	373

8. Which city is closest to Austin?

____

9. Which city would it take the longest to drive to from Austin?

____

10. Order the cities by driving distance from Austin, from least to greatest.

____

Write About It

11. Tell which method you think would be easier to use to solve Exercise 10: a number line or using the values of the digits. Explain your thinking.

____

____

Name ______________________ Date ______________

LESSON 1-4

Round Numbers to the Nearest Ten

Round the lengths of 3 pieces of wood to the nearest ten inches. The lengths are 53 inches, 58 inches, and 65 inches.

◆ Use a number line.

Round 53, 58, and 65 to the nearest ten.

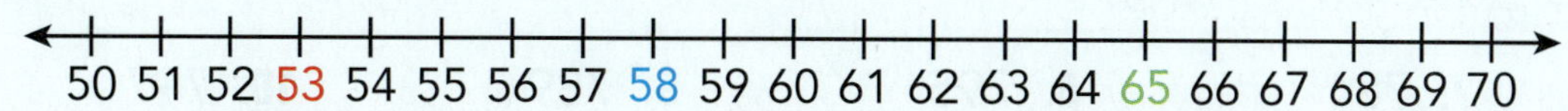

- 53 is closer to 50 than 60, so 53 rounds down to 50.
- 58 is closer to 60 than 50, so 58 rounds up to 60.
- 65 is exactly halfway from 60 to 70, so 65 rounds up to 70.

◆ Use place value.

53 The digit to the right of the tens place is 3. The digit in the tens place does not change. Round 53 to 50.

58 The digit to the right of the tens place is 8. Add 1 to the 5 in the tens place. Round 58 to 60.

65 The digit to the right of the tens place is 5. Add 1 to the 6 in the tens place. Round 65 to 70.

Find the digit to the right of the place you are rounding to.

- If that digit is less than 5, do not change the digit in the place you are rounding to.
- If that digit is 5 or greater, add 1 to the digit in the place you are rounding to.

Change the digits to the right to zeros.

The lengths are 50, 60, and 70 inches.

MORE PRACTICE

Use the number line. Round to the nearest ten.

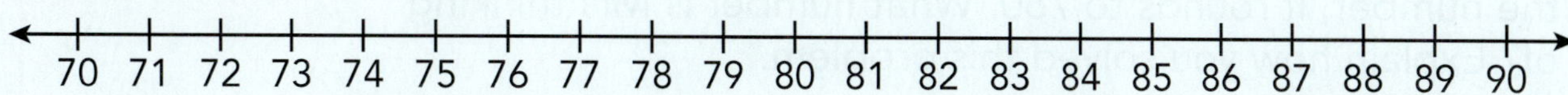

1. 76 ______ **2.** 75 ______ **3.** 81 ______ **4.** 72 ______ **5.** 85 ______

Round each number to the nearest 10.

6. 562 ______ **7.** 154 ______ **8.** 928 ______ **9.** 715 ______ **10.** 887 ______

HOMEWORK

Use the number line. Round to the nearest ten.

780 781 782 783 784 785 786 787 788 789 790 791 792 793 794 795 796 797 798 799 800

1. 782 ______
2. 798 ______
3. 787 ______
4. 791 ______
5. 785 ______
6. 796 ______
7. 784 ______
8. 795 ______
9. 789 ______
10. 797 ______

Round each number to the nearest ten.

11. 37 ______
12. 11 ______
13. 55 ______
14. 72 ______
15. 99 ______
16. 123 ______
17. 246 ______
18. 368 ______
19. 482 ______
20. 515 ______

Problem Solving

21. Ben is reading a book. Rounded to the nearest ten, he reads 150 pages. What is the least number of pages he could read? ______

Write About It

22. Mia is thinking of a 3-digit number. When she rounds the number to the nearest 10, it rounds to 750. If she adds 1 to the number, it rounds to 760. What number is Mia thinking of? Explain how you solved this problem.

______

______

______

______

Name ______________________ Date ______________

LESSON 1-5

Round Numbers to the Nearest Hundred

How can you round 845 to the nearest hundred?

◆ Use a number line to round 845.

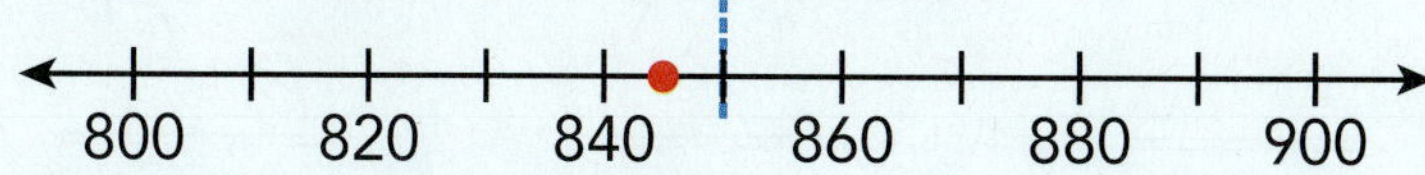

- Place a point for 845 on the number line.
- Find the point halfway between 800 and 900. 850 is halfway between 800 and 900.
- 845 is between 800 and 850, so 845 rounds down to 800.

◆ Use place value to round 845.

Find the digit to the right of the place you are rounding to.

- If that digit is less than 5, the digit in the place you are rounding to does not change.
- If it is 5 or greater, add 1 to the digit in the place you are rounding to.

Change the digits to the right to zeros.

Round 845 to the nearest hundred.

You are rounding to the hundreds place.

The digit to the right is 4. $4 < 5$, so 845 rounds to 800.

MORE PRACTICE

Use the number line. Round to the nearest hundred.

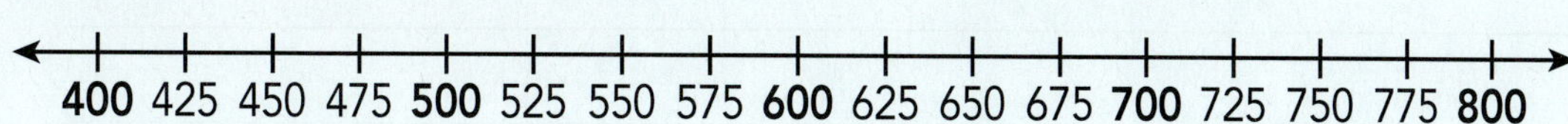

1. 725 ______ **2.** 475 ______ **3.** 450 ______ **4.** 625 ______ **5.** 555 ______

Round each number to the nearest hundred.

6. 376 ______ **7.** 658 ______ **8.** 327 ______ **9.** 203 ______ **10.** 95 ______

HOMEWORK

Use the number line. Round to the nearest hundred.

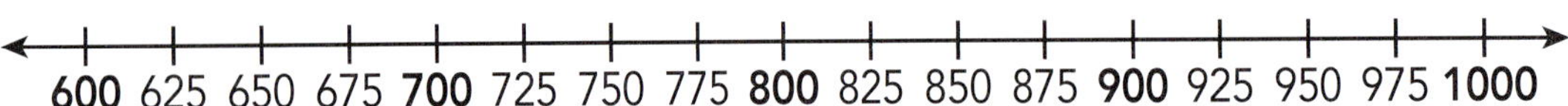

1. 770 ______ **2.** 710 ______ **3.** 650 ______ **4.** 830 ______ **5.** 790 ______

6. 723 ______ **7.** 845 ______ **8.** 803 ______ **9.** 679 ______ **10.** 750 ______

Round each number to the nearest ten and nearest hundred.

11. 561 ______ **12.** 909 ______ **13.** 755 ______ **14.** 202 ______ **15.** 11 ______

Problem Solving

16. Roaring Brook School has three hundred fifty-six third-grade students. To the nearest hundred, how many students are in the third grade at Roaring Brook School?

______

17. Joyce has to write a 500-word essay. She decides that her teacher has rounded to the nearest 100 words, so she can write between 400 and 600 words. Tell whether her thinking is correct or incorrect and explain your reasoning.

______

______

Write About It

18. A newspaper headline reads, "900 People Attend Town Hall Meeting." Do you think exactly 900 people attended? How many do you think attended? Explain your reasoning.

______

______

Name ______________________ Date ____________

LESSON 1-6

Problem Solving
Use the Four-Step Process

Olivia, Sophia, and Ava like jigsaw puzzles. Olivia has a puzzle with 513 pieces. Sophia has a puzzle with 750 pieces. Ava's puzzle has 400 pieces. Whose puzzle has the most pieces?

Read and Understand

- Olivia has a puzzle with 513 pieces.
- Sophia has a puzzle with 750 pieces.
- Ava has a puzzle with 400 pieces.
- You need to know whose puzzle has the most pieces.

Represent the Situation

A number line can be used to show the problem.

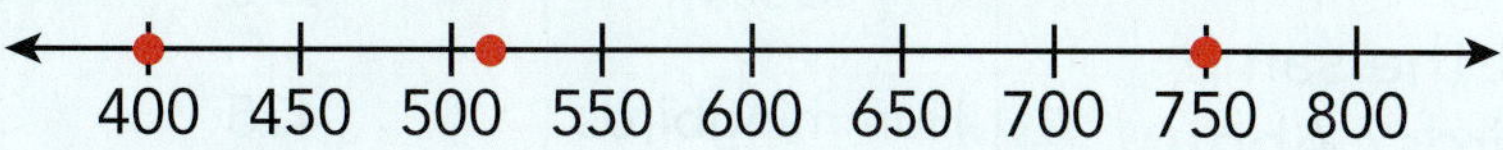

Make and Use a Plan

Use the number line to order the numbers from greatest to least: 750, 513, 400. 750 is the greatest. Sophia's puzzle has 750 pieces.

Look Back

Use place value to order the numbers. 750 > 513, 750 > 400. 750 is the greatest number.

Sophia's puzzle has the most pieces.

MORE PRACTICE

1. This week Liam spends 143 minutes drawing, 123 minutes painting, and 134 minutes making models. Which art activity does Liam spend the least amount of time on?

What do you know?

____

____

What do you need to find?

____

How can you represent the situation?

____

Make and use a plan to answer the question.

____

Use the information and the table for Exercises 2–4.

There are thousands of different kinds of birds all around the world. The table shows the numbers of different types of birds in some bird families.

Bird Family	Number of Types
Owls	180
Penguins	17
Chickens	290
Gulls	370
Hummingbirds	425
Parrots	368

2. Which bird families have about the same number of different types of birds? About what is that number? Tell what place you round to.

____

____

____

3. Which bird family has about 300 types of birds? Explain your reasoning.

____

____

____

4. Jamal is writing a report using the table. He wants to put the bird families in order from greatest to least numbers of types. He decides the order is hummingbirds, parrots, gulls, chickens, owls, and penguins. Explain his error.

____

____

____

Name ______________________________ Date ____________

Problem Solving
Use the Four-Step Process

HOMEWORK

Follow the Four-Step Process to solve this problem.

Michael is thinking of the number of days until his birthday. It is a 3-digit number.

It is the greatest number that rounds to 200 when rounded to the nearest 100.

How many days are there until Michael's birthday?

Read and Understand

1. Read the problem again. Underline key information and the problem question.

2. List the key information.

Key Information	

3. Write the question in your own words.

____

Represent the Situation

4. Make a list of the numbers it could be.

____

Make and Use a Plan

5. Find the greatest number.

____

6. Write a complete sentence to answer the question.

____

Look Back

7. Explain one way to decide if your answer is reasonable.

____

____

____

HOMEWORK

8. Ethan has 3 collections. He has 26 model cars, 112 white stones, and 156 marbles. Which collection has about 100 items?

____

9. This week Emma spends 36 minutes practicing piano on Monday, 42 minutes on Wednesday, and 57 minutes on Saturday. About how much time in all does she practice piano this week?

____

10. Isabella likes to play soccer. To warm up before a game, she runs 110 yards, does 60 stretches, and then runs 660 yards. About how far does Isabella run in her warm-up?

____

11. Farmer Dave is packing fruit from his farm to bring to farmers' markets. He puts 496 strawberries, 275 melons, and 194 peaches in crates. He puts 288 apples, 216 pears, and 504 plums in boxes. About how many pieces of fruit are in the crates? About how many pieces of fruit are in the boxes? Explain how you found your answer.

____

____

____

Write About It

12. Use this information to write and answer a question.

Mrs. Fieldstone raised $695 for the local food bank. Mr. Levy raised $659. Ms. O'Dea raised $696.

____

____

____

Name ______________________ Date ______________

LESSON 2-1

Use Addition Properties

Addition properties help you add.

Identity (Zero) Property of Addition The sum of 0 and a number is the same as that number.
For example, 26 + 0 = 26.

Commutative (Order) Property of Addition Changing the order of addends does not change the sum.
For example, 0 + 26 = 26 + 0.

Associative (Grouping) Property of Addition Changing the grouping of the addends does not change the sum.
For example, 36 + (54 + 27) = (36 + 54) + 27.

MORE PRACTICE

Identify the addition property.

1. 78 + 0 + 52 = 78 + 52

____

2. 44 + 99 = 99 + 44

____

3. (67 + 34) + 67 = (34 + 67) + 67

____

4. (70 + 81) + 2 = 70 + (81 + 2)

____

Find the missing number.

5. 98 + ______ = 98

6. 75 + 34 = 34 + ______

7. (56 + 2) + 18 = 56 + (2 + ______)

8. (25 + 41) + ______ = 25 + (41 + 1)

9. The Falcons scored 35 points in the first half and 47 points in the second half. The Terriers scored 47 points in the first half and 35 points in the second half. Which team scored more points? Explain how you know.

____

____

____

HOMEWORK

Identify the addition property.

1. $(66 + 83) + 27 = 66 + (83 + 27)$

____

2. $0 + 45 = 45$

____

3. $91 + 71 = 71 + 91$

____

4. $(53 + 44) + 5 = (44 + 53) + 5$

____

Find the missing number.

5. $62 +$ _______ $= 54 + 62$

6. $(82 + 7) + 53 = 82 + (7 +$ _______$)$

7. $0 +$ _______ $= 100$

8. $84 +$ _______ $+ 36 = 84 + 36$

Problem Solving

9. Which addition property is shown by $(50 + 72) + 3 = 50 + (72 + 3)$? Explain.

____

____

____

10. Zach walked the same number of miles Monday and Tuesday as he did Thursday and Friday. He walked 4 miles Monday, 3 miles Tuesday, and 3 miles Thursday. How many miles did Zach walk Friday?

____

11. A new bicycle costs $636 at Ike's Bikes and $663 at Mike's Bikes. Write a number sentence to compare the prices.

____

12. Which addition property is shown by $16 + 72 + \square = 16 + 72$? What is the value of $\square$?

____

Write About It

13. Explain how to use addition properties to find the value of $6 + 8 + 4$.

____

____

____

Name ______________________ Date ______________

LESSON 2-2

Explore Addition Patterns

In the addition table, the sums switch between even and odd across a row or a column. How can you explain the pattern of even and odd numbers?

+	0	1	2	3	4	5	6	7	8	9
0	0	1	2	3	4	5	6	7	8	9
1	1	2	3	4	5	6	7	8	9	10
2	2	3	4	5	6	7	8	9	10	11
3	3	4	5	6	7	8	9	10	11	12
4	4	5	6	7	8	9	10	11	12	13
5	5	6	7	8	9	10	11	12	13	14
6	6	7	8	9	10	11	12	13	14	15
7	7	8	9	10	11	12	13	14	15	16
8	8	9	10	11	12	13	14	15	16	17
9	9	10	11	12	13	14	15	16	17	18

Look at the pattern across the rows.

- Starting at 0, the even numbers are every other number.
- Starting at 1, the odd numbers are every other number.

As you add 1 more to each sum in the addition table, the sums change between even and odd.

An even number plus 1 gives you an odd number.

8 + 1 = 9

An odd number plus 1 gives you an even number.

9 + 1 = 10

MORE PRACTICE

Write even or odd. Use an addition table to help you.

1. 5 + Even = ________

2. 2 + Odd = ________

3. 1 + Odd = ________

4. 2 + Even = ________

HOMEWORK

Write even or odd. Use an addition table to help you.

1. 3 + Odd = ______

2. 3 + Even = ______

3. 4 + Even = ______

4. 4 + Odd = ______

Problem Solving

Use the addition table for Exercises 5–7.

+	0	1	2	3	4	5
0	0	1	2	3	4	5
1	1	2	3	4	5	6
2	2	3	4	5	6	7
3	3	4	5	6	7	8
4	4	5	6	7	8	9
5	5	6	7	8	9	10

5. Look down a column or across a row. Describe a pattern you see in the sums. Explain why it works.

______

______

______

6. Pick an addend. Color across the row and down the column for that addend. Describe the pattern you see. What addition property does this show?

______

______

7. Look across the 0s row. What pattern do you see? Explain why this pattern works.

______

______

Write About It

8. Jeff said adding 20 to an even number makes the sum odd, and adding 20 to an odd number makes the sum even. Is Jeff correct? Explain.

______

______

______

Name ______________________ Date ____________

LESSON 2-3

Estimate Sums

To find *about* how much, estimate the sum. Estimate: 286 + 203.

- You can use rounding to estimate.

Nearest ten

286 → 290
\+ 203 → + 200
about 490

Nearest hundred

286 → 300
\+ 203 → + 200
about 500

- You can also use front-end estimation.

286 → 200
\+ 203 → + 200
about 400

MORE PRACTICE

Estimate by rounding to the nearest ten.

1. 428 + 265 = ☐☐☐

2. 362 + 511 = ☐☐☐

3. 287 + 322 = ☐☐☐

4. 595 + 351 = ☐☐☐

Estimate by rounding to the nearest hundred.

5. 371 + 235 = ☐☐☐

6. 531 + 408 = ☐☐☐

7. 454 + 378 = ☐☐☐

8. 624 + 177 = ☐☐☐

Estimate by using front-end estimation.

9. 429 + 376 = ☐☐☐

10. 672 + 287 = ☐☐☐

11. 327 + 415 = ☐☐☐

12. 813 + 245 = ☐☐☐☐

HOMEWORK

Estimate by rounding to the nearest ten.

1. $\begin{array}{r} 364 \\ +287 \\ \hline \end{array}$ ☐☐☐

2. $\begin{array}{r} 417 \\ +342 \\ \hline \end{array}$ ☐☐☐

3. $\begin{array}{r} 429 \\ +182 \\ \hline \end{array}$ ☐☐☐

4. $\begin{array}{r} 537 \\ +368 \\ \hline \end{array}$ ☐☐☐

Estimate by rounding to the nearest hundred.

5. $\begin{array}{r} 287 \\ +416 \\ \hline \end{array}$ ☐☐☐

6. $\begin{array}{r} 337 \\ +265 \\ \hline \end{array}$ ☐☐☐

7. $\begin{array}{r} 538 \\ +327 \\ \hline \end{array}$ ☐☐☐

8. $\begin{array}{r} 594 \\ +277 \\ \hline \end{array}$ ☐☐☐

Estimate by using front-end estimation.

9. $\begin{array}{r} 362 \\ +285 \\ \hline \end{array}$ ☐☐☐

10. $\begin{array}{r} 593 \\ +248 \\ \hline \end{array}$ ☐☐☐

11. $\begin{array}{r} 611 \\ +173 \\ \hline \end{array}$ ☐☐☐

12. $\begin{array}{r} 706 \\ +295 \\ \hline \end{array}$ ☐☐☐

Problem Solving

13. A movie is attended by 268 adults and 187 students. About how many people attend the movie? Explain how you estimated.

____

____

____

14. The Wildcats scored 82, 59, and 67 points in three games. Did the Wildcats score at least 200 points in all? Explain using estimation.

____

____

____

Write About It

15. Does rounding or using front-end estimation give a better estimate of a sum? Explain.

____

____

____

Name ______________________ Date ____________

LESSON 2-4

Add with Partial Sums

Find the sum of 364 and 283.

You can break apart the addends to find the sum. Find the sum of each place value.

```
  364
+ 283
  500 ⟶ Add the hundreds: 300 + 200 = 500
  140 ⟶ Add the tens: 60 + 80 = 140
+   7 ⟶ Add the ones: 4 + 3 = 7
  647 ⟶ Add the sums of all the places: 500 + 140 + 7 = 647
```

So 364 + 283 = 647.

MORE PRACTICE

Use partial sums to add. Show each step.

1. 536 + 254

2. 318 + 265

3. 475 + 462

4. 287 + 164

5. 623 + 189

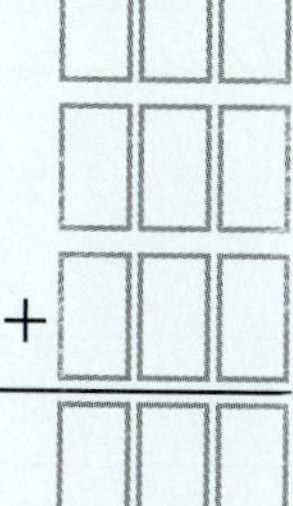

6. 786 + 145

7. 438 + 355

8. 519 + 473

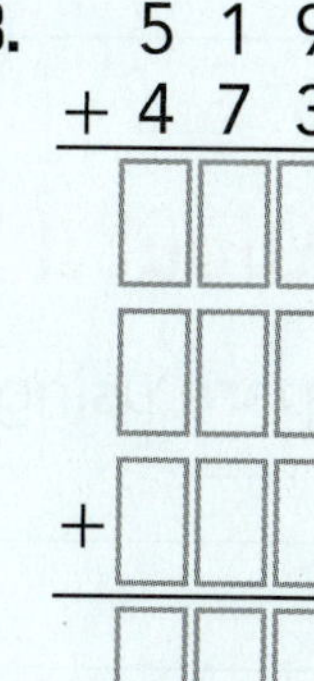

HOMEWORK

Use partial sums to add. Show each step.

1. $\begin{array}{r} 388 \\ +\ 425 \\ \hline \end{array}$

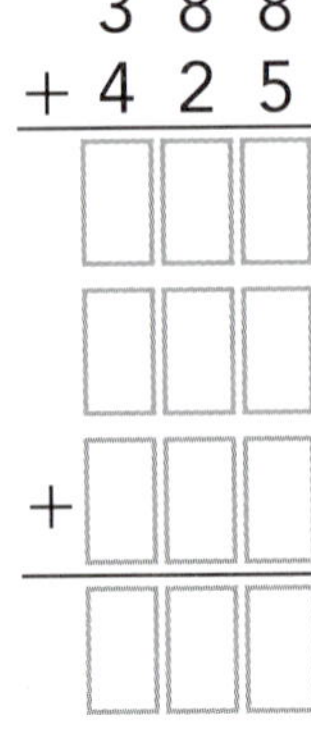

2. $\begin{array}{r} 477 \\ +\ 282 \\ \hline \end{array}$

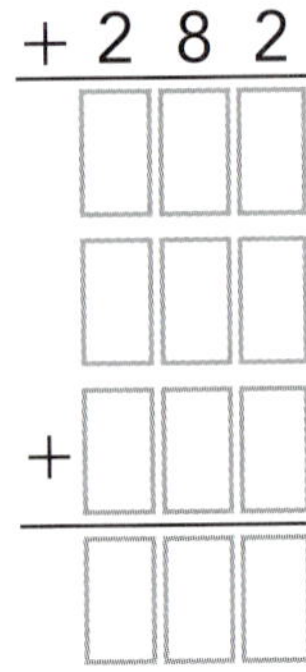

3. $\begin{array}{r} 629 \\ +\ 245 \\ \hline \end{array}$

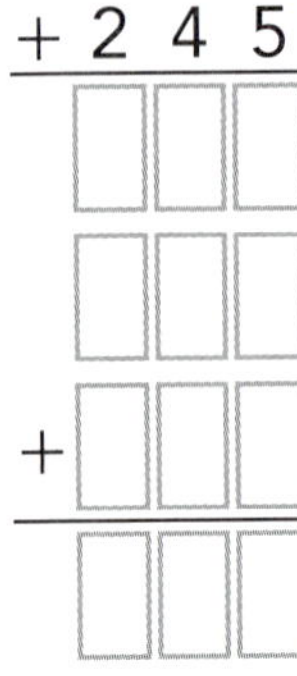

4. $\begin{array}{r} 557 \\ +\ 165 \\ \hline \end{array}$

5. $\begin{array}{r} 513 \\ +\ 248 \\ \hline \end{array}$

6. $\begin{array}{r} 365 \\ +\ 429 \\ \hline \end{array}$

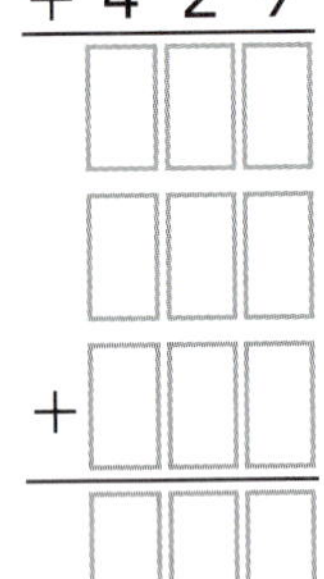

7. $\begin{array}{r} 307 \\ +\ 536 \\ \hline \end{array}$

8. $\begin{array}{r} 496 \\ +\ 189 \\ \hline \end{array}$

Problem Solving

9. The Juno spacecraft's data processing system uses 256 MB of flash memory and 128 MB of local memory. How much memory does the system use in all?

____

10. A zoo has 484 species of insects, 365 species of birds, and 268 species of reptiles. How many species of insects and reptiles does the zoo have?

____

Write About It

11. Compare using partial sums to using base ten blocks to add.

____

____

Name ____________________ Date ____________

LESSON 2-5

Use Place Value to Add: Regroup Once

Add 276 and 241.

- First estimate by rounding.

$$\begin{array}{rcr} 276 & \longrightarrow & 300 \\ +\ 241 & \longrightarrow & +\ 200 \\ & & \text{about } 500 \end{array}$$

- Then align the digits on the ones place and add.

Add the ones.

	h	t	o
	2	7	6
+	2	4	1
			7

Add the tens. Regroup by trading 10 tens for 1 hundred.

	h	t	o
	1		
	2	7	6
+	2	4	1
		1	7

Add the hundreds.

	h	t	o
	1		
	2	7	6
+	2	4	1
	5	1	7

So 276 + 241 = 517.

MORE PRACTICE

Estimate. Then add.

1. 347 + 235 = ☐☐☐

2. 461 + 373 = ☐☐☐

3. 667 + 319 = ☐☐☐

4. 193 + 245 = ☐☐☐

Add.

5. 463 + 418 = ☐☐☐

6. 537 + 247 = ☐☐☐

7. 709 + 265 = ☐☐☐

8. 343 + 271 = ☐☐☐

HOMEWORK

Estimate. Then add.

1. $\begin{array}{r} 517 \\ +346 \\ \hline \end{array}$

2. $\begin{array}{r} 287 \\ +172 \\ \hline \end{array}$

3. $\begin{array}{r} 645 \\ +261 \\ \hline \end{array}$

4. $\begin{array}{r} 434 \\ +359 \\ \hline \end{array}$

5. $\begin{array}{r} 178 \\ +415 \\ \hline \end{array}$

6. $\begin{array}{r} 724 \\ +184 \\ \hline \end{array}$

7. $\begin{array}{r} 521 \\ +349 \\ \hline \end{array}$

8. $\begin{array}{r} 606 \\ +288 \\ \hline \end{array}$

Add.

9. $\begin{array}{r} 437 \\ +258 \\ \hline \end{array}$

10. $\begin{array}{r} 336 \\ +482 \\ \hline \end{array}$

11. $\begin{array}{r} 586 \\ +361 \\ \hline \end{array}$

12. $\begin{array}{r} 272 \\ +119 \\ \hline \end{array}$

Align and add.

13. 664 + 227

14. 491 + 395

15. 338 + 247

16. 527 + 192

Problem Solving

17. Oliver's family will drive 214 miles to a cabin. Their ride home will be 25 miles longer. How many miles will Oliver's family drive in all?

____

18. Amy has 128 markers that still write. She threw away 165 markers that no longer write. How many markers did Amy have?

____

Write About It

19. Compare adding from right to left to adding partial sums.

____

____

____

Name ______________________ Date ______________

LESSON **2-6**

Use Place Value to Add: Regroup Twice

Add 447 and 365.

- First estimate by rounding.

447	→	400
+ 365	→	+ 400
	about	800

- Then add from right to left.

Add the ones. Regroup.

	h	t	o
		1	
	4	4	7
+	3	6	5
			2

Add the tens. Regroup.

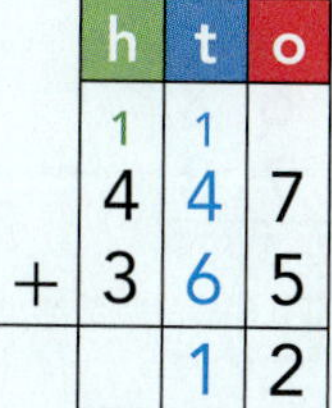

Add the hundreds.

	h	t	o
	1	1	
	4	4	7
+	3	6	5
	8	1	2

812 is close to the estimate of 800.

So 447 + 365 = 812.

MORE PRACTICE

Estimate by rounding. Then add.

1. 658 + 264 = ☐☐☐

2. 579 + 325 = ☐☐☐

3. 284 + 467 = ☐☐☐

4. 394 + 378 = ☐☐☐

Add.

5. 469 + 187 = ☐☐☐

6. 646 + 298 = ☐☐☐

7. 538 + 374 = ☐☐☐

8. 246 + 254 = ☐☐☐

9. 493 + 308 = ☐☐☐

10. 387 + 285 = ☐☐☐

11. 438 + 375 = ☐☐☐

12. 537 + 389 = ☐☐☐

HOMEWORK

Estimate by rounding. Then add.

1.
```
  5 8 4
+ 3 5 7
```

2.
```
  4 6 8
+ 3 7 4
```

3.
```
  3 2 7
+ 2 9 4
```

4.
```
  2 8 6
+ 5 1 7
```

5.
```
  4 6 2
+ 3 8 8
```

6.
```
  5 2 3
+ 1 7 9
```

7.
```
  3 9 5
+ 1 4 6
```

8.
```
  4 3 6
+ 4 8 7
```

Add.

9.
```
  5 4 8
+ 1 8 6
```

10.
```
  6 8 2
+ 1 3 8
```

11.
```
  3 6 3
+ 1 7 8
```

12.
```
  4 7 3
+ 2 6 9
```

Problem Solving

13. Last week 376 people visited an exhibit. That was 248 less than the number of people who visited the first week. How many people visited the exhibit the first week? Show your work.

14. Brooklyn bowls a 157 in her first game. In her second game, she scores 26 more points than she does in her first game. How many points does Brooklyn score in all? Show your work.

Write About It

15. Is it easier to add from right to left or to add using partial sums? Explain your answer.

Name ______________________ Date ____________

LESSON 2-7

Add with Three or More Addends

The table shows the number of points three friends score on a video game. How many points do Alexis, Trinity, and Steph score in all?

Name	Points Scored
Alexis	236
Trinity	433
Steph	158

To find how many points, add:
236 + 433 + 158.

- First estimate by rounding: 200 + 400 + 200 = 800.
- Align the addends on the ones place and add.

Add the ones. Regroup.

	h	t	o
		1	
	2	3	6
	4	3	3
+	1	5	8
			7

17 ones = 1 ten 7 ones

Add the tens. Regroup.

	h	t	o
	1	1	
	2	3	6
	4	3	3
+	1	5	8
		2	7

12 tens = 1 hundred 2 tens

Add the hundreds.

	h	t	o
	1	1	
	2	3	6
	4	3	3
+	1	5	8
	8	2	7

827 is close to the estimate of 800.

So 236 + 433 + 158 = 827.

The three friends score 827 points in all.

MORE PRACTICE

Estimate. Then add.

1.
```
  1 2 3
  4 1 7
+ 3 1 2
  □□□
```

2.
```
  2 0 2
  3 9 3
+ 1 0 9
  □□□
```

3.
```
  1 7 1
  3 1 5
+ 2 3 5
  □□□
```

4.
```
  4 9 1
  1 5 9
+ 3 1 5
  □□□
```

HOMEWORK

Add.

1. $\begin{array}{r} 293 \\ 327 \\ +\ 132 \\ \hline \end{array}$

2. $\begin{array}{r} 419 \\ 318 \\ +\ 227 \\ \hline \end{array}$

3. $\begin{array}{r} 243 \\ 198 \\ +\ 307 \\ \hline \end{array}$

4. $\begin{array}{r} 167 \\ 298 \\ +\ 399 \\ \hline \end{array}$

5. $\begin{array}{r} 127 \\ 118 \\ 198 \\ +\ 429 \\ \hline \end{array}$

6. $\begin{array}{r} 191 \\ 103 \\ 283 \\ +\ 317 \\ \hline \end{array}$

7. $\begin{array}{r} 301 \\ 105 \\ 175 \\ +\ 269 \\ \hline \end{array}$

8. $\begin{array}{r} 161 \\ 199 \\ 209 \\ +\ 242 \\ \hline \end{array}$

Problem Solving

9. Peter is keeping an exercise journal. The page shows how many minutes he performed each exercise in one week. If his goal is to exercise for 500 minutes, did Peter meet his goal? Explain.

run 170 minutes
bike 139 minutes
swim 209 minutes

____

____

____

Write About It

10. How is estimating helpful when adding three or more addends? How might it not always be accurate?

____

____

____

____

____

Name ______________________________ Date ______________

LESSON 2-8

Problem Solving
Use a Model

You can use a model to help solve a problem.

Mr. Gallo buys a pair of pants for $37 and a shirt. The shirt costs $21 more than the pants. How much does Mr. Gallo pay for the pants and shirt?

Use a bar model to organize this information.

___?___ for 1 shirt and 1 pair of pants	
$37 for 1 pair of pants	$37 + $21 for 1 shirt

Write and solve an equation to find the answer.

$\$37 + \$37 + \$21 = ?$

$\$95 = ?$

Mr. Gallo pays $95 for the pants and shirt.

MORE PRACTICE

1. Doug does 122 sit-ups on Monday. He does 25 more sit-ups on Tuesday than he does on Monday. How many sit-ups does Doug do in total on both days?

Complete the bar model to organize the information.

______ sit-ups in all	
______ sit-ups on Monday	______ + ______ sit-ups on Tuesday

Write an equation. ______________________________

Solve your equation. ______________________________

Answer the question. ______________________________

MORE PRACTICE

A museum has 76 sculptures, 216 watercolors, 124 textiles, and 284 photographs. The museum also has 102 more oil paintings than watercolors. Use this information for Exercises 2–3.

2. How many watercolors and oil paintings does the museum have in all?

______ watercolors and oil paintings	
______ watercolors	______ + ______ oil paintings

Write an equation.

____

Solve your equation.

____

Answer the question:

____

3. About how many pieces of art are in the museum?

____

____

4. At a movie fest two movies are each 126 minutes long and two more last 105 minutes each. How long is the movie fest?

______ minutes			
______ min.	______ min.	______ min.	______ min.

Answer the question:

____

5. The Eagles score 48 points in the first half and 36 points in the second half. The Ducks score 36 points in the first half and 48 points in the second half. Explain how to decide which team won without adding and comparing.

____

____

Name ______________________________ Date ______________

Problem Solving
Use a Model

HOMEWORK

The table shows the prices for some furniture at Herrera's Furniture Store. Use the table for Exercises 1–3.

Item	Price
Bed	$379
Desk	$239
Chair	$98
Dresser	$272
Bookcase	$150

1. Evelyn's family buys new furniture for her room. They buy her a bed, a chair, and two bookcases. What is the cost of Evelyn's new furniture?

Use the model to organize the information.

_______ dollars for Evelyn's furniture		
$_______	$_______	$_______ + $_______

Write an equation. ______________________________

Solve your equation. ______________________________

Answer the question:

____

2. Brandon's family buys 4 chairs and a table that costs $150 more than a desk. What is the cost of this furniture?

_______ dollars for 4 chairs and a table				
$_______	$_______	$_______	$_______	$_______ + $_______

Write an equation. ______________________________

Solve your equation. ______________________________

Answer the question:

____

3. About what is the cost of a bed and a dresser?

____

HOMEWORK

4. Kevin has a set of 405 interlocking blocks. Blake has a set with 79 more blocks than Kevin's set. When they use both sets to build things together, how many blocks do they have?

_____ blocks in all	
_____	_____ + _____

_____

The Connecticut River in New England is 407 miles long. The Pearl River in the southern United States is 4 miles longer than the Connecticut River. The Bighorn River in the western United States is 50 miles longer than the Pearl River. Organize this information before you start Exercises 5–6.

Connecticut River: _____ miles
Pearl River: _____ miles + _____ miles
Bighorn River: _____ miles + _____ miles + _____ miles

5. What is the length of the Pearl River? _____

6. What is the length of the Bighorn River? _____

Write About It

7. Puzzle 1 contains 413 more pieces than Puzzle 2. Puzzle 2 has 113 more pieces than Puzzle 3, which has 400 pieces. How many pieces are in Puzzle 1? Draw a model.

_____

Name ______________________________ Date ______________

LESSON 3-1

Estimate Differences

- You can estimate differences by rounding.
  - Estimate: 832 − 189
  - Round each number to the nearest hundred.
  - Subtract the rounded numbers.

$$\begin{array}{r} 832 \\ -189 \\ \hline \end{array} \quad \begin{array}{l} \text{rounds to} \\ \text{rounds to} \\ \text{about} \end{array} \quad \begin{array}{r} 800 \\ -200 \\ \hline 600 \end{array}$$

- You can also estimate the difference using front-end estimation.
  - Estimate: 832 − 189
  - Keep the first digit. Change the other digits to zero.
  - Subtract.

$$\begin{array}{r} 832 \\ -189 \\ \hline \end{array} \quad \begin{array}{l} \rightarrow \\ \rightarrow \\ \text{about} \end{array} \quad \begin{array}{r} 800 \\ -100 \\ \hline 700 \end{array}$$

MORE PRACTICE

Estimate by rounding to the nearest ten.

1. $\begin{array}{r} 71 \\ -45 \\ \hline \end{array}$ **2.** $\begin{array}{r} 85 \\ -54 \\ \hline \end{array}$ **3.** $\begin{array}{r} 96 \\ -78 \\ \hline \end{array}$ **4.** $\begin{array}{r} 73 \\ -16 \\ \hline \end{array}$

Estimate by rounding to the nearest hundred.

5. $\begin{array}{r} 511 \\ -425 \\ \hline \end{array}$ **6.** $\begin{array}{r} 782 \\ -199 \\ \hline \end{array}$ **7.** $\begin{array}{r} 651 \\ -249 \\ \hline \end{array}$ **8.** $\begin{array}{r} 299 \\ -187 \\ \hline \end{array}$

Estimate using front-end estimation.

9. 373 − 127 **10.** 724 − 266 **11.** 492 − 356 **12.** 351 − 214

13. Alexis estimated 525 − 414 by rounding to the nearest ten. She found 520 − 410 = 110. What mistake did Alexis make? What is the correct answer?

____

____

HOMEWORK

Estimate by rounding to the nearest ten.

1. $\begin{array}{r} 28 \\ -12 \\ \hline \end{array}$

2. $\begin{array}{r} 65 \\ -44 \\ \hline \end{array}$

3. $\begin{array}{r} 492 \\ -121 \\ \hline \end{array}$

4. $\begin{array}{r} 579 \\ -334 \\ \hline \end{array}$

Estimate by rounding to the nearest hundred.

5. $\begin{array}{r} 654 \\ -382 \\ \hline \end{array}$

6. $\begin{array}{r} 211 \\ -105 \\ \hline \end{array}$

7. $\begin{array}{r} 849 \\ -354 \\ \hline \end{array}$

8. $\begin{array}{r} 491 \\ -146 \\ \hline \end{array}$

Estimate using front-end estimation.

9. $\begin{array}{r} 995 \\ -548 \\ \hline \end{array}$

10. $\begin{array}{r} 299 \\ -150 \\ \hline \end{array}$

11. $\begin{array}{r} 457 \\ -219 \\ \hline \end{array}$

12. $\begin{array}{r} 319 \\ -192 \\ \hline \end{array}$

Problem Solving

13. An elementary school has 182 third-graders and 313 fourth-graders. About how many more fourth-graders are there than third-graders? Estimate the difference by rounding to the nearest hundred, rounding to the nearest ten, and using front-end estimation. Which method gives you an estimate that is closest to the actual difference?

____

____

14. Julia rounded to the nearest ten to estimate the difference between two numbers. The estimated difference was 10. What are four pairs of numbers she might have subtracted?

____

Write About It

15. Give two examples of when you might estimate differences in everyday life.

____

____

____

Name ______________________ Date ______________

LESSON 3-2

Relate Addition and Subtraction

This year 535 people join a charity run. Only 104 people compete in the timed run. How many runners are not timed?

535 runners	
104 timed	? not timed

◆ You know the whole and one of the parts.

part + part = whole

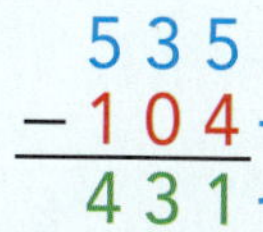

◆ You can write an addition equation and a related subtraction equation.

104 + ? = 535
535 − 104 = ?
535 − 104 = 431

One part is the number of timed runners. The other part is the number of runners who are not timed.

part + part = whole

There are 431 runners who are not timed.

◆ Use subtraction to solve the problem:

$$\begin{array}{r} 535 \\ -\,104 \\ \hline 431 \end{array}$$

◆ Use addition to check your answer:

$$\begin{array}{r} 431 \\ +\,104 \\ \hline 535 \end{array}$$

MORE PRACTICE

Write the addition equation that can be used to check the answer to each subtraction problem.

1. 905 − 198 = ?

_____ + 198 = _____

2. 330 − 177 = ?

_____ + 177 = _____

3. 843 − 212 = ?

_____ + _____ = _____

4. 646 − 238 = ?

_____ + _____ = _____

Add or subtract. Then check your answer using the inverse operation.

5. 433 − 231 = ☐☐☐ ; ☐☐☐ + 231 = ☐☐☐

6. 721 + 108 = ☐☐☐ ; ☐☐☐ − 108 = ☐☐☐

7. 478 − 277 = ☐☐☐ ; ☐☐☐ + 277 = ☐☐☐

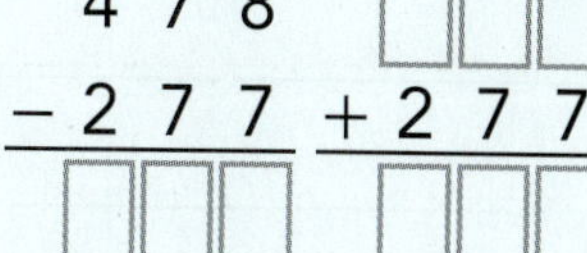

HOMEWORK

Add or subtract. Then check your answer using the inverse operation.

1. $\begin{array}{r} 474 \\ +123 \\ \hline \square\square\square \end{array}$ $\begin{array}{r} \square\square\square \\ -123 \\ \hline \square\square\square \end{array}$

2. $\begin{array}{r} 699 \\ -289 \\ \hline \square\square\square \end{array}$ $\begin{array}{r} \square\square\square \\ +289 \\ \hline \square\square\square \end{array}$

3. $\begin{array}{r} 101 \\ +354 \\ \hline \square\square\square \end{array}$ $\begin{array}{r} \square\square\square \\ -354 \\ \hline \square\square\square \end{array}$

Add or subtract. Then check your answer using the inverse operation.

4. $\begin{array}{r} 548 \\ -118 \\ \hline \square\square\square \end{array}$ + ______

5. $\begin{array}{r} 858 \\ +\ \ 31 \\ \hline \square\square\square \end{array}$ − ______

6. $\begin{array}{r} 469 \\ -233 \\ \hline \square\square\square \end{array}$ + ______

7. $\begin{array}{r} 60 \\ +138 \\ \hline \square\square\square \end{array}$ − ______

8. $\begin{array}{r} 875 \\ -341 \\ \hline \square\square\square \end{array}$ + ______

9. $\begin{array}{r} 802 \\ +127 \\ \hline \square\square\square \end{array}$ − ______

Problem Solving

Complete each bar model, and solve the problem.

10. Abby has 375 minutes of talk time on her phone. She has used 152 minutes. How many minutes does she have left?

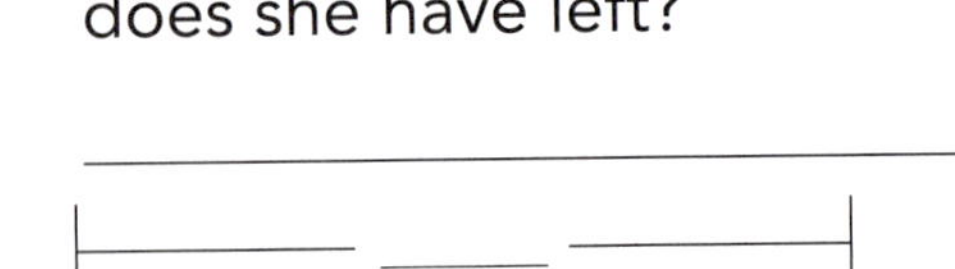

11. Eric is saving money to buy a computer that costs $348. He has saved $132. How much more money does Eric need to save?

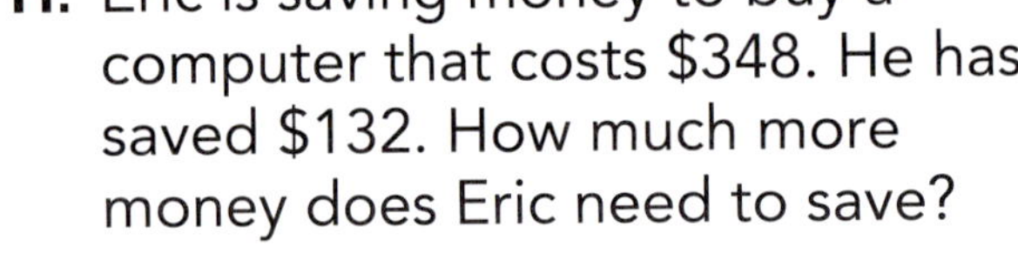

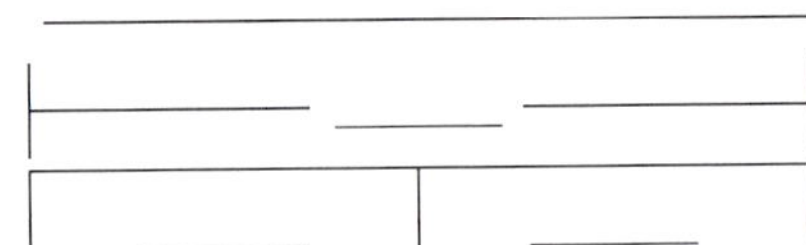

Write About It

12. Sam solved the problem 465 − 144 and got the answer 321. He checked the answer using the equation 321 − 144 = 465, but it did not check. What mistake did Sam make?

____

____

Name ______________________ Date ______________

LESSON 3-3

Subtract with Partial Differences

One way to subtract is to use partial differences.

Find 748 − 572.

- Start with 748. Subtract the hundreds in 572. 748 − 500 = 248

  So far 500 has been subtracted.

- Now start with 248. Subtract the tens in 572.

  You need to subtract 7 tens, but there are only 4 tens.

  First subtract 4 tens. 248 − 40 = 208

  Then subtract the remaining 3 tens. 208 − 30 = 178

  So far 500 + 40 + 30 = 570 has been subtracted.

- Next start with 178. Subtract the ones in 572. 178 − 2 = 176

  500 + 40 + 30 + 2 = 572 has been subtracted.

MORE PRACTICE

Subtract using partial differences. Complete every step.

1. 548 − 233 = ?

548 − 200 = ______

______ − 30 = ______

______ − 3 = ______

2. 625 − 331 = ?

625 − 300 = ______

______ − 20 = ______

______ − 10 = ______

______ − 1 = ______

3. 409 − 144 = ?

409 − 100 = ______

______ − 40 = ______

______ − 4 = ______

4. 754 − 321

______

______

______

______

5. 568 − 284

______

______

______

______

6. 375 − 108

______

______

______

______

HOMEWORK

Subtract using partial differences. Show your work.

1. 462 − 163

2. 247 − 188

3. 610 − 377

Match each subtraction to the correct sum of the numbers you need to subtract.

4. 872 − 279	200 + 40 + 30 + 3 + 6
5. 943 − 279	200 + 70 + 2 + 7
6. 387 − 279	200 + 50 + 20 + 3 + 6
7. 653 − 279	200 + 70 + 7 + 2

Problem Solving

8. Joy wants to solve 234 − 185 using partial differences. Show what smaller problems Joy can break it up into.

9. Carlos subtracted 529 − 248 using partial differences. The numbers he subtracted were 200, 20, and 8. What mistake did Carlos make?

Write About It

10. Explain to a friend how to subtract using partial differences.

Name ____________________ Date ____________

LESSON 3-4

Subtract Three-Digit Numbers

Subtract: 326 − 247.

- First estimate the difference by rounding.

$$\begin{array}{r} 326 \\ -247 \\ \hline \end{array} \rightarrow \begin{array}{r} 300 \\ -200 \\ \hline \text{about } 100 \end{array}$$

- Then subtract. Align on the ones place.

Subtract the ones. Regroup the tens.

	h	t	o
		1	16
	3	~~2~~	~~6~~
−	2	4	7
			9

16 ones = 1 ten 6 ones

Subtract the tens. Regroup the hundreds.

	h	t	o
		11	
	2	~~1~~	16
	~~3~~	~~2~~	~~6~~
−	2	4	7
		7	9

11 tens = 1 hundred 1 ten

Subtract the hundreds.

	h	t	o
		11	
	2	~~1~~	16
	~~3~~	~~2~~	~~6~~
−	2	4	7
	0	7	9

Even though there is a 0 in the hundreds column, you don't write 079. Write: 79.

So 326 − 247 = 79.

MORE PRACTICE

Subtract and check.

1. 785 − 414 = ☐71

2. 642 − 408 = 23☐

3. 775 − 316 = 4☐9

4. 912 − 682 = ☐☐☐

5. 574 − 249 = ☐☐☐

6. 871 − 469 = ☐☐☐

7. 766 − 575 = ☐☐☐

8. 351 − 169 = ☐☐☐

9. 818 − 127 = ☐☐☐

HOMEWORK

Subtract and check.

1.
$$\begin{array}{r} 544 \\ -\ 393 \\ \hline \end{array}$$

2.
$$\begin{array}{r} 996 \\ -\ 588 \\ \hline \end{array}$$

3.
$$\begin{array}{r} 641 \\ -\ 325 \\ \hline \end{array}$$

4.
$$\begin{array}{r} 422 \\ -\ 319 \\ \hline \end{array}$$

5.
$$\begin{array}{r} 631 \\ -\ 129 \\ \hline \end{array}$$

6.
$$\begin{array}{r} 522 \\ -\ 362 \\ \hline \end{array}$$

Align and subtract.

7. 712 − 649 = ______
8. 928 − 781 = ______
9. 818 − 525 = ______
10. 342 − 116 = ______
11. 541 − 307 = ______
12. 316 − 218 = ______

Problem Solving

13. Michael found that the difference between two numbers is 259. What could the two numbers be? How did you find the numbers?

____

____

____

14. The bar model shows the number of trees at a park. How many birch trees are there? How many times did you need to regroup?

508 trees	
227 maple trees	______ birch trees

____

Write About It

15. How does rounding help you when you are subtracting two numbers? Give an example.

____

____

____

Name ______________________ Date ____________

LESSON 3-5

Subtract Across Zeros

Subtract: 420 − 182.

- First estimate the difference by rounding.

420	→	400
− 182	→	− 200
	about	200

- Then subtract. Align on the ones place.

Subtract the ones. Regroup the tens.

	h	t	o
		1	10
	4	2	0
−	1	8	2
			8

10 ones = 1 ten 0 ones

Subtract the tens. Regroup the hundreds.

	h	t	o
		11	
	3	1	10
	4	2	0
−	1	8	2
		3	8

11 tens = 1 hundred 1 ten

Subtract the hundreds.

	h	t	o
		11	
	3	1	10
	4	2	0
−	1	8	2
	2	3	8

238 is close to the estimate of 200, so the answer is reasonable.

- Add to check.

```
  238  ✓
+ 182
  420
```

420 − 182 = 238

MORE PRACTICE

Estimate by rounding. Then find the difference.

1.
```
   9
 8 10 10
 9  0  0
−7  3  6
 1  □  4
```

2.
```
   9
 5 10 10
 6  0  0
−3  3  6
 2  6  □
```

3.
```
   9
 1 10 10
 2  0  0
−1  7  2
 0  □  8
```

4.
```
   9
 3 10 10
 4  0  0
−2  8  7
 1  □  3
```

5.
```
  500
− 219
  □□□
```

6.
```
  800
− 152
  □□□
```

7.
```
  700
− 372
  □□□
```

8.
```
  350
− 169
  □□□
```

HOMEWORK

Find the difference. Check your answer.

1. $\begin{array}{r} 800 \\ -\ 411 \\ \hline \end{array}$

2. $\begin{array}{r} 900 \\ -\ 127 \\ \hline \end{array}$

3. $\begin{array}{r} 600 \\ -\ 321 \\ \hline \end{array}$

4. $\begin{array}{r} 470 \\ -\ 189 \\ \hline \end{array}$

5. $\begin{array}{r} 200 \\ -\ 102 \\ \hline \end{array}$

6. $\begin{array}{r} 500 \\ -\ 173 \\ \hline \end{array}$

7. $\begin{array}{r} 850 \\ -\ 453 \\ \hline \end{array}$

8. $\begin{array}{r} 700 \\ -\ 292 \\ \hline \end{array}$

9. $\begin{array}{r} 600 \\ -\ 468 \\ \hline \end{array}$

Problem Solving

10. A ferry can hold up to 400 cars. So far 167 cars have already been loaded onto the ferry. How many more cars will the ferry hold? Write an addition sentence you can use to check your answer.

____

11. The table shows the number of calories in one piece of each fruit. How many more calories are in one watermelon than in one banana and one pineapple combined?

Fruit	Calories
Banana, medium	105
Watermelon	920
Pineapple	453

____

Write About It

12. John bought a bicycle that cost $259. He gave the cashier three $100 bills. How much change did he receive? John wants to check to see if the answer is reasonable by rounding. To what place should he round? Why?

____

____

____

Name ______________________ Date ______________

LESSON 3-6

Problem Solving
Write an Equation

Sarah is driving 197 miles from San Antonio to Houston. Then she is driving 239 miles from Houston to Dallas. How much shorter would her trip be if she drove 274 miles straight from San Antonio to Dallas?

- Read and understand.
  - What are you asked to find?

    How much shorter would the trip be if Sarah drove straight to Dallas?
  - Is this a one-step problem or a two-step problem?

    It is a two-step problem.
  - What operations will you use to solve the problem?

    In Step 1 you will add. In Step 2 you will subtract.
- Write equations and solve the problem.

Distance from San Antonio to Houston	+	Distance from Houston to Dallas	=	Total Distance driven
197	+	239	=	436
Total Distance Driven	–	Distance from San Antonio to Dallas	=	Shorter trip distance by driving directly to Dallas
436	–	274	=	162

Sarah's trip would be 162 miles shorter if she drove straight to Dallas from San Antonio.

MORE PRACTICE

1. At a craft fair, Matt earned $120 and had expenses of $12 and $9. How much did he earn after expenses?

   What are you asked to find? ______________________

   What equation can you write to solve the problem?

   ____

MORE PRACTICE

2. Jackie, Olivia, and Ava work at a store. Jackie can mop the floors in 25 minutes. Olivia can wash the windows in 20 minutes. Ava can mop the floors and wash the windows in 35 minutes. How much faster can Ava do both tasks than Jackie and Olivia together?

What are you asked to find?

____

List the steps you would use to solve this problem.

____

____

____

What operations do you need to solve the problem?

____

The table shows the height in feet of the four tallest buildings in Boston. Use the table for Exercises 3–5.

Building	Height
200 Clarendon	790
Prudential Center Tower	749
Federal Reserve Bank of Boston	614
One Boston Place	601

3. How much taller is the Prudential Center Tower than One Boston Place?

____

4. About how much taller is 200 Clarendon than the Prudential Center Tower? Explain how you estimated.

____

____

____

5. Write another word problem using addition or subtraction that you can solve using the table. Then solve the problem.

____

____

____

Name ______________________ Date ____________

Problem Solving
Write and Solve an Equation

HOMEWORK

1. There were 856 cats in animal shelters in one state. On a Saturday 129 cats were adopted. The next morning 12 kittens were born at the shelters. How many cats are now at the animal shelters?

What are you asked to find?

____

List the steps you would use to solve this problem.

____

____

____

A hardware store is having a sale. The sign shows the sale prices. Use the sign for Exercises 2–3.

Sale	
Ladder	$92
Drill	$88
Grill	$96
Shelves	$85

2. Hannah buys a ladder and a grill. She pays with two $100 bills. How much change will Hannah get back?

What are two ways to solve this problem?

____

____

____

What is the answer? ________

3. Daniel has $270. He wants to buy three different items that are on sale. Which three can Daniel buy?

____

How did you find the answer?

____

____

____

HOMEWORK

4. A cafeteria has 225 chairs. New chairs were added last week. Before the chairs were added, there were only 180 chairs. How many chairs were added? What equation can you write to find the answer?

____

5. The table shows the weight in pounds of three animals. How much more does the polar bear weigh than the brown bear and giant panda combined?

Animal	Weight (lb)
Brown bear	275
Polar bear	960
Giant panda	195

What are the steps that you take to solve this problem? What is the answer?

____

____

____

____

How can you use estimation to check that your answer is reasonable?

____

____

____

____

Write About It

6. Dan's grandmother gave him $100. Then he earned $37 babysitting and $22 running errands. Dan wants to know how much money he now has. He added $37 + $22 and got $59. Then he subtracted from $100: $100 − $59 = $41. What mistake did Dan make? Explain. What is the correct answer?

____

____

____

Name ______________________ Date ____________

LESSON 4-1

Represent Multiplication as Repeated Addition

There are 2 stacks of books. Each stack has 3 books. How many books are there in all?

You can add or multiply to join equal groups.

$3 + 3 = 6$

addition equation

The are 3 books in each group.

$2 \times 3 = 6$

multiplication equation

There are 2 equal groups of 3.

There are 6 books in all.

MORE PRACTICE

Find how many in all.

1. $6 + 6 + 6 =$ ______

3 groups of 6 = ______

$3 \times 6 =$ ______

2. $3 + 3 + 3 + 3 + 3 =$ ______

5 groups of 3 = ______

$5 \times 3 =$ ______

3. $4 + 4 + 4 + 4 =$ ______

4 groups of 4 = ______

$4 \times 4 =$ ______

4. $5 + 5 =$ ______

2 groups of 5 = ______

$2 \times 5 =$ ______

Write an addition equation and a multiplication equation to find how many in all.

5.  

______

______

6.     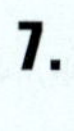

______

______

7.     

______

______

HOMEWORK

Find how many in all.

1. $3 + 3 + 3 + 3 =$ ______

4 groups of $3 =$ ______

$4 \times 3 =$ ______

2. $2 + 2 + 2 + 2 + 2 =$ ______

5 groups of $2 =$ ______

$5 \times 2 =$ ______

Write an addition equation and a multiplication equation to find how many in all.

3. 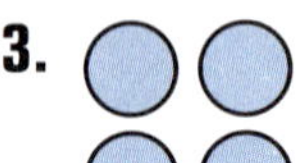 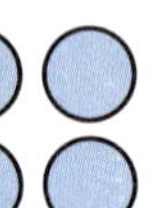 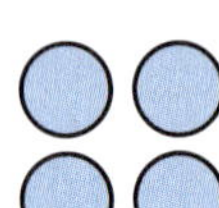 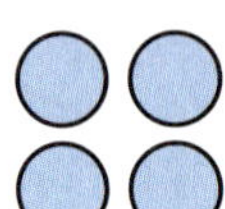 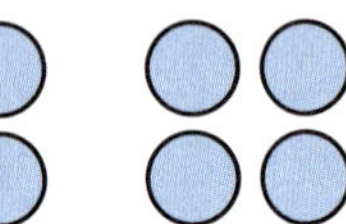

____

____

4. 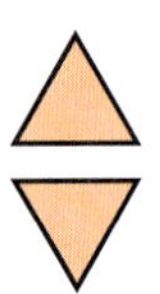 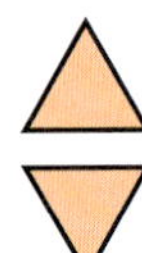 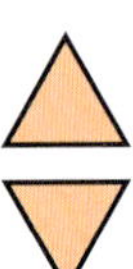

____

____

Complete each equation.

5. $7 + 7 + 7 = 3 \times$ ______

6. $9 + 9 + 9 + 9 + 9 =$ ______ $\times 9$

Problem Solving

7. Rachel has 5 cases. She puts 5 dolls in each case. How many dolls does she have? Write an addition equation and a multiplication equation to solve.

____

8. Can you write the equation $6 + 6 + 6 + 6$ as a multiplication equation? Explain why or why not.

____

Write About It

9. Can you always use addition to join groups? Can you always use multiplication to join groups? Explain why or why not.

____

____

Name ______________________ Date ____________

LESSON 4-2

Represent Multiplication on a Number Line

You can use a number line and skip count to multiply.

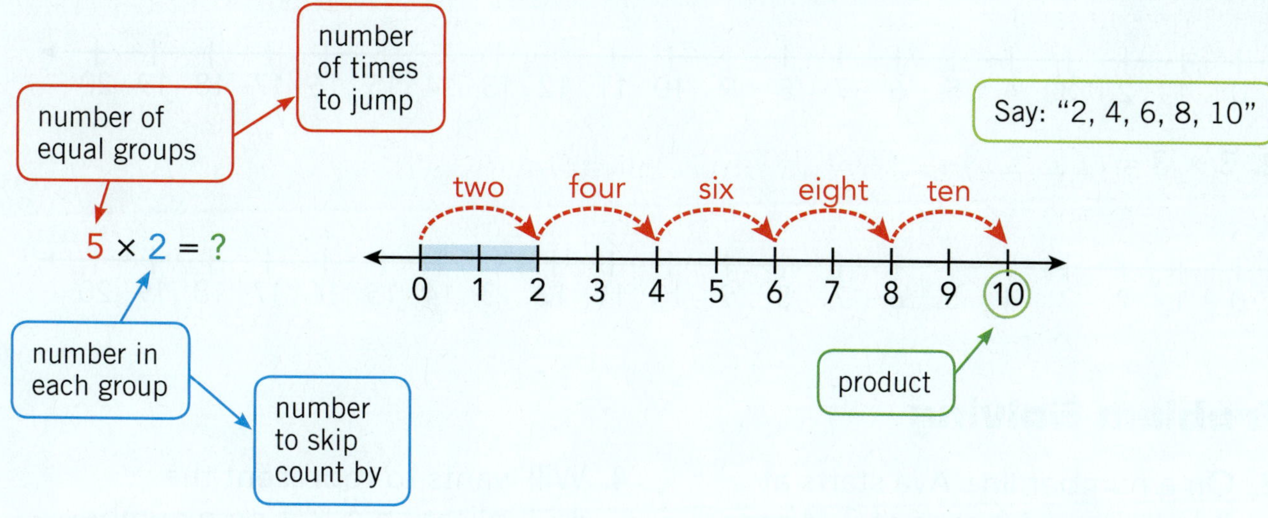

Each arrow shows one jump. There are 5 jumps. The length of each jump is 2. You land on 10.

5 × 2 = 10

MORE PRACTICE

Find the product. Draw jumps on the number line.

How many jumps?
How long is each jump?

1. 3 × 5 = ______

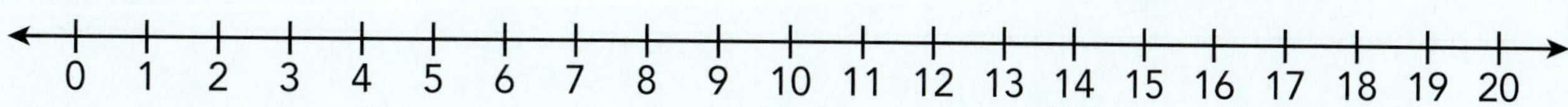

2. 2 × 6 = ______

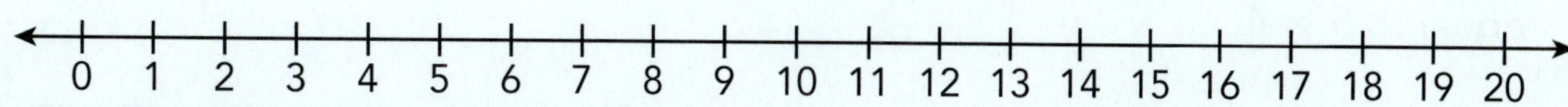

3. 4 × 5 = ______

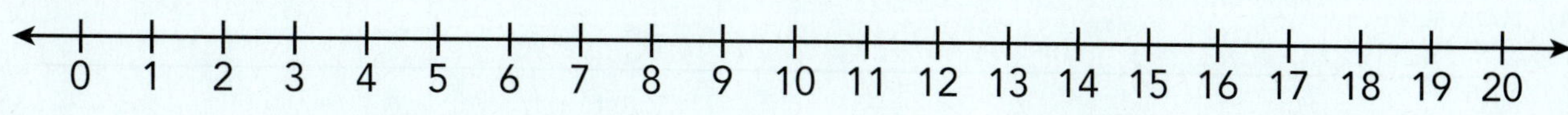

HOMEWORK

Find the product. Draw jumps on the number line.

How many jumps?
How long is each jump?

1. $9 \times 2 =$ ______

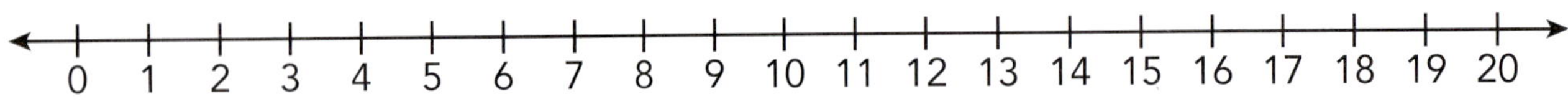

2. $3 \times 3 =$ ______

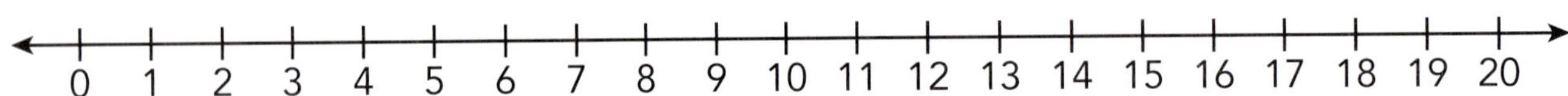

Problem Solving

3. On a number line Ava starts at 0 and draws 6 jumps of 2. Write an equation to show what multiplication Ava models on her number line.

______

4. Will wants to represent the multiplication 4×7 on a number line. How many jumps should Will draw? How long should each jump be? Where will he land?

______

5. Thomas has 4 boxes with 4 action figures in each box. Use the number line to represent the situation. How many action figures does Thomas have?

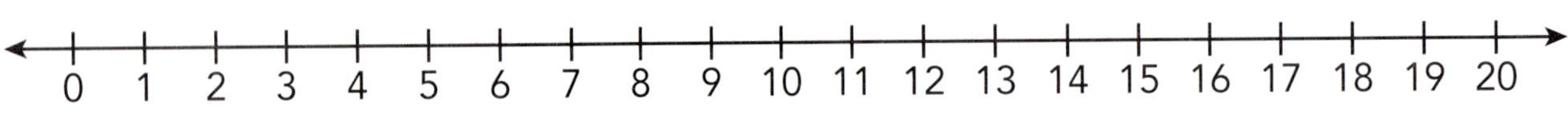

______

Write About It

6. Explain how you can use number lines to show that 4×5 is equal to 5×4.

______

______

______

______

Name ______________________ Date ____________

LESSON 4-3

Represent Multiplication as Arrays

In this array each of the 3 rows has 4 counters. How many counters are in the array?

An array is a set of objects arranged in rows and columns. Rows go across, and columns go down.

- You can add the number of objects in each row. $4 + 4 + 4 = 12$
- You can skip count by 4s three times. 4, 8, 12
- You can multiply the number of rows by the number of objects in each row to find the product.

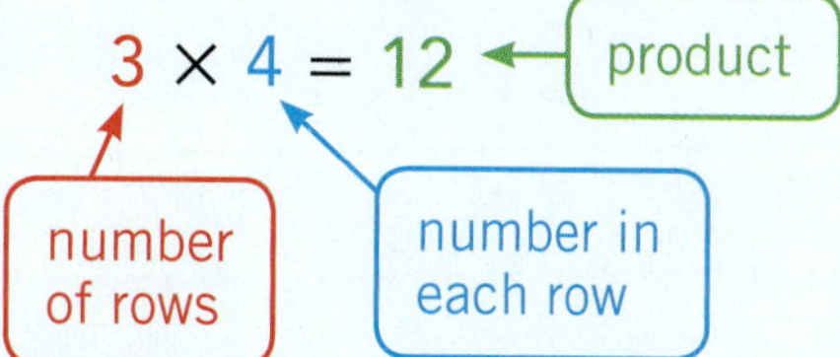

There are 12 counters in the array.

MORE PRACTICE

Write an addition equation, skip counting, and a multiplication equation for each array.

1\.

___ + ___ + ___ + ___ = ___

___, ___, ___, ___

___ × ___ = ___

2\.

___ + ___ + ___ + ___ = ___

___, ___, ___, ___

___ × ___ = ___

3\. Draw an array to show 3×8. Then write the product.

$3 \times 8 =$ ___

HOMEWORK

Write an addition equation, skip counting, and a multiplication equation for each array.

1. 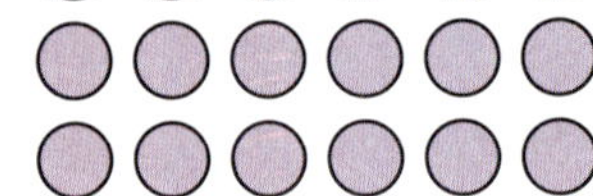

_____ + _____ + _____ = _____

_____, _____, _____

_____ × _____ = _____

2. _____ + _____ = _____

_____, _____

_____ × _____ = _____

Draw an array to show each equation. Write the product.

3. $3 \times 9 =$ _____

4. $4 \times 6 =$ _____

Problem Solving

5. Hazel has a page of stickers with 8 rows of 4 stickers each. Write a multiplication equation for the situation. Then find how many stickers are on the page.

Equation: _____

_____

6. Logan makes 8 rows of trains with 2 trains in each. His brother makes 4 rows with 4 trains in each. Who has more trains? How many more?

_____

_____

Write About It

7. Write a multiplication story for this array. Then solve it.

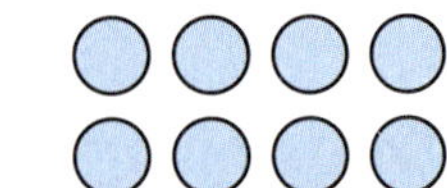

_____

_____

_____

Name ______________________ Date ______________

LESSON 4-4

Multiply with the Commutative Property

Array 1

4 groups of 2 cupcakes

$2 + 2 + 2 + 2 = 8$

factor × factor = product

$4 \times 2 = 8$

Array 2

2 groups of 4 cupcakes

$4 + 4 = 8$

factor × factor = product

$2 \times 4 = 8$

The arrays have the same number of cupcakes. This is true because of the Commutative Property of Multiplication.

Commutative Property of Multiplication

Changing the order of factors does not change the product.

MORE PRACTICE

Find the product for each array.

1. ★★ ★★ ★★ ★★ ★★ ★★★★★ ★★★★★

$5 \times 2 =$ ______

$2 \times 5 =$ ______

2. ●●● ●●● ●●● ●●● ●●●● ●●●● ●●●●

$4 \times 3 =$ ______

$3 \times 4 =$ ______

3. What property of multiplication explains why 5×8 and 8×5 have the same product?

____

HOMEWORK

Write a multiplication equation for each array.

1.

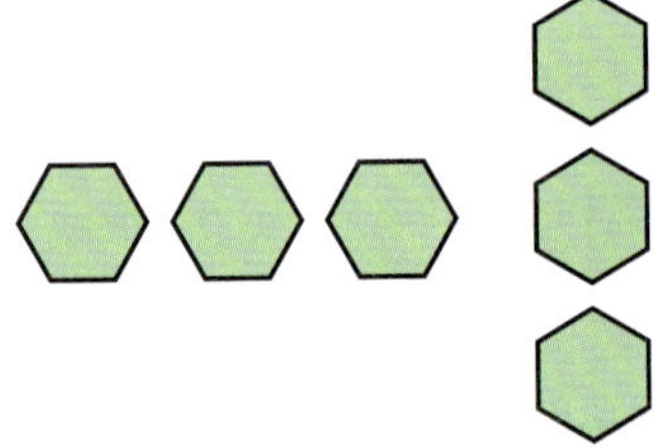

_____ × _____ = _____

_____ × _____ = _____

2.

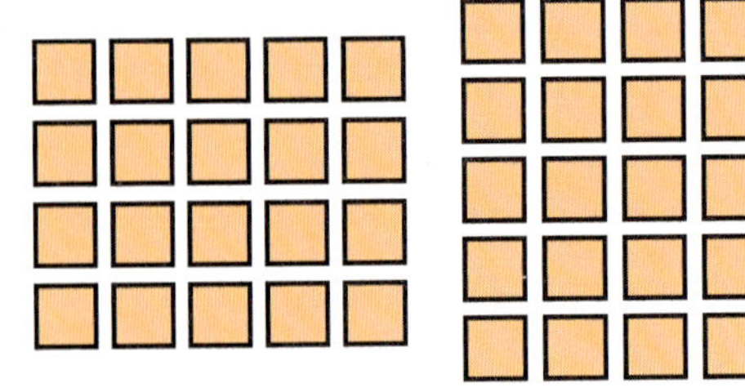

_____ × _____ = _____

_____ × _____ = _____

Complete. Use the Commutative Property of Multiplication.

3. $3 \times 2 =$ _____ $\times 3$ **4.** $9 \times 2 =$ _____ $\times 9$ **5.** $5 \times 1 =$ _____ $\times 5$

Find the products.

6. $5 \times 2 =$ ☐☐ $2 \times 5 =$ ☐☐

7. $1 \times 7 =$ ☐☐ $7 \times 1 =$ ☐☐

8. $3 \times 6 =$ ☐☐ $6 \times 3 =$ ☐☐

9. $3 \times 8 =$ ☐☐ $8 \times 3 =$ ☐☐

Problem Solving

10. Lena has 2 rows of 6 pennies. Ava has the same number of pennies in 6 rows. How many pennies does Ava have in each row?

____

11. An array showing 15 has 5 rows and 3 columns. A different array showing 15 has 3 rows. How many columns are in that array?

____

Write About It

12. An array with 7 rows and 3 columns represents a greater number than an array with 3 rows and 7 columns. True or false? Explain your reasoning.

____

____

Name ______________________ Date ____________

LESSON 4-5

Represent Division by Sharing

Share 12 erasers into 3 equal groups.

You can use division to find the number of equal groups or the number in each group.

To divide 12 erasers into 3 equal groups, make 3 groups with the same number of erasers in each group.

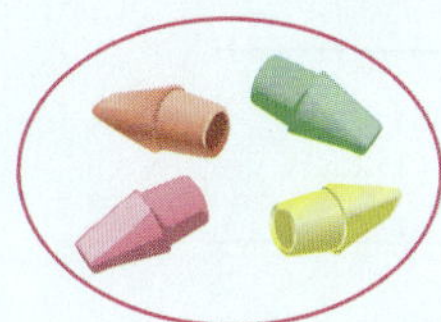

You can write an equation to show this division.

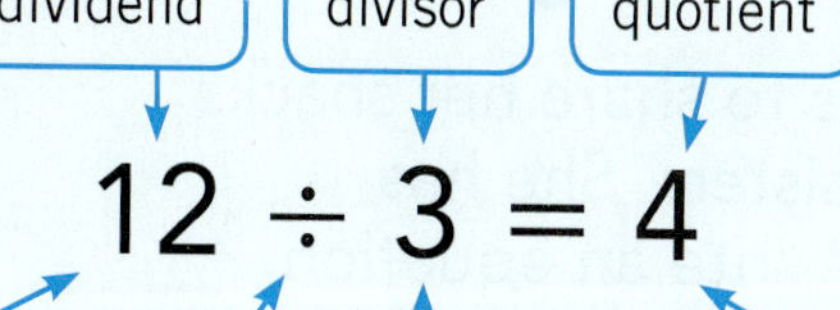

Each group has 4 erasers.

MORE PRACTICE

Divide to share. Find how many in each group. Write a division equation.

1. 8 in all
4 equal groups
_____ in each group
_____ ÷ _____ = _____

2. 14 in all
7 equal groups
_____ in each group
_____ ÷ _____ = _____

3. 16 in all
2 equal groups
_____ in each group
_____ ÷ _____ = _____

4. 12 in all
6 equal groups
_____ in each group
_____ ÷ _____ = _____

5. 15 in all
3 equal groups
_____ in each group
_____ ÷ _____ = _____

6. 24 in all
6 equal groups
_____ in each group
_____ ÷ _____ = _____

HOMEWORK

Write a division equation. Find how many in each group.

1. 24 in all
   4 equal groups
   ____ in each group
   ____ ÷ ____ = ____

2. 14 in all
   7 equal groups
   ____ in each group
   ____ ÷ ____ = ____

3. 16 in all
   4 equal groups
   ____ in each group
   ____ ÷ ____ = ____

Complete each equation.

4. $10 \div 5 =$ ____
5. $18 \div 2 =$ ____
6. $27 \div 3 =$ ____
7. $24 \div 3 =$ ____
8. $20 \div 5 =$ ____
9. $32 \div 8 =$ ____

Problem Solving

10. Kiana wants to share her snacks with her 2 sisters. She has 21 snacks. Write an equation, and tell how many snacks each sister gets.

    ____

11. Preston makes an array of 25 marbles. He says that the number of marbles in each row and each column is the same. Is Preston correct? Explain.

    ____

12. Some numbers can be divided equally into groups in more than one way. Complete the table showing ways to divide 24 into equal groups. Describe any pattern you notice.

    ____
    ____
    ____

Number in All = 24	
Number of Equal Groups	Number in Each Group
3	
4	
6	
8	

Write About It

13. How are the equations $7 \times 4 = 28$ and $28 \div 7 = 4$ related?

    ____
    ____

Name ______________________________ Date ______________

LESSON 4-6

Represent Division by Repeated Subtraction

Here are three ways to find the number of equal groups of 3 in 15.

- You can use repeated subtraction to zero.

$15 - 3 = 12$
$12 - 3 = 9$
$9 - 3 = 6$
$6 - 3 = 3$
$3 - 3 = 0$

Subtract 3 five times.
5 groups of 3 in 15

- You can count back on a number line.

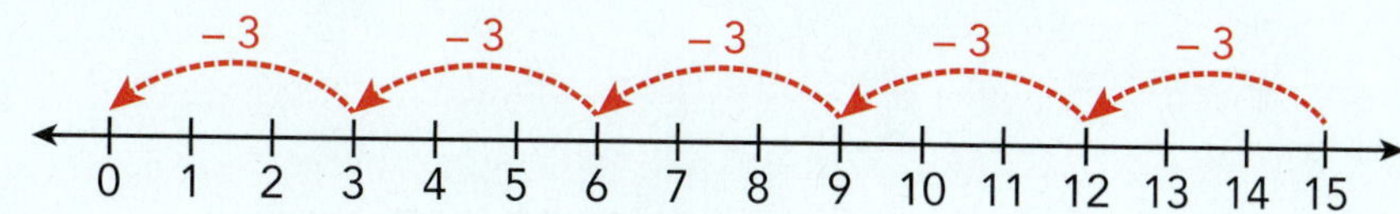

Count back 3 five times.
5 groups of 3 in 15

- You can write a division equation.

$15 \div 3 = 5$

15: number in all
3: number in each group
5: number of equal groups

The equation shows 15 divides into 5 equal groups of 3.
There are 5 groups of 3 in 15.

There are 5 equal groups of 3 in 15.

MORE PRACTICE

Subtract to find how many groups. Complete the equations.

1. 27 in all
9 in each group
27 − 9 = ______
______ − 9 = ______
______ − 9 = ______
______ groups
______ ÷ 9 = ______

2. 10 in all
5 in each group
10 − 5 = ______
______ − 5 = ______
______ groups
______ ÷ 5 = ______

3. 16 in all
4 in each group
16 − 4 = ______
______ − 4 = ______
______ − 4 = ______
______ − 4 = ______
______ groups
______ ÷ 4 = ______

HOMEWORK

Find how many groups. Complete the equations.

1. 18 in all
9 in each group

18 − 9 = ______

______ − 9 = ______

______ groups

______ ÷ 9 = ______

2. 21 in all
7 in each group

21 − 7 = ______

______ − 7 = ______

______ − 7 = ______

______ groups

______ ÷ 7 = ______

3. 9 in all
3 in each group

9 − 3 = ______

______ − 3 = ______

______ − 3 = ______

______ groups

______ ÷ 3 = ______

Solve each equation.

4. 30 ÷ 5 = ______

5. 36 ÷ 6 = ______

6. 42 ÷ 7 = ______

Problem Solving

7. Posters have 4 pins in each. There are 20 pins. Write an equation to represent the situation. How many posters are there?

Equation: ______________________

Answer: ______________________

8. Kaylee is making first-aid kits. She has 24 rolls of tape. She needs to put 3 rolls in each kit. Can she make 10 kits? Explain.

____

____

9. Zach writes these subtractions to solve a problem. What division equation can Zach use to solve the same problem?

____

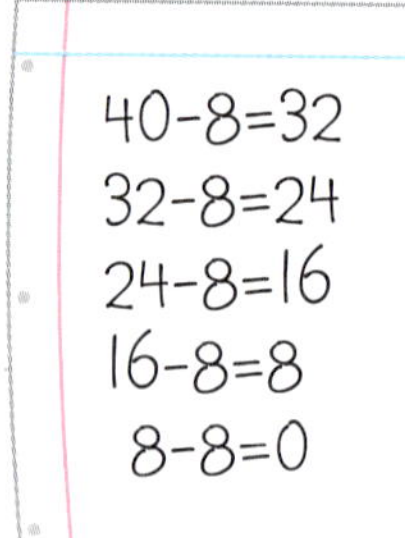

Write About It

10. How is division like subtraction? How is it different?

____

____

Name ______________________ Date ____________

LESSON 4-7

Problem Solving
Write an Equation

When James arranges some pennies, he has 4 rows and 6 columns. How many pennies does James have?

You can write an equation to help find the answer.

♦ Use counters to represent the situation with an array.

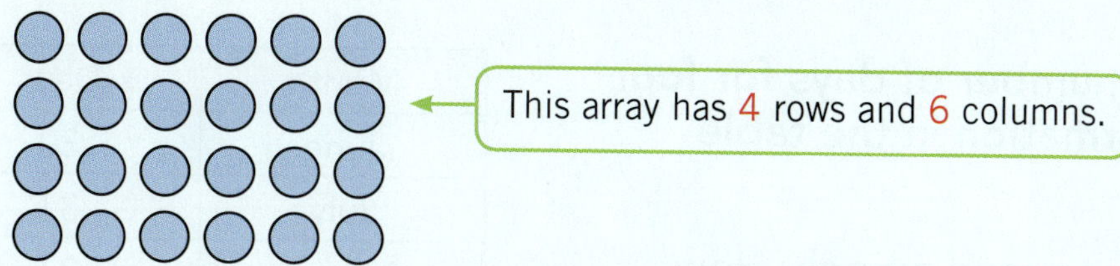

♦ Write an equation to represent the problem.

Let p equal the unknown number of pennies.

The array shows that the number of pennies is equal to 4×6.

$p = 4 \times 6$

♦ Solve the equation to find the answer.

$p = 24$ ← James has 24 pennies in all.

MORE PRACTICE

Justin is playing a game. He puts 5 rows of 4 cards on the table. How many cards does Justin put on the table?

1. Draw an array to represent the situation.

2. Use the array to write an equation.

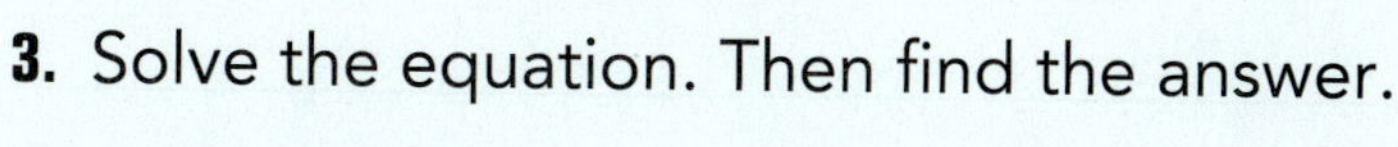

3. Solve the equation. Then find the answer.

____

____

MORE PRACTICE

Grace has 32 candles. She is putting the same number of candles on each of 8 tables. How many candles does Grace put on each table?

4. Write and solve an equation to find the answer.

____

5. Write the answer to the question.

____

The table shows the number of days for four months. Use the information in the table for Exercises 6–8.

Month	Days
June	30
July	31
August	31
September	30

6. Dylan takes 5 days to read a book. How many books can he read during June? Write and solve an equation to find out.

____

7. Arla reads a book in 7 days. Why does she finish reading the same number of books both in June and in August?

____

____

____

8. Kayla and her family go to a lake on 8 weekends during these 4 months. They go the same number of weekends each month. How many weekends a month do they go to the lake?

____

9. Four sisters want to share 36 stickers equally. How many stickers will each sister receive? Explain how to draw a diagram to find the answer.

____

____

____

____

Name ______________________ Date ____________

Problem Solving
Write an Equation

HOMEWORK

David and Nolan are collecting cans of food for a local charity. David puts 40 cans in boxes that hold 8 cans each. Nolan puts 54 cans in boxes that hold 9 cans each. How many boxes in all do both David and Nolan use?

1. What do you need to find first? How can you do that?

____

____

____

2. Write an equation to show how many boxes David uses.

____

3. Solve the equation.

____

4. How many boxes does David use?

____

5. Write an equation to show how many boxes Nolan uses.

____

6. Solve the equation.

____

7. How many boxes does Nolan use?

____

8. Write an equation to find the number of boxes that David and Nolan use in all.

____

9. Solve the equation.

____

10. How many boxes do David and Nolan use together?

____

HOMEWORK

11. Sophia is having a party. She may put 8 chairs at each of 6 tables. But she may also put 6 chairs at each of 8 tables. Which way uses more chairs? Explain.

____

____

____

The model represents the multiplication equation $3 \times 6 = 18$. Use the model for Exercises 12–14.

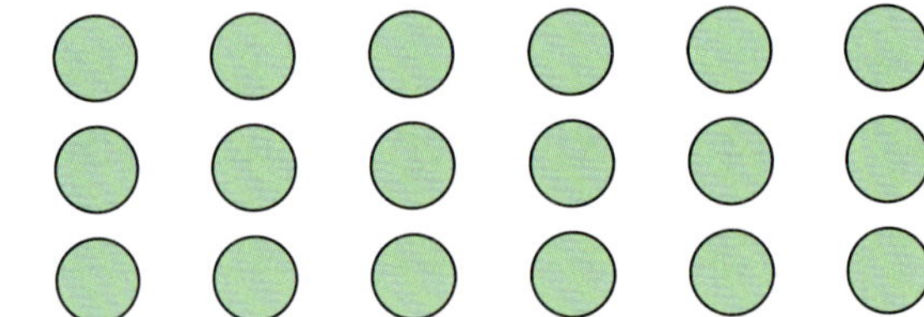

12. Write another multiplication equation with the same factors.

____

13. Write a repeated addition equation for the model.

____

14. Change the model to represent the division $18 \div 3 = 6$. Explain your work.

____

____

____

Write About It

15. Chloe makes 24 sandwiches. She wants to put the same number of sandwiches in each of 3 picnic baskets. Name two strategies Chloe can use to solve her problem. Explain how to use one of the strategies to find the answer.

____

____

____

____

Name ____________________ Date ____________

LESSON 5-1

Multiply by 2

This apple has 5 seed pockets called carpels. Each carpel has 2 seeds. How many seeds are in this apple?

To find the number of seeds, multiply: 5×2.

- There are 5 groups with 2 seeds in each group.

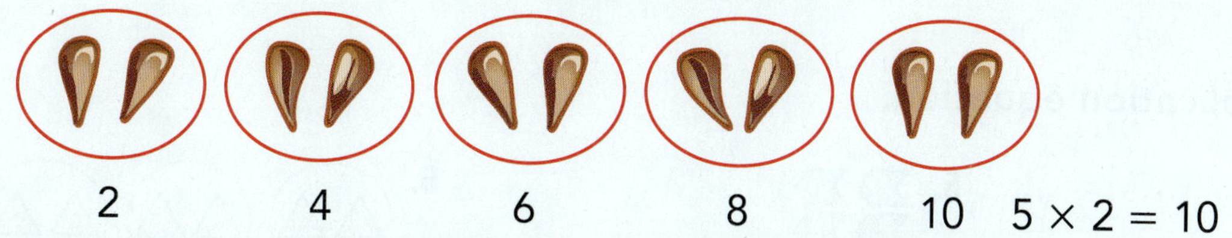

$5 \times 2 = 10$

- Another way to find 5×2 is by using an array. There are 5 rows with 2 circles in each row.

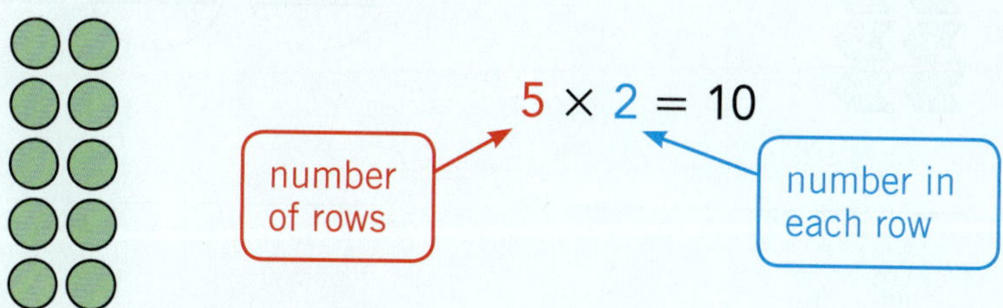

There are 10 seeds in all.

MORE PRACTICE

Find the product.

1.

3 twos = ______

$3 \times 2 =$ ______

2.

7 twos = ______

$7 \times 2 =$ ______

3.

6 twos = ______

$6 \times 2 =$ ______

4.

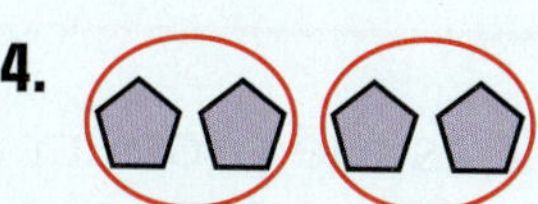

2 twos = ______

$2 \times 2 =$ ______

HOMEWORK

Multiply to find the product.

1. 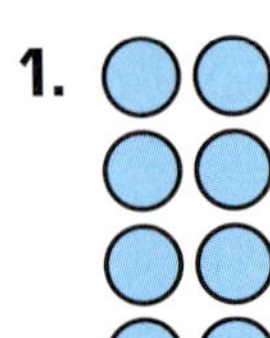

$4 \times 2 =$ ______

2. 

$5 \times 2 =$ ______

3. 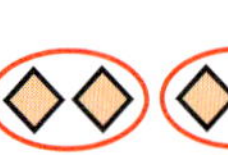 

$8 \times 2 =$ ______

Write a multiplication equation.

4. 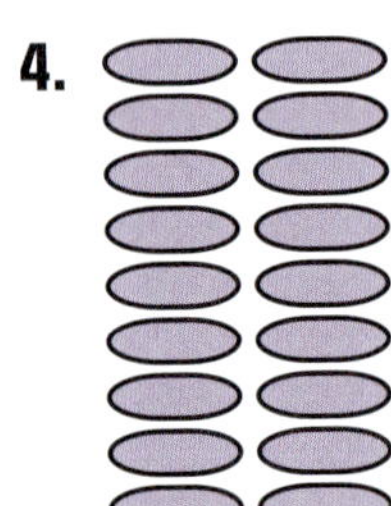

______

5. 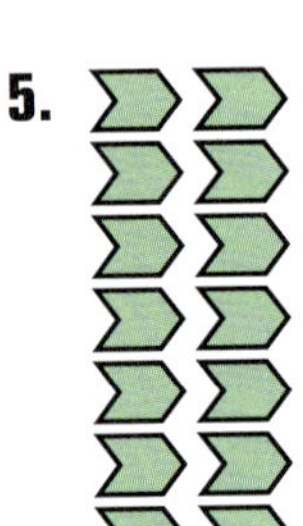

______

6. 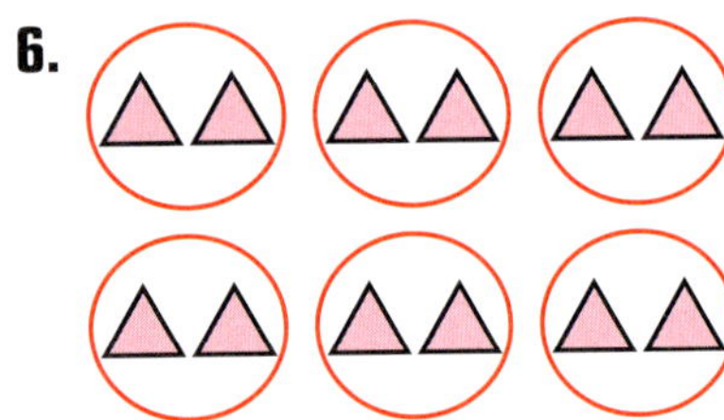

______

Find the product.

7. $\begin{array}{r} 2 \\ \times 0 \\ \hline \end{array}$

8. $\begin{array}{r} 2 \\ \times 8 \\ \hline \end{array}$

9. $\begin{array}{r} 2 \\ \times 1 \\ \hline \end{array}$

10. $\begin{array}{r} 2 \\ \times 4 \\ \hline \end{array}$

11. $\begin{array}{r} 2 \\ \times 10 \\ \hline \end{array}$

12. $\begin{array}{r} 2 \\ \times 5 \\ \hline \end{array}$

Problem Solving

13. Chelsea has 4 pairs of white socks and 2 pairs of black socks. How many socks does Chelsea have?

______

14. A bottle of water costs \$2. If David buys 8 bottles of water, how much money will he spend?

______

Write About It

15. When one factor is 2, is the product always even? Explain.

______

______

Name ______________________ Date ______________

LESSON 5-2

Multiply by 5

Max is buying batteries. There are 5 batteries in each package. How many batteries are in 3 packages?

To find the number of batteries in all, find $3 \times 5 =$ _?_.

- There are 3 groups with 5 batteries in each group.

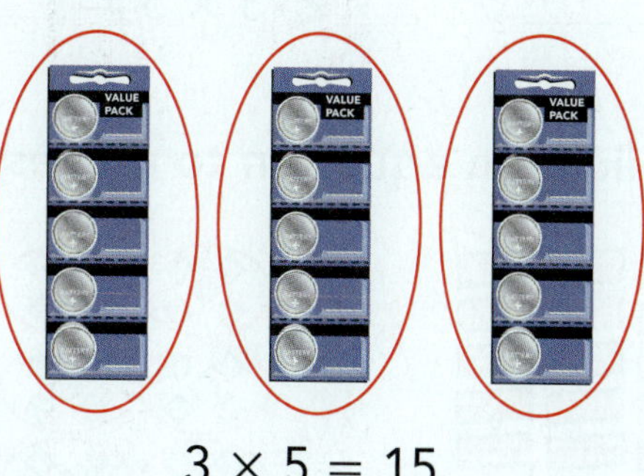

$3 \times 5 = 15$

- Another way to find the product is to skip count by 5s three times.

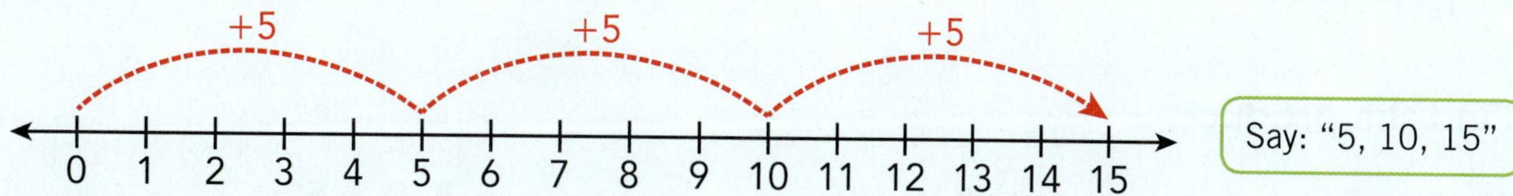

Say: "5, 10, 15"

There are 15 batteries in 3 packages.

MORE PRACTICE

Find the product.

1.

2 fives = ______

$2 \times 5 =$ ______

2.

8 fives = ______

$8 \times 5 =$ ______

3. $0 \times 5 =$ ______ **4.** $7 \times 5 =$ ______ **5.** $1 \times 5 =$ ______ **6.** $9 \times 5 =$ ______

7. $4 \times 5 =$ ______ **8.** $6 \times 5 =$ ______ **9.** $10 \times 5 =$ ______ **10.** $5 \times 5 =$ ______

HOMEWORK

Find the product by skip counting.

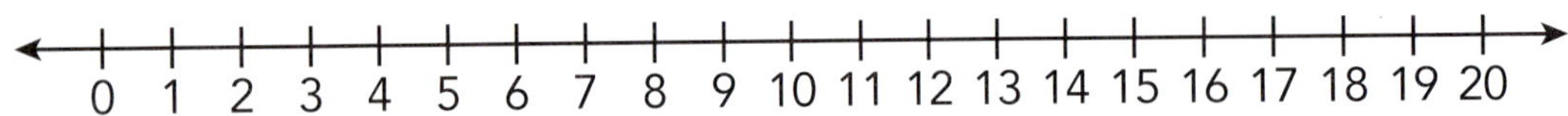

1. 1 × 5 = ______ **2.** 3 × 5 = ______ **3.** 4 × 5 = ______

Write a multiplication equation to represent each model.

4. 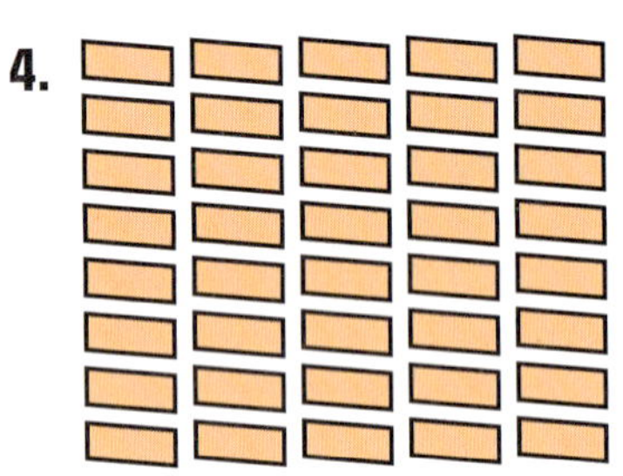

______

5. 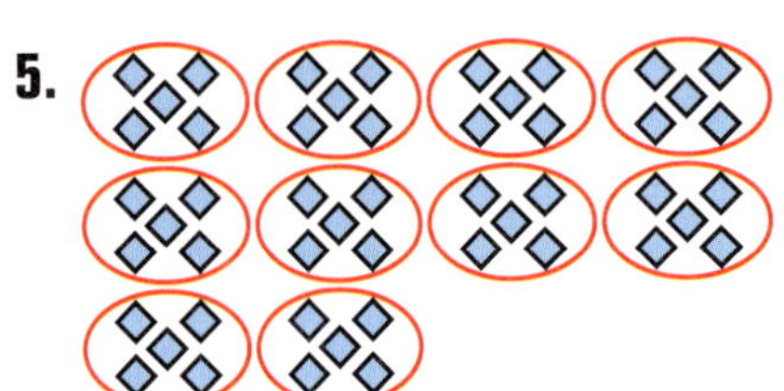

______

6. 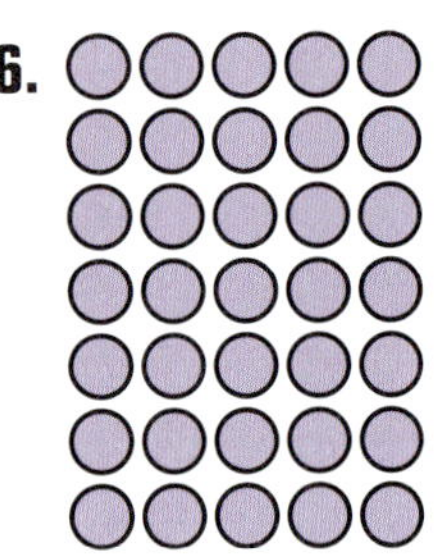

______

Find the product.

7. 5 × 5 = ______ **8.** 9 × 5 = ______ **9.** 0 × 5 = ______

Problem Solving

10. Tristan is making pancakes. He can make 5 pancakes with one batch of batter. How many pancakes can he make with 7 batches of batter? Show your work.

______

______

11. Shannon has 30 pencils. Can she give 4 of her friends 6 pencils and keep 6 for herself? Explain.

______

______

______

Write About It

12. Alex skip counts by 5s from 0 to 50. Explain the pattern Alex sees in odd and even numbers.

______

______

Name ______________________________ Date ______________

LESSON
5-3

Multiply by 9

Each group of volunteers has 9 people. There are 4 groups of volunteers. How many volunteers are there in all?

To find the number of volunteers in all, find 4×9.

- You can make an array with 4 rows of 9 and multiply.

$4 \times 9 = 36$

number of rows → 4; number in each row → 9; product → 36

- You can also skip count by 9s.

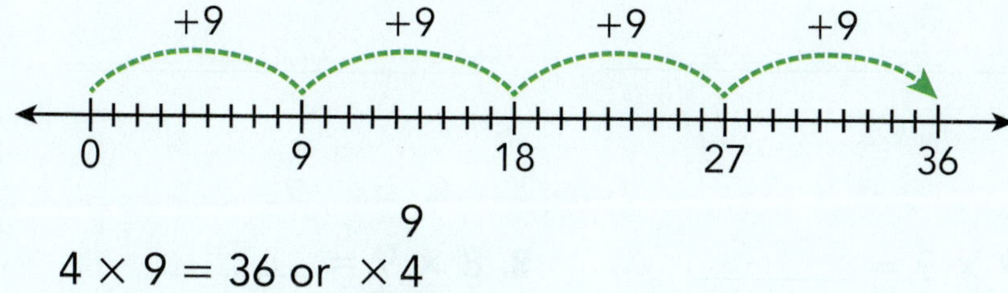

$4 \times 9 = 36$ or $\begin{array}{r} 9 \\ \times 4 \\ \hline 36 \end{array}$

There are 36 volunteers in all.

MORE PRACTICE

Find the product.

1.

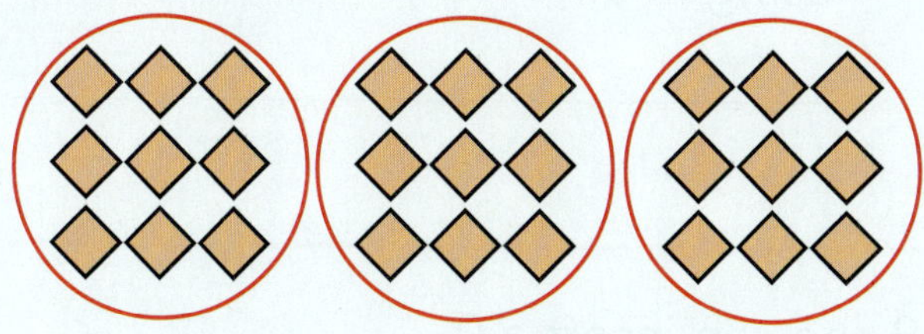

3 nines = ______

$3 \times 9 =$ ______

2.

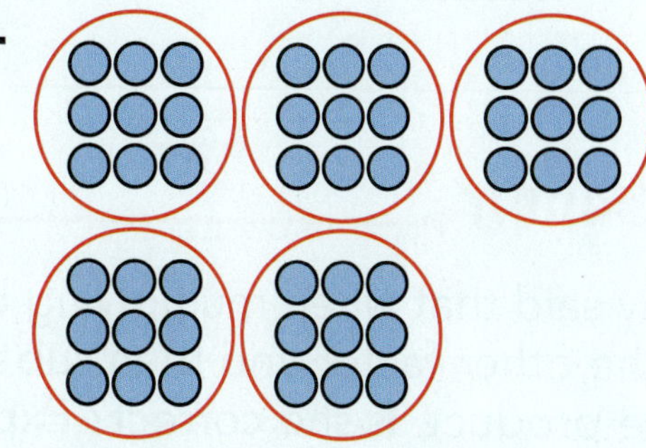

5 nines = ______

$5 \times 9 =$ ______

HOMEWORK

Find the product by skip counting.

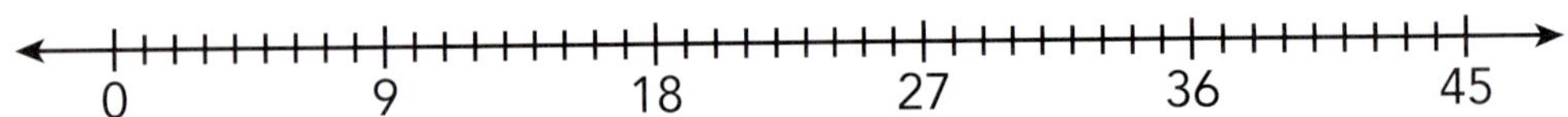

1. $4 \times 9 =$ ______
2. $3 \times 9 =$ ______
3. $2 \times 9 =$ ______

Write a multiplication equation.

4. ______
5. ______
6. ______

Find the product.

7. $0 \times 9 =$ ______
8. $9 \times 9 =$ ______
9. $8 \times 9 =$ ______
10. $5 \times 9 =$ ______
11. $1 \times 9 =$ ______
12. $10 \times 9 =$ ______

Problem Solving

13. Andrew scored 2 goals per week. Mark scored 4 goals per week. How many goals did they score in all in 9 weeks?

______

14. A group of 10 friends are making tile mosaics. Each friend uses 9 tiles. How many tiles are they using in all?

______

Write About It

15. Tammy said that when multiplying by 9 she can insert a 0 after the other factor and then subtract the other factor to get the product. Is she correct? Explain.

______

______

Name ______________________ Date ______________

LESSON 5-4

Multiply by 1 and 0

Jose collects eggs from his chickens. He gets 1 egg from each of 6 chickens on Monday. How many eggs does Jose collect on Monday?

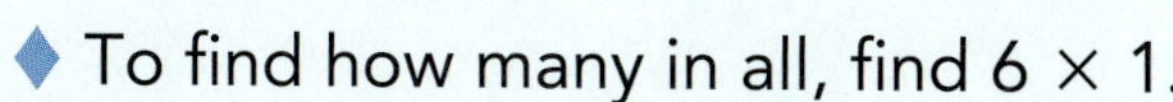

- To find how many in all, find 6 × 1.

  6 × 1 = 6

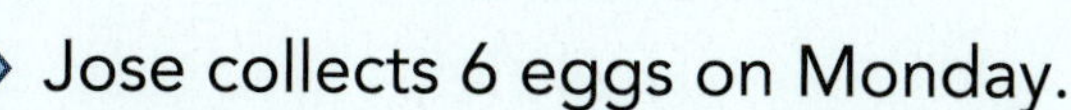

Jose collects 6 eggs on Monday.

On Tuesday, Jose gets 0 eggs from each of his 6 chickens. How many eggs does he collect on Tuesday?

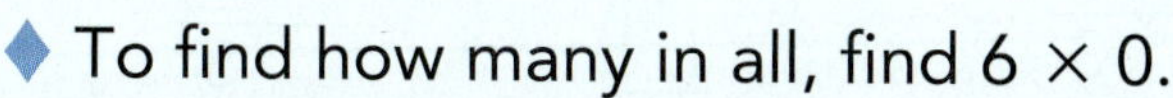

- To find how many in all, find 6 × 0.

  6 × 0 = 0

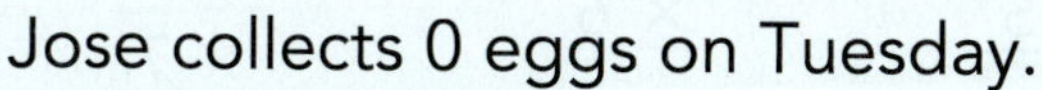

Jose collects 0 eggs on Tuesday.

Identity Property of Multiplication

The product of 1 and a number is the same as that number.

Zero Property of Multiplication

The product of 0 and a number is 0.

MORE PRACTICE

Find the product.

1. 2 × 0 = ______ **2.** 7 × 0 = ______ **3.** 9 × 1 = ______

4. 8 × 0 = ______ **5.** 4 × 1 = ______ **6.** 0 × 1 = ______

7. How can you use repeated addition to explain the Zero Property of Multiplication?

____

____

HOMEWORK

Write a multiplication equation.

1. 4 groups of 0 ______

2. 9 groups of 1 ______

Find the product.

3. $10 \times 1 =$ ______

4. $5 \times 0 =$ ______

5. $2 \times 0 =$ ______

Complete each multiplication.

6. $\square \times 1 = 0$

7. $1 \times \square = 1$

8. $1 \times 2 = \square$

9. $\square \times 3 = 3$

10. $1 \times 4 = \square$

11. $1 \times \square = 5$

12. $\square \times 2 = 0$

13. $\square \times 3 = 0$

14. $0 \times 4 = \square$

15. $1 \times 5 = \square$

16. $1 \times 6 = \square$

17. $\square \times 7 = 0$

Problem Solving

18. Mona needs a pair of pants and a shirt for each day of her 9-day trip. Mona has packed 7 shirts and 7 pants so far. How many more of each does she need to pack?

______

19. Todd has 7 shells that he collected on his last vacation. He wants to put each shell in its own box. How many boxes will Todd need?

______

Write About It

20. Marcus says that 0 multiplied by any number is 0, so $0 \times 1 = 0$. Jackson says that any number multiplied by 1 is that number, so $0 \times 1 = 1$. Who is correct? Explain.

______

______

Name ______________________ Date ______________

LESSON 5-5

Multiply by 10

Decapods are animals with 10 legs.

How many legs are on 5 decapods?

To find how many legs, find 5 × 10.

- There are 5 groups of 10. Skip count by 10s five times.

  10, 20, 30, 40, 50

- You can also use an array to find the product. There are 5 rows with 10 objects in each row. Multiply.

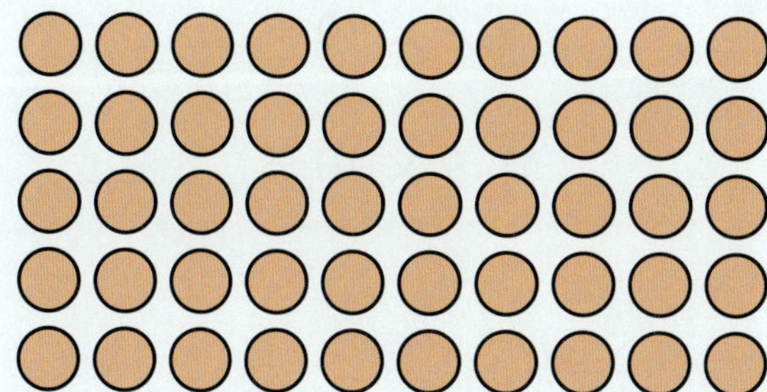

$5 \times 10 = 50$ or $\begin{array}{r} 10 \\ \times\ 5 \\ \hline 50 \end{array}$

There are 50 legs on 5 decapods.

MORE PRACTICE

Find the product.

1.

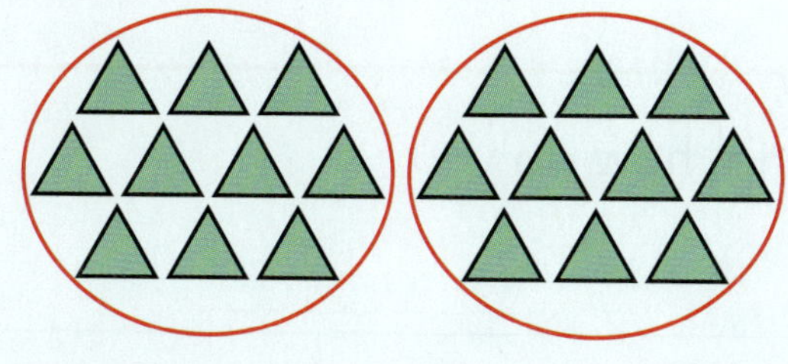

2 tens = ______

2 × 10 = ______

2.

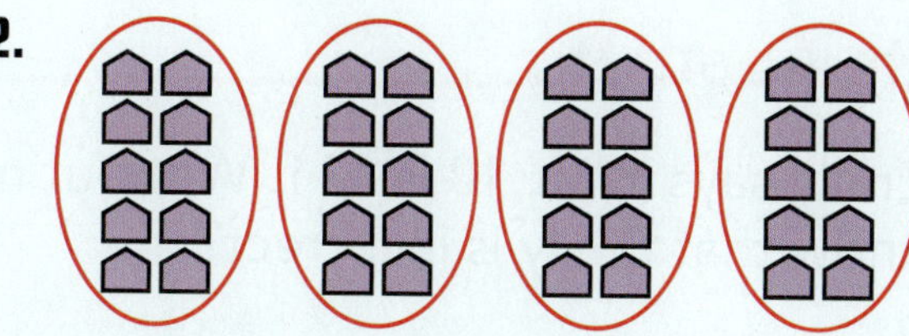

4 tens = ______

4 × 10 = ______

HOMEWORK

Multiply to find the product.

1.

$2 \times 10 =$ ______

2. 

$8 \times 10 =$ ______

3. 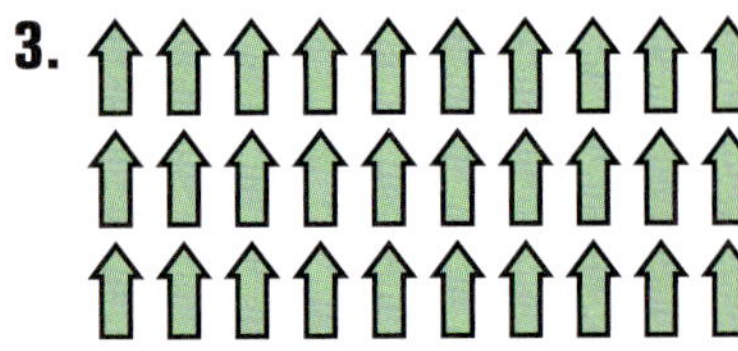

$3 \times 10 =$ ______

Skip count and write a multiplication equation.

4. 5 groups of 10

______

______

5. 7 groups of 10

______

______

Find the product.

6. $1 \times 10 =$ ______
7. $10 \times 10 =$ ______
8. $6 \times 10 =$ ______
9. $4 \times 10 =$ ______
10. $3 \times 10 =$ ______
11. $9 \times 10 =$ ______

Problem Solving

12. Ricardo is filling ice trays. Each ice tray holds 10 ice cubes. He fills 3 ice trays on Monday and 3 more trays on Tuesday. How many ice cubes will Ricardo have in all?

______

13. In Tonya's garden there are 3 rows of tomatoes, 4 rows of beans, and 1 row of peas. There are 10 plants in each row. How many plants are there in all?

______

Write About It

14. Emily says 11×10 is 111. Without multiplying, how do you know that Emily is incorrect?

______

______

Name ______________________ Date ______________

LESSON 5-6

Find Patterns in the Multiplication Table

Look at the 5s and 10s columns.

×	0	1	2	3	4	5	6	7	8	9	10
0	0	0	0	0	0	0	0	0	0	0	0
1	0	1	2	3	4	5	6	7	8	9	10
2	0	2	4	6	8	10	12	14	16	18	20
3	0	3	6	9	12	15	18	21	24	27	30
4	0	4	8	12	16	20	24	28	32	36	40
5	0	5	10	15	20	25	30	35	40	45	50
6	0	6	12	18	24	30	36	42	48	54	60
7	0	7	14	21	28	35	42	49	56	63	70
8	0	8	16	24	32	40	48	56	64	72	80
9	0	9	18	27	36	45	54	63	72	81	90
10	0	10	20	30	40	50	60	70	80	90	100

- All the products in the 5s column have a 0 or 5 in the ones place.
- All the products in the 10s column have a 0 in the ones place.
- The products in the 10s column are double the products in the 5s column.
- The products in the 5s column change between even and odd, but all the products in the 10s column are even.

Can you find other patterns?

MORE PRACTICE

Look at the products for the fact. Write *even, odd,* or *both.*

1. 7s ________ **2.** 1s ________ **3.** 10s ________

4. Patrick said that the product of any number and 4 is always double the product of that number and 2. Is Patrick correct? Explain.

____

____

HOMEWORK

Problem Solving

Use the multiplication table for Exercises 1–4.

1. Shade the diagonal from 0 to 100. What do you notice about the products you shaded?

______

______

______

______

______

×	0	1	2	3	4	5	6	7	8	9	10
0	0	0	0	0	0	0	0	0	0	0	0
1	0	1	2	3	4	5	6	7	8	9	10
2	0	2	4	6	8	10	12	14	16	18	20
3	0	3	6	9	12	15	18	21	24	27	30
4	0	4	8	12	16	20	24	28	32	36	40
5	0	5	10	15	20	25	30	35	40	45	50
6	0	6	12	18	24	30	36	42	48	54	60
7	0	7	14	21	28	35	42	49	56	63	70
8	0	8	16	24	32	40	48	56	64	72	80
9	0	9	18	27	36	45	54	63	72	81	90
10	0	10	20	30	40	50	60	70	80	90	100

2. Choose one of the products you colored. What do you notice about the product in the box just below it and the product in the box to its right?

______

______

______

3. Go down the 7s column and across the 6s row. Shade where they meet. Then go down the 6s column and across the 7s row. Shade where they meet. Describe what you see. Explain why.

______

______

______

Write About It

4. How does the multiplication table demonstrate the Identity Property of Multiplication?

______

______

Name ______________________ Date ______________

LESSON 5-7

Solve for Unknowns

Grace and Cara are decorating picture frames. There are 14 frames. Each girl should decorate the same number. How many frames should each girl decorate?

To find the number of frames each girl should decorate, think: What number times 2 equals 14?

You must find the unknown number. You can write an equation with the unknown on either the left or the right side of the equal sign.

?	×	2	=	14
number in each group		number of groups		total
7	×	2	=	14

14	=	?	×	2
total		number in each group		number of groups
14	=	7	×	2

The unknown number is 7.

Grace and Cara should each decorate 7 frames.

MORE PRACTICE

Find the unknown number.

1. ______ × 3 = 9

2. 3 × ______ = 15

3. 4 × 4 = ______

4. 20 = ______ × 4

5. ______ × 1 = 9

6. ______ = 5 × 6

7. 0 × 5 = ______

8. 20 = 2 × ______

9. ______ × 9 = 27

HOMEWORK

Find the unknown number.

1. $0 = \_\_\_\_ \times 9$
2. $\_\_\_\_ \times 5 = 45$
3. $4 \times 3 = \_\_\_\_$
4. $5 \times \_\_\_\_ = 20$
5. $\_\_\_\_ = 4 \times 7$
6. $\_\_\_\_ \times 8 = 48$
7. $2 \times 5 = \_\_\_\_$
8. $4 \times \_\_\_\_ = 8$
9. $27 = \_\_\_\_ \times 9$

Problem Solving

10. Abby baked bread. She used 3 cups of flour for each loaf. How many loaves did she bake if she used 12 cups of flour?

11. Nolan has 4 sets of water colors. Each set has 8 colors. How many total colors would he have if he bought 2 more sets?

12. An animal shelter has 10 cats. Each day 20 cans of food are used for the cats. If each cat eats the same amount of food, how many cans of food does each cat eat in a day?

13. Laura has 27 beads in all. Each bead is blue, red, or yellow. Laura has the same number of each color. How many blue beads does she have? Explain.

Write About It

14. Describe how to use skip counting to find the unknown in $\underline{?} \times 5 = 35$. How could you check your answer?

Name ______________________________ Date ______________

LESSON 5-8

Problem Solving
Use a Model

There are 8 teams in a tennis tournament. Each team has 2 players. How many tennis players are there in the tournament?

To find the number of players, use a model to multiply: $8 \times 2 =$? .

Models include arrays, making equal groups, number lines, and bar models. Any of these models can be used to find the product.

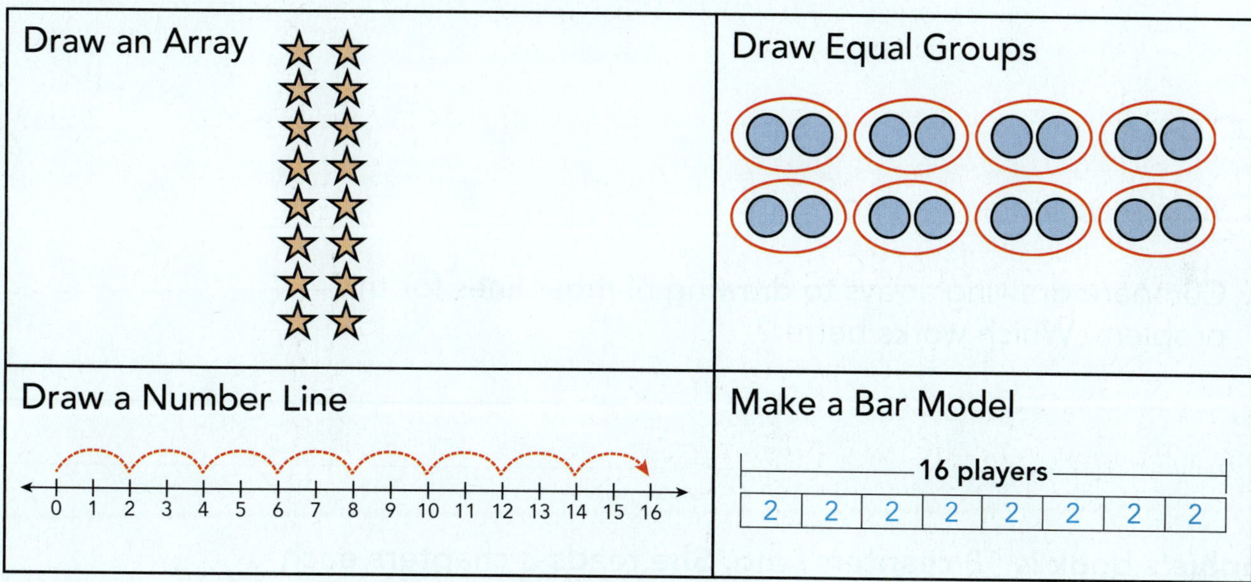

There are 16 tennis players in the tournament.

MORE PRACTICE

In a game, each player receives 5 cards. There are 3 people playing. Use this information for Exercises 1–3.

1. Write an equation to find the number of cards being used. __________

2. Make an array to represent your equation.

3. There are __________ cards being used.

MORE PRACTICE

Adam buys 6 bags of 9 apples. Mark buys 7 bags of 8 plums. Use this information for Exercises 4–7.

4. Write two equations to show how many pieces of fruit each boy buys. ______________________________

5. Draw two arrays to represent your equations.

6. Who buys more pieces of fruit? __________

7. Compare drawing arrays to drawing number lines for this problem. Which works better?

____

____

Sophie's book is 18 chapters long. She reads 3 chapters each day. Use this information for Exercises 8–11.

8. Write an equation you can use to find the number of days it will take Sophie to read the book. __________

9. Complete the number line to represent your equation.

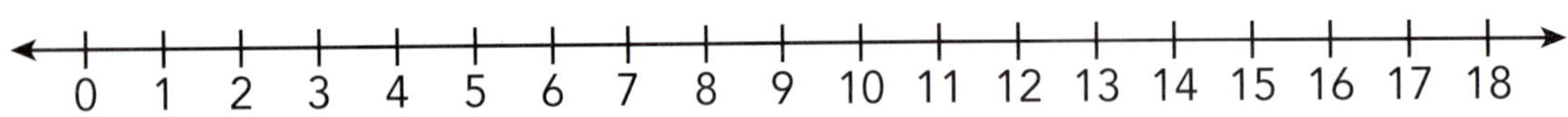

10. It will take ______ days for Sophie to read the book.

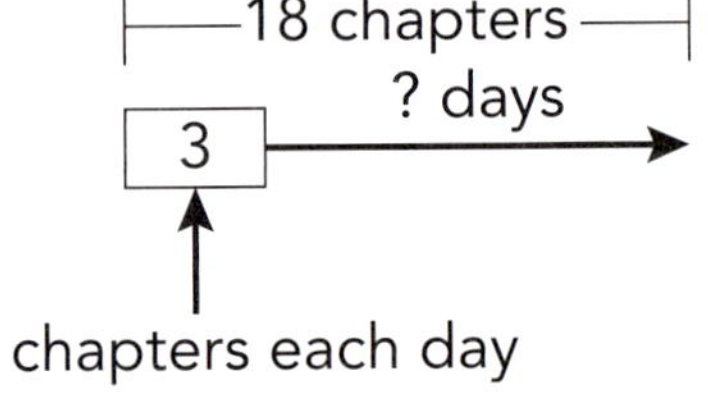

11. Sophie made this bar model to find how many days it would take her to read this book. How are both models useful for this problem?

____

____

Name ______________________ Date ____________

Problem Solving
Use a Model

HOMEWORK

Dalton is given 7 packs of stickers. Each pack contains 5 stickers. Use this information for Exercises 1–5.

1. Write an equation to find how many stickers Dalton is given. ______________________

2. Make an array to represent your equation.

3. Complete the number line to show the number of stickers that Dalton is given.

4. How many stickers is Dalton given? ____________

5. Which model was better for finding the number of stickers that Dalton is given? Explain your answer.

____

____

____

Serenity buys 80 colored markers for drawings. Each box has 10 markers. Use this information for Exercises 6–9.

6. Write an equation to find the number of boxes of markers that Serenity buys. ____________

HOMEWORK

7. Draw a bar model to represent your equation.

8. Do you think a bar model is the best model for this problem? Explain why or why not.

9. Serenity buys _____ boxes of markers.

Think about the problems you have solved in this lesson.

10. Does the size of the factors matter when you decide which model to use? Circle one. Yes No

11. If both factors are large, which models would you not choose? Which ones would you choose? Why?

12. If both factors are small, which models would you not choose? Which models would you choose? Why?

Write About It

13. Which two models did you find the best models to use for missing factors?

Name ______________________ Date ______________

LESSON 6-1

Break Apart to Multiply

Use the Distributive Property to find 5×4.

Distributive Property

Multiplying a number by a sum is the same as multiplying the number by each addend of the sum and then adding the products.

Break apart one factor. Then multiply by the other factor.

- Rename 4 as a sum. $5 \times 4 = ?$
  $5 \times (2 + 2) = ?$

- Use the Distributive Property to rewrite $5 \times (2 + 2)$. $(5 \times 2) + (5 \times 2) = ?$

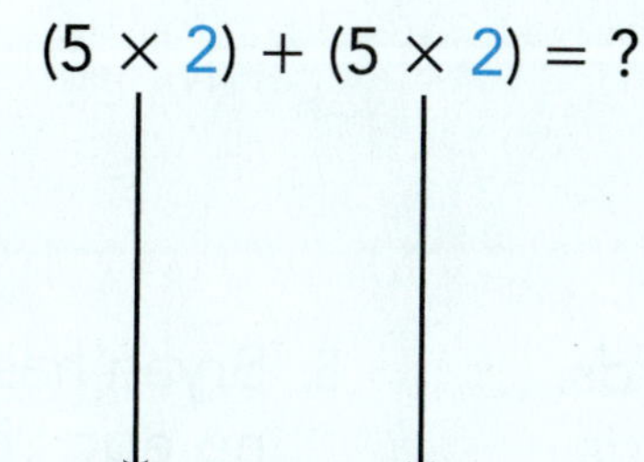

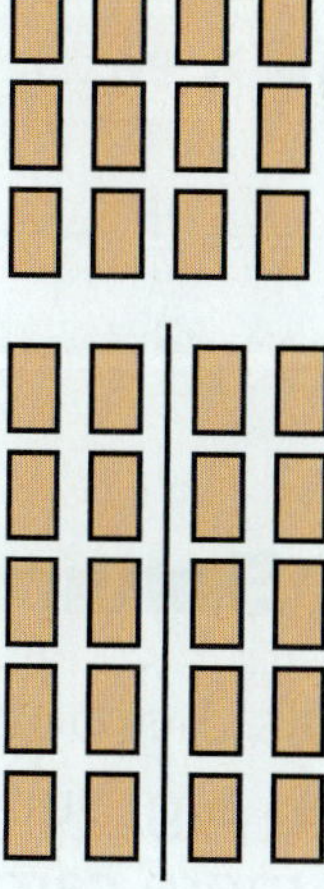

- Find both products. $10 + 10 = ?$
- Find the sum. $10 + 10 = 20$

So $5 \times 4 = 20$.

MORE PRACTICE

Use the Distributive Property to find the product.

1. $2 \times 6 = ?$

$2 \times (3 +$ ______ $) = ?$

$(2 \times$ ______ $) + ($ ______ $\times 3) = ?$

______ + ______ = ______

2. $5 \times 5 = ?$

$5 \times (3 +$ ______ $) = ?$

$(5 \times$ ______ $) + ($ ______ $\times 2) = ?$

______ + ______ = ______

HOMEWORK

Find the product.

1. $5 \times 6 = ?$

$\_\_\_ \times (\_\_\_ + 2) = ?$

$(\_\_\_ \times \_\_\_) + (\_\_\_ \times \_\_\_) = ?$

$\_\_\_ + \_\_\_ = \_\_\_$

2. $3 \times 7 = ?$

$\_\_\_ \times (5 + \_\_\_) = ?$

$(\_\_\_ \times \_\_\_) + (\_\_\_ \times \_\_\_) = ?$

$\_\_\_ + \_\_\_ = \_\_\_$

3.

$3 \times 6 = (3 \times \_\_\_) + (3 \times \_\_\_)$

$= \_\_\_ + \_\_\_$

$= \_\_\_$

4. 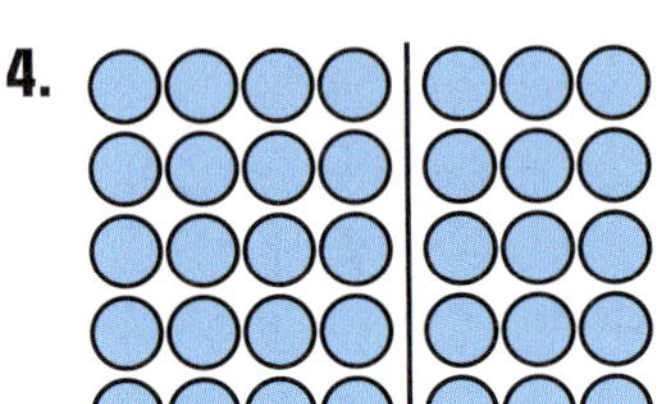

$5 \times 7 = (5 \times \_\_\_) + (5 \times \_\_\_)$

$= \_\_\_ + \_\_\_$

$= \_\_\_$

Problem Solving

5. Megan has 3 groups of 6 cards. Tiffany has 6 groups of 3 cards. Who has more cards? Explain.

____

____

6. Bryan has 3 egg cartons. There are no eggs in each carton. How many eggs are there in all? Explain.

____

____

Write About It

7. What is the error in this problem? Correct the error.

$(8 \times 6) \longrightarrow 8 \times (5 + 1) = ?$

$(8 \times 5) + (1 \times 5) = ?$

$40 + 5 = 45$

____

____

Name ______________________ Date ______________

LESSON 6-2

Multiply by 3

Austin has 6 packages of light bulbs. Each package has 3 light bulbs. How many light bulbs does Austin have in all?

To find how many light bulbs in all, find 6×3.

- There are 6 groups of 3.

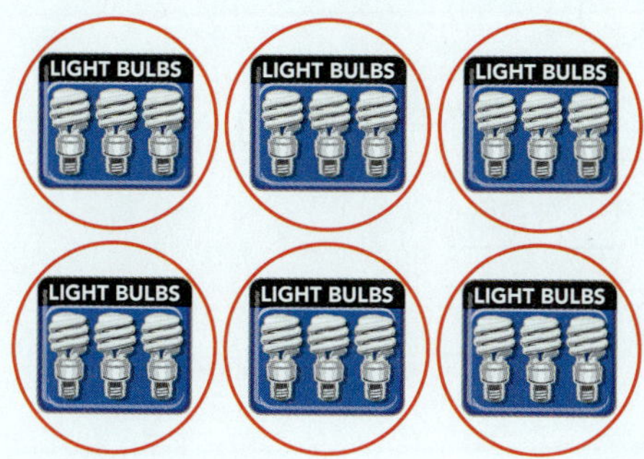

$6 \times 3 = 18$

- You can also use the Distributive Property. Break apart 3 as the sum of 2 and 1.

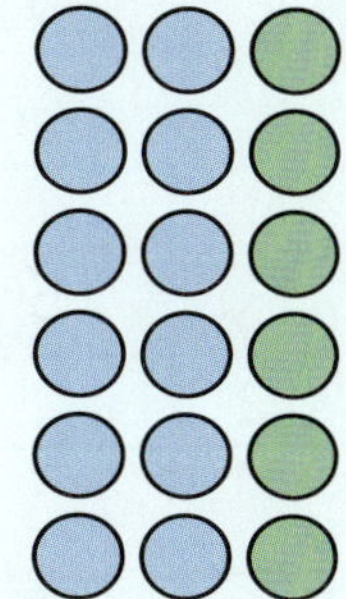

$$\begin{aligned} 6 \times 3 &= 6 \times (2 + 1) \\ &= (6 \times 2) + (6 + 1) \\ &= 12 + 6 \\ &= 18 \end{aligned}$$

Austin has 18 light bulbs in all.

MORE PRACTICE

Find the product.

1.

7 threes = ______

$7 \times 3 =$ ______

2.

5 threes = ______

$5 \times 3 =$ ______

3.

4 threes = ______

$4 \times 3 =$ ______

4. Zoe buys 2 cans of tennis balls. Each can contains 3 tennis balls. Faith buys 3 more cans of tennis balls than Zoe. How many tennis balls does Faith buy? ______

HOMEWORK

Find each product.

1. 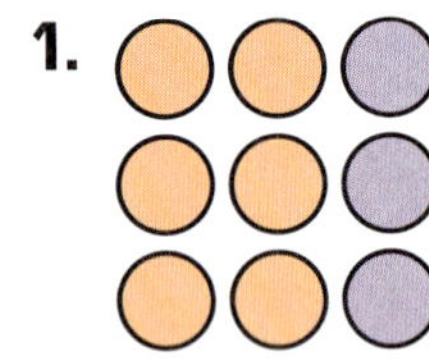

$4 \times 3 = (4 \times 2) + (4 \times 1)$

$4 \times 2 =$ ______

$4 \times 1 =$ ______

$4 \times 3 =$ ______

2. 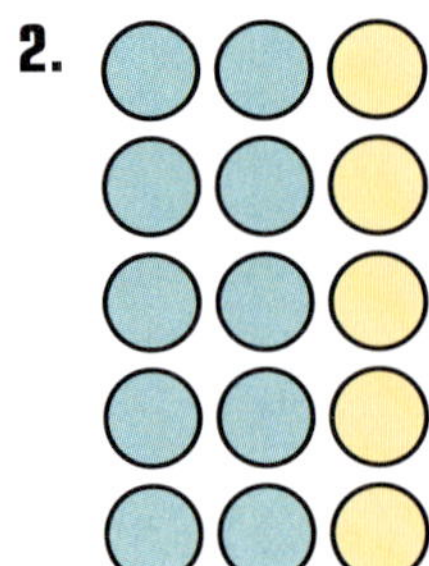

$5 \times 3 = (5 \times 2) + (5 \times 1)$

$5 \times 2 =$ ______

$5 \times 1 =$ ______

$5 \times 3 =$ ______

3. $9 \times 3 =$ ______

4. $8 \times 3 =$ ______

5. $3 \times 3 =$ ______

6. $2 \times 3 =$ ______

7. $7 \times 3 =$ ______

8. $1 \times 3 =$ ______

9. $6 \times 3 =$ ______

10. $0 \times 3 =$ ______

11. $10 \times 3 =$ ______

Problem Solving

12. Each ride at a fair costs $3. Kaleb goes on 4 rides. How much money does Kaleb spend on the rides? ______

13. Braden jogs 3 miles each day. A week is 7 days. How many miles does Braden run in 1 week? ______

Write About It

14. Explain how knowing the product of 3×3 can help you to find the product of 6×3.

______

______

Name ______________________ Date ______________

LESSON 6-3

Multiply by 4

Laurel has 6 packages of bottled water. Each package contains 4 bottles. How many bottles of water does Laurel have?

To find the number of bottles in all, multiply: $6 \times 4 = \underline{?}$.

- There are 6 groups with 4 bottles in each group.
  - You can break the 4 into 2 groups of 2.
  - Multiply: $6 \times 4 = (6 \times 2) + (6 \times 2)$
  - Then add: $12 + 12 = 24$

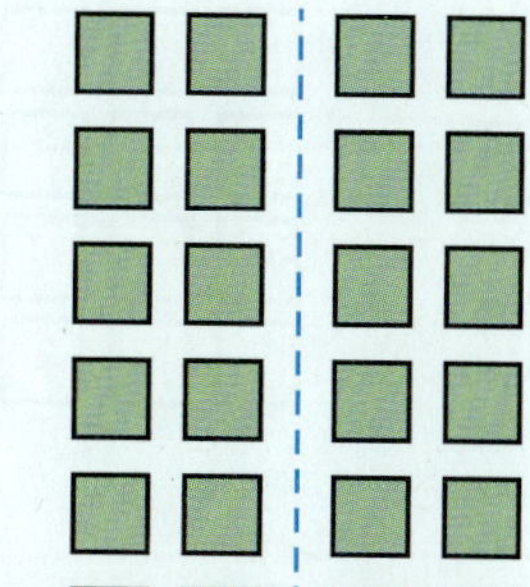

$6 \times 2 = 12$ $6 \times 2 = 12$

- Another way to find the product is to skip count by 4s. Count by 4s six times: 4, 8, 12, 16, 20, 24.

  So $6 \times 4 = 24$.

Laurel has 24 bottles of water.

MORE PRACTICE

Find the product.

1.

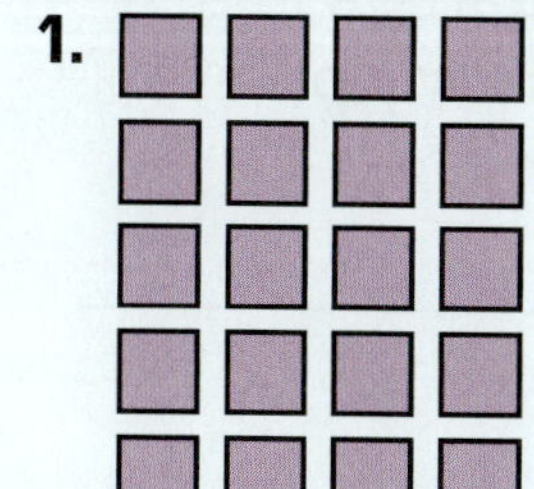

5 fours = ______

$5 \times 4 =$ ______

2.

3 fours = ______

$3 \times 4 =$ ______

3.

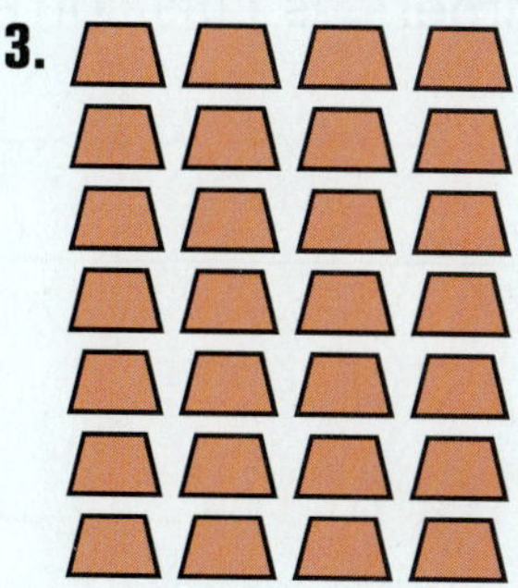

7 fours = ______

$7 \times 4 =$ ______

HOMEWORK

Shade the array to break apart the 4s fact. Find the product.

To multiply by 4, think of a 2s fact and then double it.

1. 

$4 \times 4 =$ ______

2. $7 \times 4 =$ ______

3. $8 \times 4 =$ ______

Find the product.

4. $3 \times 4 =$ ______ **5.** $6 \times 4 =$ ______ **6.** $9 \times 4 =$ ______ **7.** $1 \times 4 =$ ______

8. 4×0 **9.** 4×2 **10.** 4×5 **11.** 4×10 **12.** 4×9 **13.** 4×7

Problem Solving

14. There are 2 rows of 4 drummers in the band. Luis said there are 6 drummers. Is Luis correct? Explain.

______

______

15. The Beagles scored 7 points in each quarter of their football game. There are 4 quarters in a football game. How many points did the Beagles score?

______

Write About It

16. Explain how to use 6×2 to find the product of 6×4. Include the product in your explanation.

______

______

Name ______________________ Date ______________

LESSON
6-4

Multiply by 6

A touchdown is worth 6 points. The Tigers score 3 touchdowns. How many points do the Tigers score in all?

To find how many points in all, multiply: $3 \times 6 = \underline{?}$ or $\begin{array}{r} 6 \\ \times\ 3 \\ \hline \end{array}$.

- You can use a 5s fact and a 1s fact and add the products.

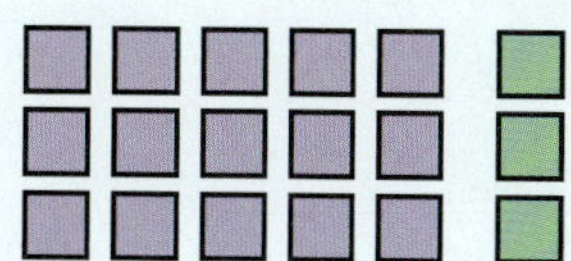

5 columns of 3 → 3 × 5 = 15

1 column of 3 → 3 × 1 = 3

Add: 15 + 3 = 18.

- You can also use a 3s fact and then double it.

3 columns of 3 → 3 × 3 = 9

3 columns of 3 → 3 × 3 = 9

Add: 9 + 9 = 18.

So 3 × 6 = 18.

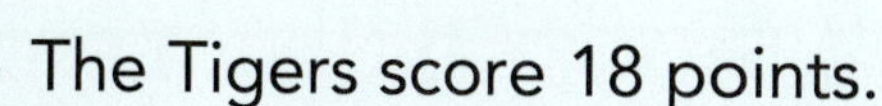

The Tigers score 18 points.

MORE PRACTICE

Shade the array to match the facts. Then find the product.

1. 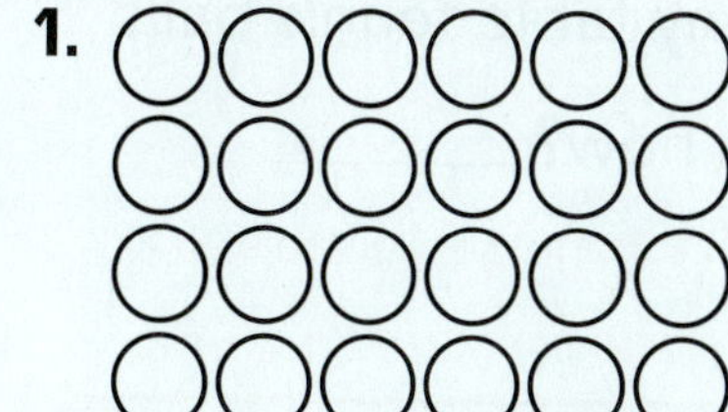

4 × 5 = ______

4 × 1 = ______

4 × 6 = ______

2. 

5 × 5 = ______

5 × 1 = ______

5 × 6 = ______

3. 

8 × 3 = ______

8 × 6 = ______

HOMEWORK

Shade the array to match the facts. Then find the product.

1. 

$6 \times 5 =$ ______

$6 \times 1 =$ ______

$6 \times 6 =$ ______

2. $7 \times 3 =$ ______

$7 \times 6 =$ ______

3. $2 \times 3 =$ ______

$2 \times 6 =$ ______

Find the product.

4. $9 \times 6 =$ ______

5. $3 \times 6 =$ ______

6. $1 \times 6 =$ ______

7. $10 \times 6 =$ ______

8. 6×4

9. 6×0

10. 6×3

11. 6×5

12. 6×8

13. 6×7

Problem Solving

14. Seth set up 8 rows of chairs that have 3 chairs in each row. Then he set up the same number of chairs in 4 rows. How many chairs are in each row? ______

15. Ellison buys 3 packs of table tennis balls. Each pack contains 6 balls. She already has 4 table tennis balls. How many table tennis balls does she have now? ______

Write About It

16. Maddie writes $6 + 6 + 6 + 6 + 6 = 4 \times 6$. Is Maddie's equation correct? Explain your answer.

______

______

Name ______________________ Date ______________

LESSON 6-5

Multiply by 7

David starts a project that will take 6 weeks. There are 7 days in a week. How many days will David's project take?

To find how many days David's project will take, find 6×7.

You can use a 5s fact and a 2s fact.

- Make an array of 6 rows with 7 in each row.
- Break apart the array.

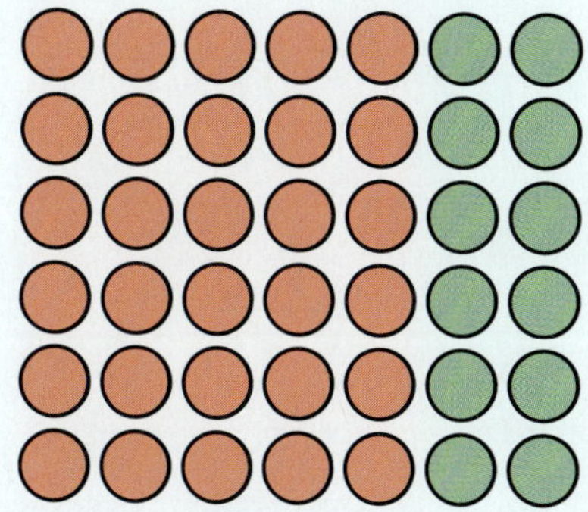

$6 \times 5 = 30$

$6 \times 2 = 12$

- Add: $30 + 12 = 42$.

So $6 \times 7 = 42$.

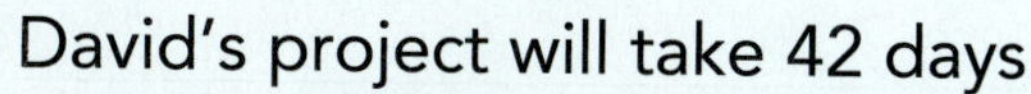

David's project will take 42 days.

MORE PRACTICE

Find the product.

1.

$4 \times 7 =$ ______

2.

$3 \times 7 =$ ______

3.

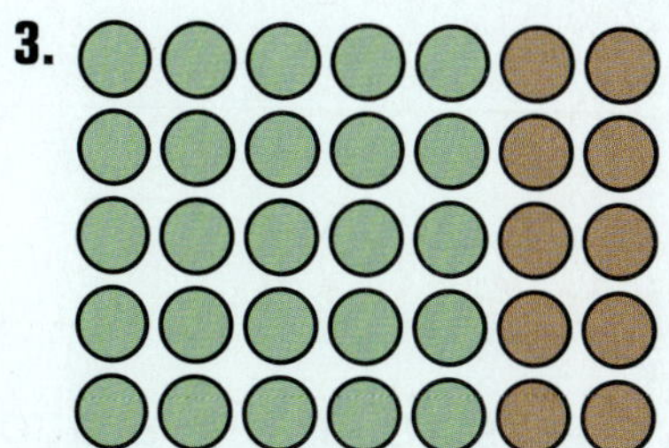

$5 \times 7 =$ ______

4. $\begin{array}{r} 7 \\ \times\ 8 \\ \hline \end{array}$

5. $\begin{array}{r} 7 \\ \times\ 9 \\ \hline \end{array}$

6. $\begin{array}{r} 7 \\ \times\ 0 \\ \hline \end{array}$

7. $\begin{array}{r} 7 \\ \times\ 7 \\ \hline \end{array}$

HOMEWORK

Find the product.

1. $2 \times 7 =$ ______

2. $1 \times 7 =$ ______

3. $6 \times 7 =$ ______

4. $4 \times 7 =$ ______

5. $3 \times 7 =$ ______

6. $0 \times 7 =$ ______

7. $\begin{array}{r} 7 \\ \times\ 8 \\ \hline \end{array}$

8. $\begin{array}{r} 7 \\ \times\ 10 \\ \hline \end{array}$

9. $\begin{array}{r} 7 \\ \times\ 7 \\ \hline \end{array}$

10. $\begin{array}{r} 7 \\ \times\ 6 \\ \hline \end{array}$

Problem Solving

11. A race has 4 heats. Each heat will have 7 runners. How many runners will compete?

______

12. Each baseball cap costs $7. How much money will 8 baseball caps cost?

______

13. Rylee writes 7 pages in her journal each week. She has already filled 42 pages in her journal. How many pages will she have filled in 3 more weeks?

______

14. It takes Colton 15 minutes to walk to the park. Each lap around the park takes 7 minutes. How many minutes will it take Colton to walk to the park and then walk 6 laps?

______

Write About It

15. Ava is going on vacation for 17 days. She says her vacation will last between 2 and 3 weeks. There are 7 days in a week. Is Ava correct? Explain.

______

______

Name ______________________ Date __________

LESSON 6-6

Multiply by 8

Multiply: $4 \times 8 = \underline{?}$

- You can use an array with 4 rows and 8 in each row.

4 rows of 8

$4 \times 8 = 32$

- You can also use a multiplication fact for 4 and then double it.

4 rows of 4

$4 \times 4 = 16$

4 rows of 4

$4 \times 4 = 16$

Add the partial products: $16 + 16 = 32$.

So $4 \times 8 = 32$.

MORE PRACTICE

Find the product.

1.

$5 \times 8 =$ ______

2.

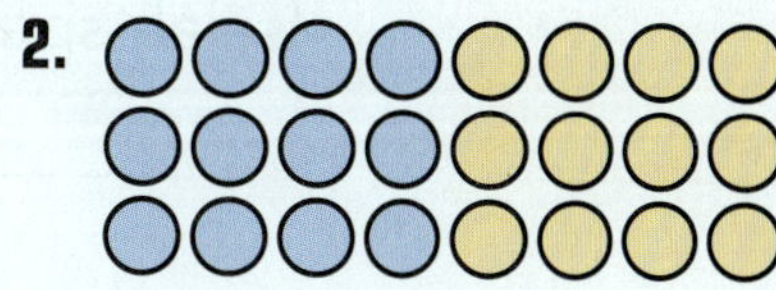

$3 \times 8 =$ ______

3.

$2 \times 8 =$ ______

4. $0 \times 8 =$ ______

5. $1 \times 8 =$ ______

6. $4 \times 8 =$ ______

7. $\begin{array}{r} 8 \\ \times\ 7 \\ \hline \end{array}$

8. $\begin{array}{r} 8 \\ \times\ 6 \\ \hline \end{array}$

9. $\begin{array}{r} 8 \\ \times\ 10 \\ \hline \end{array}$

10. $\begin{array}{r} 8 \\ \times\ 8 \\ \hline \end{array}$

HOMEWORK

Find the product.

1. 

$4 \times 8 =$ ______

2. $6 \times 8 =$ ______

3. $0 \times 8 =$ ______

4. 8×5

5. 8×2

6. 8×0

7. 8×7

8. 8×1

9. 8×9

Problem Solving

10. Sadie has 4 boxes of pencils. Each box contains 8 pencils. She has 5 other pencils. How many pencils does Sadie have?

______

11. Luke draws 7 rows of 7 circles. Kyle draws 6 rows of 8 squares. Who draws more shapes? Explain.

______

12. Sara has 4 packs of baseball cards and 2 packs of football cards. Each pack has 8 cards. How many cards does Sara have?

______

13. Isaiah buys 3 used computer games for $8 each. He buys a new game for $25. How much does Isaiah spend in all?

______

Write About It

14. How does knowing how to multiply by 2s help you to multiply by 8s? Give an example using 9×8.

______

______

______

______

Name ______________________ Date ____________

LESSON 6-7

Use a Bar Model to Multiply

Gabriel has 5 stacks of quarters. Each stack contains 8 quarters. How many quarters does Gabriel have?

You can use a bar model to see the parts of the problem.

- Identify what you know. There are 5 stacks of quarters.

  Each stack has 8 quarters.

- Make a bar model to show 5 × 8 = ?

?

8	8	8	8	8

The bar model shows repeated addition or multiplication.

- Multiply: 5 × 8 = 40.

40 quarters

8	8	8	8	8

Gabriel has 40 quarters.

MORE PRACTICE

Complete the bar model to solve the problem.

1. Each page in Jackson's photo album has 8 photos. Jackson has 4 pages filled. How many photos are in Jackson's photo album?

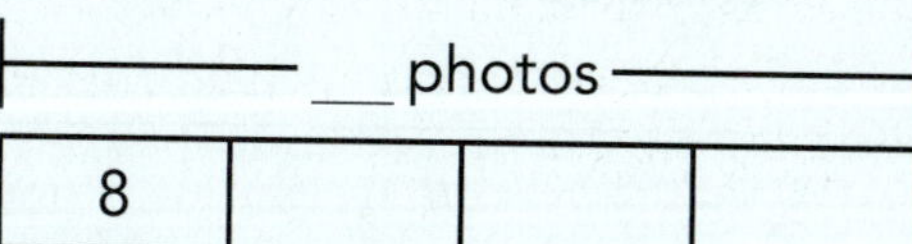

____

2. Ashlyn has 5 rows of 5 trees in her yard. How many trees does Ashlyn have in her yard?

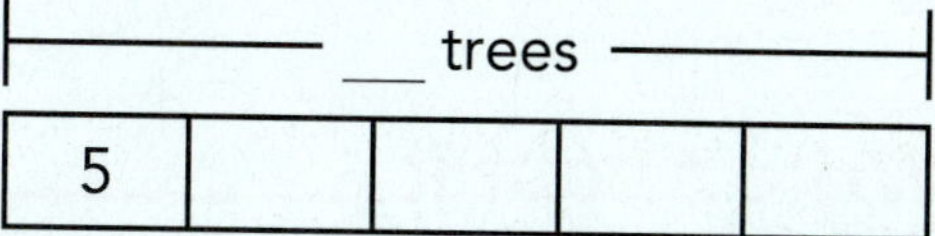

____

3. Cole has 6 bobble heads on each shelf in his room. He has 3 shelves. How many bobble heads does Cole have in all?

__ bobble heads

6		

____

HOMEWORK

Write an equation and complete each bar model to solve each problem.

1. A gallon is equal to 8 pints. A sports cooler holds 5 gallons. How many pints are there in 5 gallons?

   ____ pints

8				

   ____

2. Skylar plays an amusement park game and wins 7 tickets each time she plays. She plays 4 games. How many tickets does Skylar win in all?

   ____ tickets

7			

   ____

3. Devin scores 5 three-point field goals in his basketball game. How many points does Devin score from three-point field goals?

   ____ points

   ____

Problem Solving

4. Each lunch special at the Fine Diner costs $9. A group of 6 friends each ordered the lunch special. How much did the friends spend in all? Draw a bar model.

   ____

Write About It

5. How does using a bar model help you to multiply? Explain by giving an example.

   ____

   ____

   ____

Name ______________________ Date ____________

LESSON 6-8

Problem Solving
Make a Table

A team gets 3 points for a win and 1 point for a tie. The Bears have won 5 games and tied once. How many points do the Bears have?

You can make a table to organize this information. Let W stand for win and T stand for tie.

Bears Points						
Win or Tie	W1	W2	W3	W4	W5	T1
Number of Points	3	3	3	3	3	1

Use the table to find the total points scored by the Bears.

- Multiply the number of wins made by the number of points each win is worth.

  $5 \times 3 = 15$

- Add the point the Bears scored from its tied game.

  $15 + 1 = 16$

The Bears have 16 points in all.

MORE PRACTICE

1. In an experiment, the temperature increases 6°F every hour. The temperature was 68°F when the experiment started. Complete the table to organize the information.

Experiment Temperatures					
Length in Hours	0	1	2	3	4
Temperature (in °F)					

Write and solve an equation to show the total increase.

____

Write and solve an equation to show the temperature after 4 hours. ______________________________

MORE PRACTICE

Complete the table. Use equations to answer the questions.

2. The Lions scored 4 goals in each of their first 5 games. The team scored only 2 goals in its sixth game. How many goals did the Lions score in all?

Goals Scored						
Game	1	2	3	4	5	6
Goals Scored						

How many goals did the Lions score in the first 5 games?

____

How many goals did the Lions score in all? ______________

The Lions scored ________ goals in all.

3. From Sunday to Friday, Antonio jogs 6 miles each day. On Saturdays, Antonio jogs 9 miles. How many miles does Antonio jog in a week?

Miles Jogged							
Day	Sun.	Mon.	Tues.	Wed.	Thurs.	Fri.	Sat.
Miles Jogged							

How many miles does Antonio jog from Sunday to Friday?

____

How many miles does Antonio jog all week? ______________

Antonio jogs ________ miles in a week.

4. There are 7 rows of chairs. Every row has 8 chairs except for the last row, which has 4 chairs. How many chairs are there?

Chairs							
Row	1	2	3	4	5	6	7
Number of Chairs							

How many chairs are in the first 6 rows? ______________

How many chairs are there in total? ______________

There are ________ chairs.

Name ______________________ Date ____________

Problem Solving
Make a Table

HOMEWORK

The table shows the prices for some of the events at a fair. Use the table for Exercises 1–3.

Fair Prices	
Event	Price
Ride	$5
Petting Zoo	$4
Animal Feeding	$3
Games	$2

1. Jesse goes on 4 rides and visits the petting zoo. How much money does Jesse spend at the fair?

Make a table to organize the information.

Jesse at the Fair					
Event	R1	R2	R3	R4	PZ
Cost in Dollars					

How much does Jesse spend on rides? ____________

How much does Jesse spend on rides and the petting zoo?

____

Jesse spends $______ at the fair.

2. Amanda plays 7 games and feeds the animals. How much does Amanda spend?

Amanda at the Fair								
Event	G1	G2	G3	G4	G5	G6	G7	AF
Cost in Dollars								

How much does Amanda spend on games? ____________

How much does Amanda spend on games and animal feeding? ______________________

Amanda spends $______ at the fair.

3. Nate goes to the fair with $20. He goes on 3 rides.

How much money does Nate spend on rides?

____

How much money will Nate have left after going on 3 rides?

____

HOMEWORK

4. The temperature increased 3°F each hour from 7 A.M. to 12 noon. The temperature at 7 A.M. was 49°F. What was the temperature at 12 noon?

Temperatures from 7:00 A.M. to 12:00 noon						
Time	7:00	8:00	9:00	10:00	11:00	12:00
Temperature						

Write and solve an equation to show the total increase from 7:00 to 12:00. ______

Write and solve an equation to show the temperature at 12 noon. ______

The temperature at 12 noon was ______°F.

5. Joe makes 6 two-point field goals and scores 8 points on free throws. Make a table to show how many points Joe scored.

______

Write About It

6. The first team to reach 60 points wins a contest. In each of the first 4 events, the blue team scored 8 points. The blue team is in first place. How many points does the Blue team need to win? Explain how to make a table to find the answer.

______

______

______

Name ________________________________ Date ______________

LESSON 6-9

Use the Associative Property to Multiply

There are 2 third-grade classrooms at a school. Each classroom has 4 rows of 5 desks. How many desks are in the 2 classrooms?

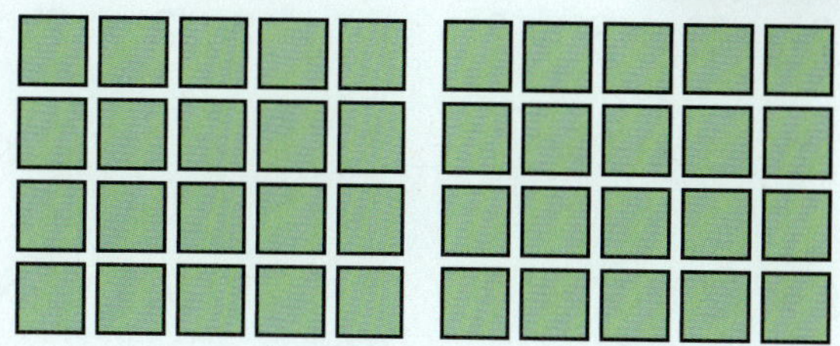

To find how many desks, multiply: $2 \times 4 \times 5 = \underline{?}$.

Associative Property of Multiplication

Changing the grouping of the factors does not change the product.

- To multiply three factors:
  - Group the first two factors using parentheses. $(2 \times 4) \times 5 = ?$
  - Multiply these factors first. $8 \times 5 = ?$
  - Complete the multiplication. $8 \times 5 = 40$
- You can also use the Commutative and Associative Properties to make the multiplication easier.
  - Change the order of the factors. $4 \times 2 \times 5 = ?$
  - Group the last two factors using parentheses. $4 \times (2 \times 5) = ?$
  - Multiply these factors first. $4 \times 10 = ?$
  - Complete the multiplication. $4 \times 10 = 40$

So $2 \times 4 \times 5 = 40$.

There are 40 desks in the 2 classrooms.

MORE PRACTICE

Write the missing number.

1. $8 \times 3 \times 7 = 8 \times (\_\_\_\_ \times 7)$

2. $6 \times 3 \times 4 = (\_\_\_\_ \times 3) \times 4$

3. $4 \times 5 \times 3 = (4 \times 5) \times \_\_\_\_$

4. $6 \times 8 \times 7 = 6 \times (8 \times \_\_\_\_)$

HOMEWORK

Find the product.

1. $(2 \times 5) \times 3 = ?$

   ______ $\times 3 =$ ______

2. $(3 \times 2) \times 7 = ?$

   ______ $\times 7 =$ ______

3. $(4 \times 2) \times 7 = ?$

   ______ $\times 7 =$ ______

4. $6 \times (2 \times 2) = ?$

   ______ $\times$ ______ $=$ ______

5. $9 \times (3 \times 2) = ?$

   ______ $\times$ ______ $=$ ______

6. $8 \times (2 \times 5) = ?$

   ______ $\times$ ______ $=$ ______

Multiply. Show your grouping.

7. $5 \times 2 \times 5 =$ ______
8. $3 \times 4 \times 2 =$ ______
9. $9 \times 2 \times 2 =$ ______
10. $2 \times 4 \times 6 =$ ______
11. $3 \times 3 \times 7 =$ ______
12. $4 \times 2 \times 9 =$ ______

Problem Solving

13. Which is greater: $2 \times 4 \times 6$ or $6 \times 3 \times 3$? Explain how you can tell without finding the products.

____

____

____

____

14. Steve eats 2 bags of carrots each day. There are 8 carrots in each bag. How many carrots does Steve eat in 5 days? Show your work.

____

____

____

Write About It

15. How is the Associative Property of Multiplication different from the Commutative Property of Multiplication? Give an example of each using $4 \times 3 \times 2$.

____

____

____

____

Name ______________________ Date ______________

LESSON 6-10

Find More Multiplication Patterns

Look at the products of 3s and 6s in the multiplication table. Describe the even and odd number patterns that you see.

×	0	1	2	3	4	5	6	7	8	9
0	0	0	0	0	0	0	0	0	0	0
1	0	1	2	3	4	5	6	7	8	9
2	0	2	4	6	8	10	12	14	16	18
3	0	3	6	9	12	15	18	21	24	27
4	0	4	8	12	16	20	24	28	32	36
5	0	5	10	15	20	25	30	35	40	45
6	0	6	12	18	24	30	36	42	48	54
7	0	7	14	21	28	35	42	49	56	63
8	0	8	16	24	32	40	48	56	64	72
9	0	9	18	27	36	45	54	63	72	81

Look at the products from left to right.

- Starting at 0, when 3 is multiplied by an even number, the product is even.
- Starting at 1, when 3 is multiplied by an odd number, the product is odd.

The product of a number and 3 alternates between even and odd.

- Starting at 0, when 6 is multiplied by any number, the product is even.

The product of a number and 6 is always even.

MORE PRACTICE

Write *even* or *odd*.

1. Even × 4 = ________

2. Even × 7 = ________

3. Odd × 9 = ________

4. Odd × 8 = ________

5. 10 × Even = ________

6. 1 × Odd = ________

HOMEWORK

Write *even* or *odd*.

1. Odd × 7 = ______

2. Even × 5 = ______

3. Odd × 6 = ______

4. Even × 2 = ______

Problem Solving

Use the multiplication table for Exercises 5–7.

×	0	1	2	3	4	5	6	7	8	9	10
0	0	0	0	0	0	0	0	0	0	0	0
1	0	1	2	3	4	5	6	7	8	9	10
2	0	2	4	6	8	10	12	14	16	18	20
3	0	3	6	9	12	15	18	21	24	27	30
4	0	4	8	12	16	20	24	28	32	36	40
5	0	5	10	15	20	25	30	35	40	45	50
6	0	6	12	18	24	30	36	42	48	54	60
7	0	7	14	21	28	35	42	49	56	63	70
8	0	8	16	24	32	40	48	56	64	72	80
9	0	9	18	27	36	45	54	63	72	81	90
10	0	10	20	30	40	50	60	70	80	90	100

5. Shade a row and column using 3 and 4. How are 3 × 4 and 4 × 3 related? Explain how you know.

____

____

____

____

____

6. Shade the 9s row or column. How can you use the multiplication table to represent the Distributive Property?

____

____

____

____

Write About It

7. Is the multiplication table helpful to find the products of two 1-digit numbers by using the Distributive Property? Explain why or why not.

____

____

____

Name ______________________ Date ______________

LESSON 6-11

Multiply by Multiples of 10

Cassidy buys 4 boxes of blocks. Each box contains 60 blocks. How many blocks did Cassidy buy in all?

To find how many blocks, multiply: $4 \times 60 = \underline{?}$.

- You can use the Associative Property of Multiplication.

  Break apart 60 into 6×10.

  $$\begin{aligned} 4 \times 60 &= 4 \times (6 \times 10) \\ &= (4 \times 6) \times 10 \\ &= 24 \times 10 \\ &= 240 \end{aligned}$$

- You can show the multiplication on a number line.

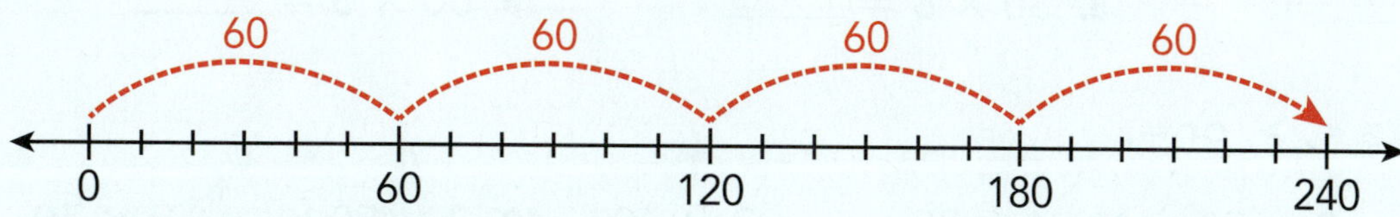

  Skip count: 60, 120, 180, 240.

- You can use a basic fact and a pattern of multiples of 10.

  $4 \times 6 = 4 \times 6$ ones $= 24$

  $4 \times 60 = 4 \times 6$ tens $= 240$

Cassidy buys 240 blocks in all.

MORE PRACTICE

Complete the multiplication.

1. $5 \times 70 = 5 \times (7 \times$ ______)

= (5 × ______) × ______

= ______ × ______

= ______

2. $8 \times 30 = 8 \times (3 \times$ ______)

= (8 × ______) × ______

= ______ × ______

= ______

HOMEWORK

Complete the multiplication.

1. $2 \times 80 = 2 \times (8 \times$ ____$)$
   $= ($____ $\times$ ____$) \times$ ____
   $=$ ____ $\times$ ____
   $=$ ____

2. $5 \times 60 = 5 \times (6 \times$ ____$)$
   $= ($____ $\times$ ____$) \times$ ____
   $=$ ____ $\times$ ____
   $=$ ____

3. $7 \times 7 =$ ____
   $7 \times 70 =$ ____

4. $9 \times 5 =$ ____
   $9 \times 50 =$ ____

Multiply.

5. $4 \times 40 =$ ____
6. $7 \times 50 =$ ____
7. $9 \times 30 =$ ____
8. $80 \times 8 =$ ____
9. $30 \times 8 =$ ____
10. $60 \times 3 =$ ____

Compare. Write <, >, or =.

11. 6×60 ____ 8×50
12. 4×30 ____ 3×40
13. 3×50 ____ 2×70

Problem Solving

14. A puzzle has 500 pieces. Hope has 3 groups of 80 pieces left to put together. How many pieces has she put together? Show your work.

    ____

15. Each hour, 60 people are allowed into an art exhibit. After 9 hours, how many people will be allowed to see the art exhibit?

    ____

Write About It

16. How does knowing multiplication facts help you multiply a 1-digit number by a 2-digit multiple of 10?

    ____

    ____

Name ______________________ Date ______________

LESSON 7-1

Relate Multiplication and Division

Brian has 24 model cars in his bookcase. He has 6 models on each shelf. How many shelves are there?

To find how many shelves, find 24 ÷ 6.

Every division fact has a related multiplication fact. Multiplication and division undo each other.

24	÷	6	=	?	→	?	×	6	=	24
↑		↑		↑		↑		↑		↑
dividend		divisor		quotient		factor		factor		product

Use the related fact 4 × 6 = 24 to find 24 ÷ 6 = 4.

There are 4 shelves.

MORE PRACTICE

Match each model to the fact it shows.

1. 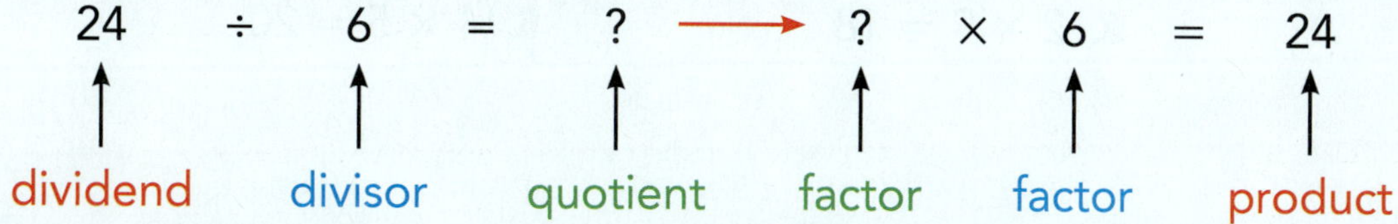

2. 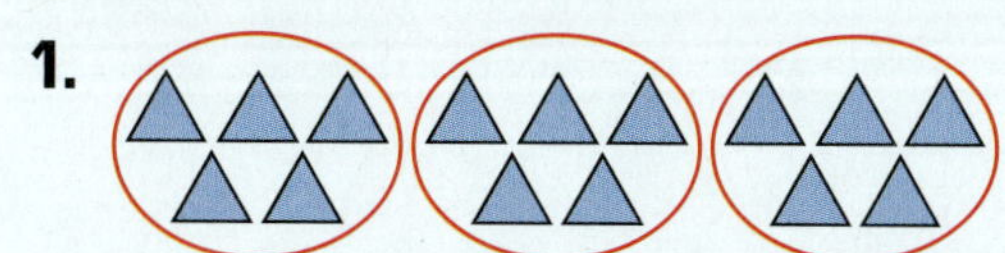

3. 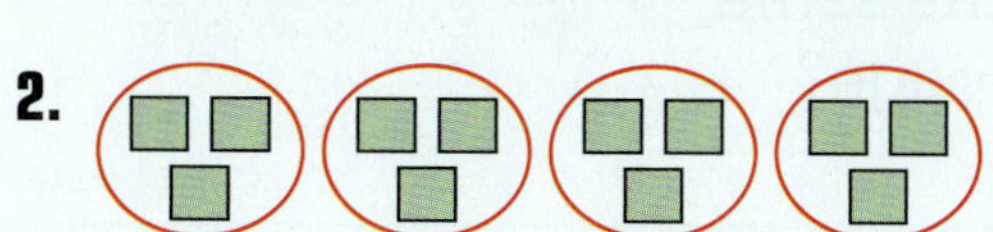

4. 

8 ÷ 2 = 4

18 ÷ 6 = 3

15 ÷ 5 = 3

12 ÷ 3 = 4

HOMEWORK

Write a multiplication fact for each model. Use the fact to complete the division equation.

1. 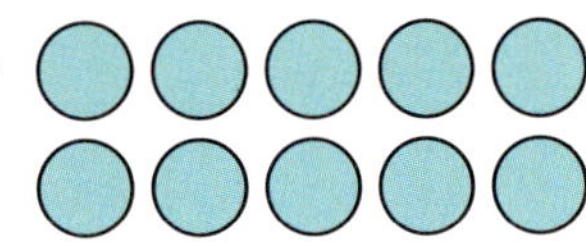

____

$10 \div 5 =$ _______

2. 

____

$12 \div 4 =$ _______

3. _______________

$8 \div 4 =$ _______

Draw a model to represent the multiplication fact. Then write the related division fact.

4. $3 \times 8 = 24$

5. $2 \times 9 = 18$

6. $4 \times 5 = 20$

Complete each equation.

7. $3 \times 2 =$ _______

_______ $\div 2 = 3$

8. $6 \times 2 =$ _______

_______ $\div 2 = 6$

9. $9 \times 3 =$ _______

_______ $\div 3 = 9$

Problem Solving

10. Ken has 30 cards on 5 pages. Each page has the same number of cards. How many cards are on each page?

____

Write About It

11. How does knowing multiplication help you to learn division?

____

____

Name ______________________________ Date ______________

LESSON
7-2

Divide by 2

Alicia writes 14 pages in her journal in 2 days.
She writes the same number of pages each day.
How many pages does Alicia write each day?

To find how many pages, divide: $14 \div 2 = \underline{?}$.

- You can draw a model to find how many in each group.

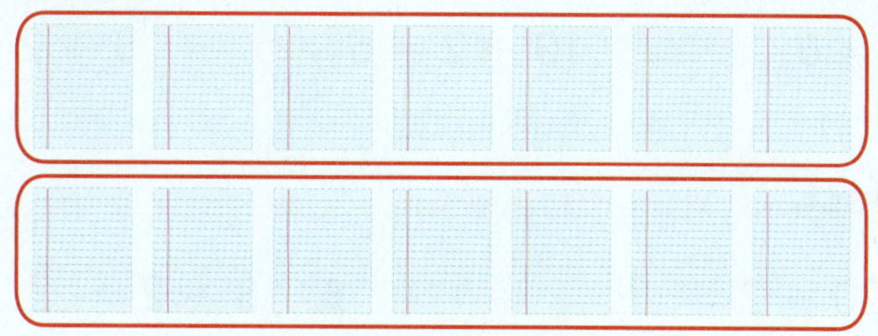

- You can also use a related multiplication fact.

$\underline{?} \times 2 = 14 \longrightarrow 7 \times 2 = 14$

So, $14 \div 2 = 7$ or $2\overline{)14}$ with quotient 7.

Alicia writes 7 pages each day.

MORE PRACTICE

Write a division equation and a multiplication equation for each model.

1. 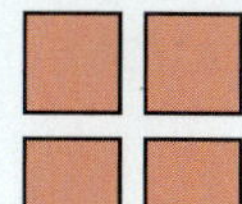

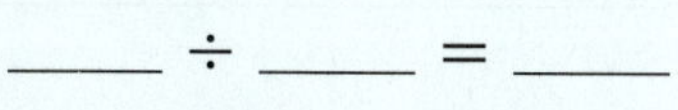

____ ÷ ____ = ____

____ × ____ = ____

2. 
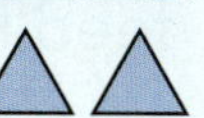

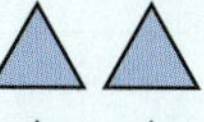
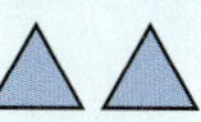
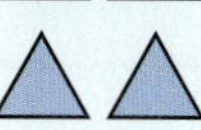

____ ÷ ____ = ____

____ × ____ = ____

3.

____ ÷ ____ = ____

____ × ____ = ____

HOMEWORK

Match the model to the fact it represents.

1. 

2. 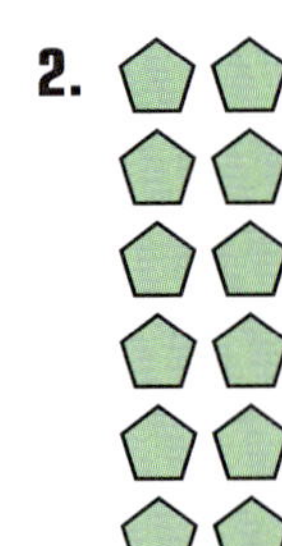

3. 

$14 \div 2 = 7$ $12 \div 2 = 6$ $10 \div 2 = 5$ $8 \div 2 = 4$

Write a related multiplication fact.

4. $4 \div 2 =$? ______________

5. $20 \div 2 =$? ______________

6. $18 \div 2 =$? ______________

Find the quotient.

7. $6 \div 2 =$ ______

8. $12 \div 2 =$ ______

9. $16 \div 2 =$ ______

10. $2\overline{)8}$

11. $2\overline{)14}$

12. $2\overline{)20}$

Problem Solving

13. Amanda scores 12 points in 2 games. She scores the same number of points in each game. How many points does Amanda score in each game?

____

14. Antonio fed his cat 6 times in the last 2 days. He feeds his cat the same number of times each day. How many times does Antonio feed his cat each day?

____

Write About It

15. How can you find $14 \div 2$ by counting back from 14?

____

____

Name ______________________ Date ______________

LESSON 7-3

Divide by 3

There are 15 birds resting on 3 branches of a tree. Each branch has the same number of birds resting on it. How many birds are on each branch?

To find how many birds are on each branch, find $15 \div 3$.

Divide to separate into equal groups.

- You can draw an array to show $15 \div 3 = \underline{?}$.
  - Draw 1 circle in each of 3 rows.
  - Keep drawing 1 circle in each row until you have 15 circles.
  - Count the number of columns.

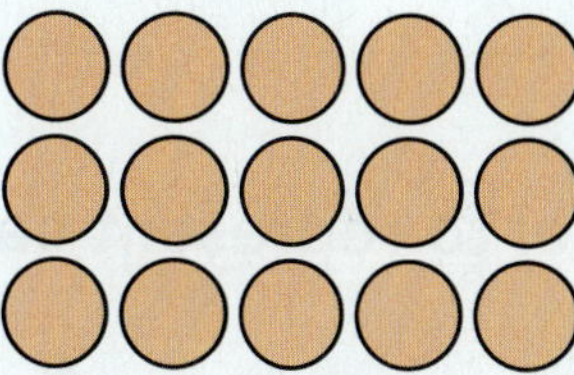

  There are 5 columns, so $15 \div 3 = 5$.

- You can also use a related multiplication fact: $\underline{?} \times 3 = 15$.

  Because $5 \times 3 = 15$, you know that $15 \div 3 = 5$.

  You can write $15 \div 3 = 5$ or $3\overline{)15}$ with quotient 5.

There are 5 birds on each branch of the tree.

MORE PRACTICE

Write a division equation for each model.

1. 

____ ÷ ____ = ____

2. 

____ ÷ ____ = ____

3. 

____ ÷ ____ = ____

4. Lillian paints 9 pictures that are arranged in 3 equal rows.

How many pictures are in each row? ______________________

HOMEWORK

Match each division equation to the related multiplication equation.

1. $6 \div 3 = \underline{?}$	$10 \times 3 = 30$
2. $12 \div 3 = \underline{?}$	$4 \times 3 = 12$
3. $18 \div 3 = \underline{?}$	$2 \times 3 = 6$
4. $30 \div 3 = \underline{?}$	$8 \times 3 = 24$
	$6 \times 3 = 18$

Draw a model to represent each division equation.

5. $9 \div 3 = 3$

6. $15 \div 3 = 5$

7. $27 \div 3 = 9$

Find the quotient.

8. $24 \div 3 = \_\_\_\_$

9. $12 \div 3 = \_\_\_\_$

10. $3\overline{)30}$

11. $3\overline{)21}$

Problem Solving

12. Delaney's book has 21 chapters. There are 3 parts with the same number of chapters per part. How many chapters are in each part?

____

13. Pablo draws a comic strip that has 12 pictures in 3 rows. Each row has the same number of pictures. How many pictures are in each row?

____

Write About It

14. How can you use what you have learned to find $36 \div 3$?

____

____

Name ______________________ Date ______________

LESSON 7-4

Divide by 4

Twenty people are using the tennis courts at the park. Four people are playing on each court. How many tennis courts are being used?

To find how many tennis courts are being used, divide: 20 ÷ 4.

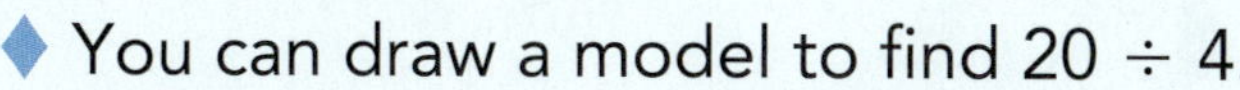

- You can draw a model to find 20 ÷ 4.
  - Draw 1 square in each of 4 rows.
  - Keep adding squares to each row until you have 20 squares.
  - Count the number of columns.

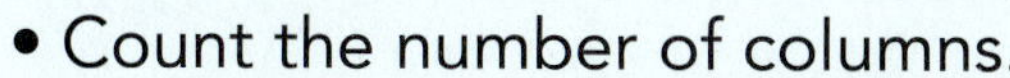

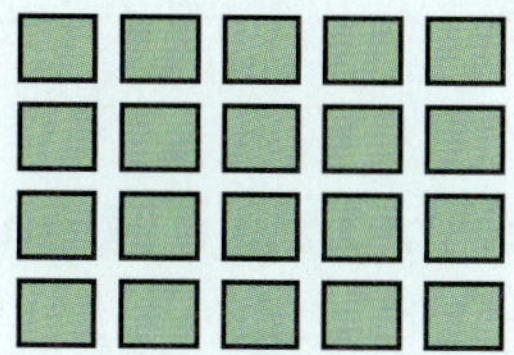

There are 5 columns of 4, so 20 ÷ 4 = 5.

- You can also use a related multiplication fact.

? × 4 = 20

5 × 4 = 20

Multiplication and division are related operations. They undo each other.

You can write 20 ÷ 4 = 5 or $\begin{array}{r}5\\4\overline{)20}\end{array}$.

There are 5 tennis courts being used.

MORE PRACTICE

Write a division equation for each model.

1. 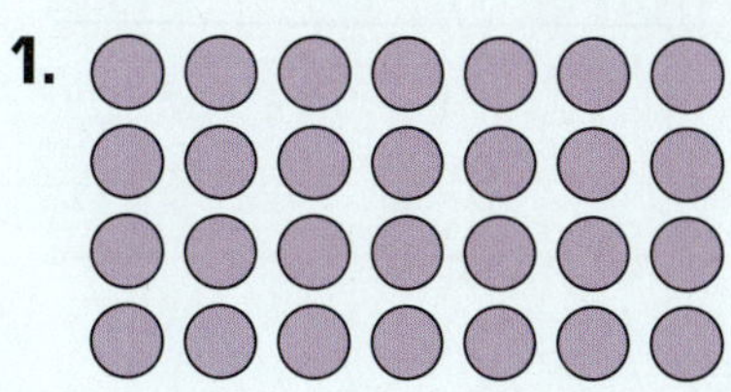

___ ÷ ___ = ___

2. 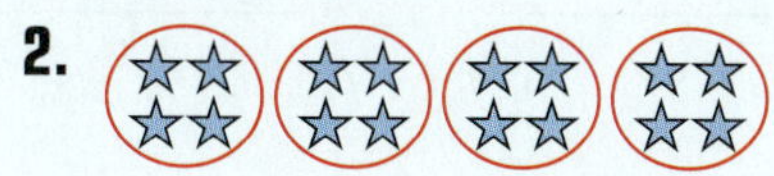

___ ÷ ___ = ___

3. 

___ ÷ ___ = ___

4. How can you use a multiplication fact to find 32 ÷ 4?

____

____

HOMEWORK

Match the model to the fact it represents.

1.

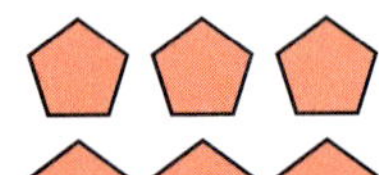

2.

3.

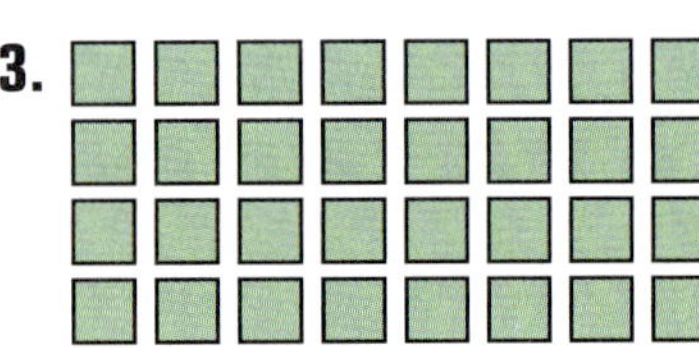

$24 \div 4 = 6$ $\quad 12 \div 4 = 3$ $\quad 16 \div 4 = 4$ $\quad 32 \div 4 = 8$

Write a related multiplication fact.

4. $8 \div 4 =$ ___?___ ______________

5. $20 \div 4 =$ ___?___ ______________

6. $40 \div 4 =$ ___?___ ______________

7. $36 \div 4 =$ ___?___ ______________

Find the quotient.

8. $4\overline{)28}$

9. $4\overline{)16}$

10. $4\overline{)12}$

11. $4\overline{)24}$

Problem Solving

12. Sonia has a rock collection. She took 24 rocks and put 4 rocks in each box. How many boxes did Sonia use? Show your work.

____

13. Chris has 28 carrot sticks. He keeps 8. He gives the same number of carrot sticks to 4 friends. How many carrot sticks does each friend receive?

____

Write About It

14. How do the dividends for divisors of 4 compare to the dividends for divisors of 2 when the quotients are the same? Give an example using a quotient of 3.

____

____

Name ______________________ Date ______________

LESSON 7-5

Divide by 5

Layla buys 30 strawberries. She divides the strawberries equally into 5 bags. How many strawberries does Layla put into each bag?

To find how many strawberries are in each bag, divide: 30 ÷ 5.

- You can draw a model. Draw 30 objects separated into 5 equal groups. There are 6 objects in each group, so 30 ÷ 5 = 6.

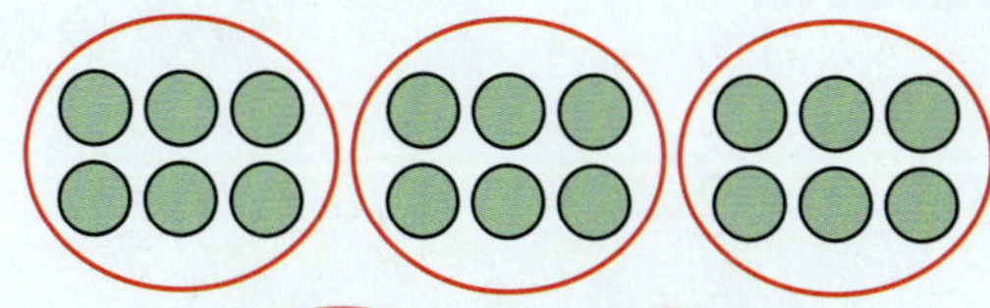

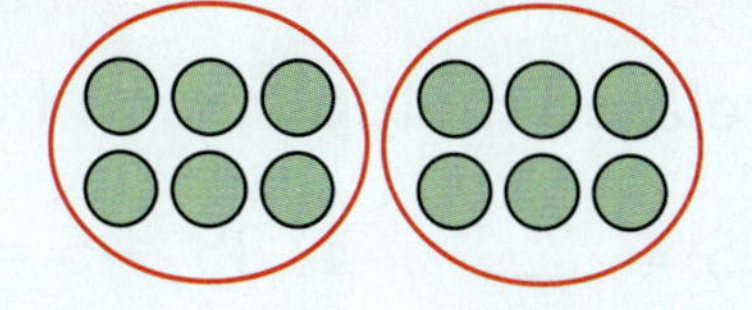

- You can also use a related multiplication fact.

6 × 5 = 30 ← *Think* _?_ × 5 = 30

So 30 ÷ 5 = 6 or $5\overline{)30}$ = 6.

Layla puts 6 strawberries into each bag.

MORE PRACTICE

Write a division equation for each model.

1.

_____ ÷ _____ = _____

2.

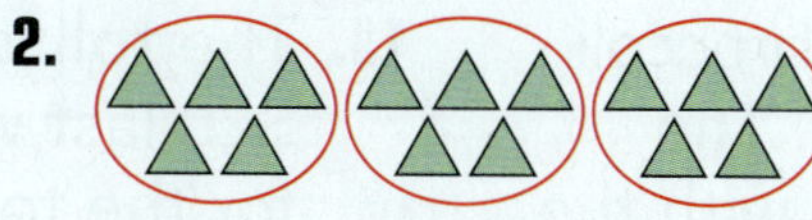

_____ ÷ _____ = _____

3.

_____ ÷ _____ = _____

4. Two division equations have the same quotient. One divisor is 3 and the other divisor is 5. If both quotients are 10, what are the dividends? Explain your reasoning.

____

____

____

HOMEWORK

Match each model to the fact it represents.

1. 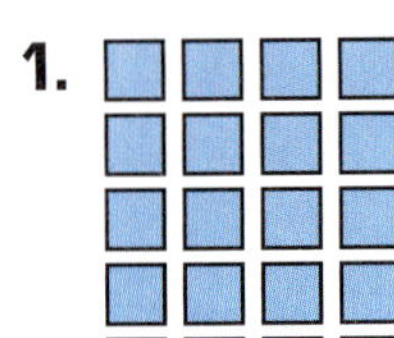

2. 

3. 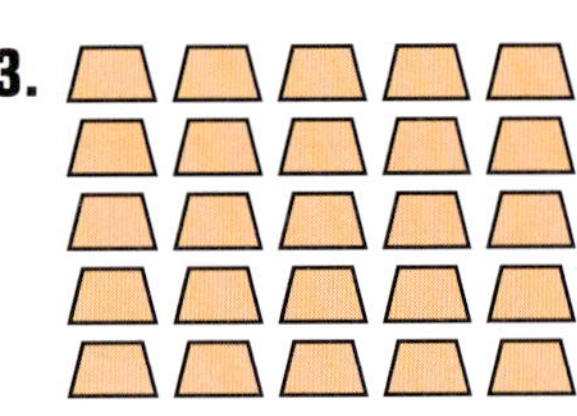

$45 \div 5 = 9$ $20 \div 5 = 4$ $25 \div 5 = 5$ $30 \div 5 = 6$

Write a related multiplication fact.

4. $15 \div 5 = \underline{?}$ ____________

5. $35 \div 5 = \underline{?}$ ____________

6. $50 \div 5 = \underline{?}$ ____________

7. $10 \div 5 = \underline{?}$ ____________

Find the quotient.

8. $5\overline{)20}$

9. $5\overline{)30}$

10. $5\overline{)40}$

11. $5\overline{)45}$

Problem Solving

12. Michelle has 15 pieces of broccoli and 25 pieces of pepper. The vegetables are in 5 bags with the same number of pieces in each bag. How many pieces are in each bag?

____

13. The toll is $5. Mr. Waters spent $20 last week and $25 this week for the toll. How many times was Mr. Waters charged for the toll in the last two weeks?

____

Write About It

14. Without multiplying or dividing, Devon knew the equation $35 \div 5 = 8$ was incorrect. How did Devon know that?

____

____

____

Name ______________________ Date ____________

LESSON 7-6

Problem Solving
Use Drawings to Solve Problems

There are 24 students on 4 teams participating in a robotics competition. Each team has the same number of students. How many students are on each team?

- You can use equal sharing to represent 24 ÷ 4 = ___?___.
  - Draw 4 squares to represent the teams.
  - Draw circles to represent the students. Share the circles equally in the 4 squares.
  - Six circles go in each square.

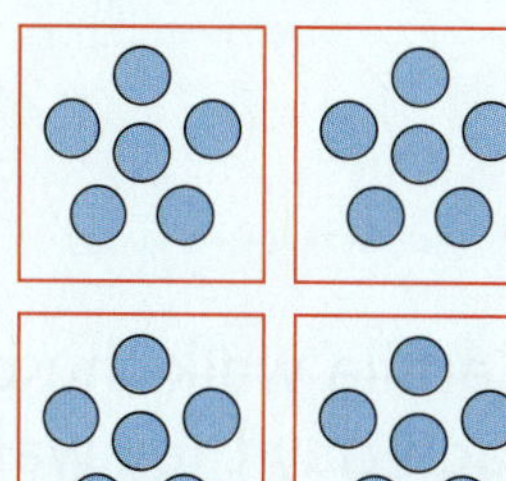

There are 6 students on each team.

- You can use a bar model to represent 24 ÷ 4 = ___?___.
  - Draw a bar model to show the total number of students in 4 equal parts.
  - Then use a related multiplication fact to solve. Because 6 × 4 = 24, each bar shows 6.

24 students			
?	?	?	?

24 students			
6	6	6	6

There are 6 students on each team.

- You can draw an array to find the number of students on each team to represent 24 ÷ 4 = ___?___.
  - Draw an array with 4 rows.
  - Draw a circle to represent each student. There should be the same number of circles for each row. Draw circles until you have 24 total.
  - There are 6 circles in each row.

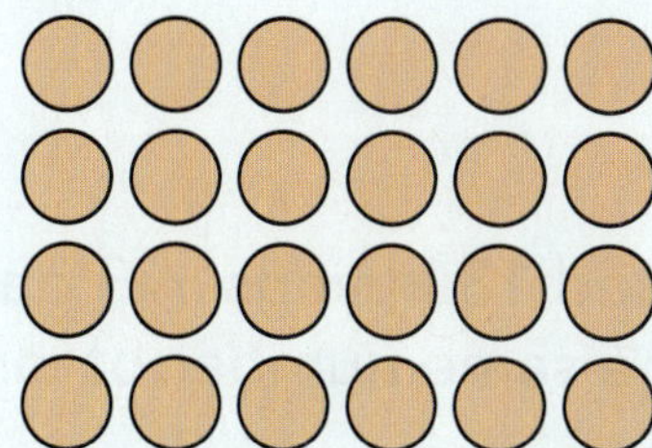

There are 6 students on each team.

MORE PRACTICE

Solve. Use a model that works best for you.

1. Sam has 45 stickers. He puts 5 stickers on each page of his sticker book. He says he needs 8 pages for all of the stickers. Jacob said that Sam needs 9 pages for all of the stickers. Who is correct? Explain why.

___

2. Jana and Camila walk the beach 16 times during their 4-day vacation. Each day they walk the beach the same number of times. Jana said they walk the beach 4 times each day. Camila said they walk the beach 3 times each day. Who is correct? Explain why.

___

3. The bill at a restaurant is $32. Four friends will equally split the cost. How much will each friend spend? ______

4. Riley pitched 18 innings in 3 games for her softball team. She pitched the same number of innings in each game. How many innings did Riley pitch in each game? ______

Name ______________________ Date ____________

Problem Solving
Use Drawings to Solve Problems

HOMEWORK

Solve. Use a model that works best for you.

1. Caitlin has 16 trophies on 4 shelves. She has the same number of trophies on each shelf. Use equal sharing to model the number of trophies on each shelf.

   What equation does your model represent?

   ____

   How many trophies does Caitlin have on each shelf? ________

2. Jayla and two of her friends go to the movies. They pay $21 in all. They share the cost equally. Make a bar model to represent the cost to each person.

   What equation does your bar model represent?

   ____

   What is the cost to each person? ________

3. Trent has 20 plants. He is going to plant them in 5 equal rows. Make an array to model the number of plants in each row.

   What equation does your array represent?

   ____

   How many plants are in each row? ________

HOMEWORK

Solve. Use a model that works best for you.

4. It costs $36 to buy 4 tickets. How much does one ticket cost? ______

5. Each box contains 3 paintbrushes. How many boxes are filled if there are 15 paintbrushes? ______

6. A match of 3 rounds lasts a total of 6 minutes. Each round is the same number of minutes. How many minutes long is each round? ______

7. A builder has a board that is 18 inches long. He will cut the board into 2 equal pieces. What will be the length of each piece after the cut? ______

Write About It

8. Giselle packed 2 outfits for each day of her trip. She packed 10 outfits. Which model would you use to find the number of days her trip will last? How many days is Giselle's trip?

______

______

Name ______________________ Date ____________

LESSON 8-1

Divide by 6

Brandon has 24 rose bushes in his garden. They are planted 6 in a row. How many rows of rose bushes does Brandon have?

To find the number of rows of rose bushes, find 24 ÷ 6.

- You can draw a model. The model shows there are 4 rows when 24 rose bushes are planted 6 in a row.

- You can also use a related multiplication fact:

  $\underline{?} \times 6 = 24$

  Because $4 \times 6 = 24$, you know $24 \div 6 = 4$.

  You can write $24 \div 6 = 4$ or $6\overline{)24}$ with quotient 4.

There are 4 rows of rose bushes.

MORE PRACTICE

Write a division equation for each model.

1. 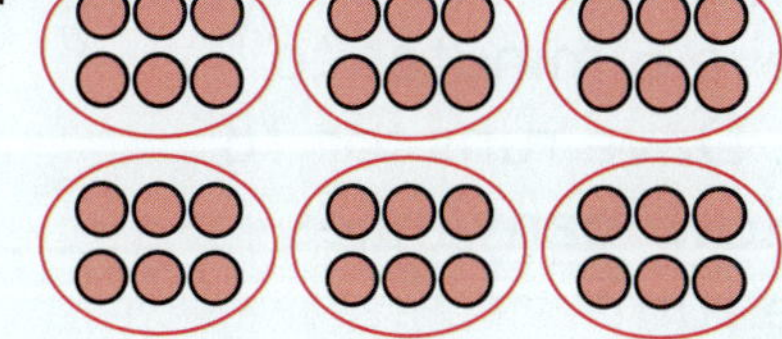

____

2. 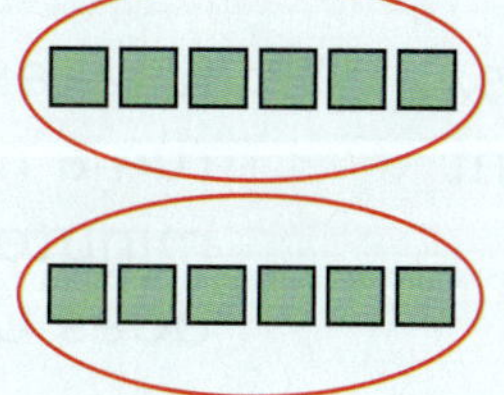

____

3. 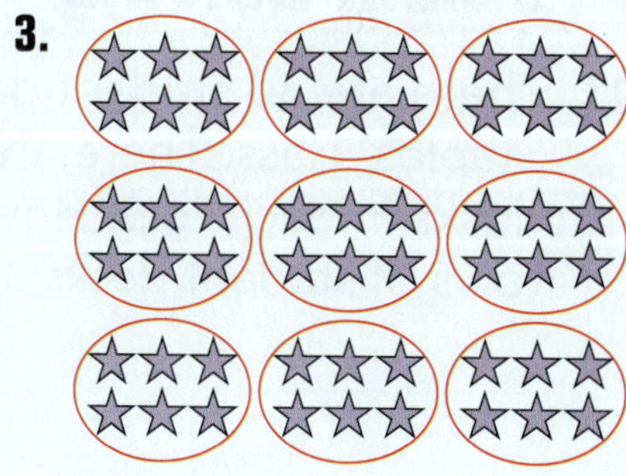

____

4. Explain how to use a number line to divide 30 ÷ 6. Include the quotient in your explanation.

____

____

____

HOMEWORK

Write a division equation and a multiplication equation for each model.

1. 

______

______

2. 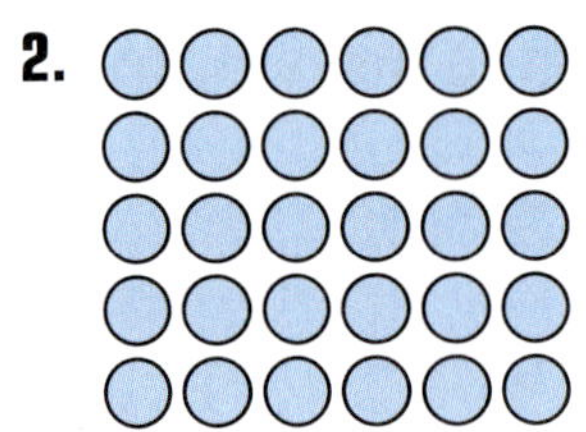

______

______

3. 

______

______

Match the division fact to its related multiplication fact.

4. $18 \div 6 = \underline{?}$

5. $42 \div 6 = \underline{?}$

6. $54 \div 6 = \underline{?}$

$9 \times 6 = 54$ $7 \times 6 = 42$ $3 \times 6 = 18$

Find the quotient.

7. $6\overline{)48}$

8. $6\overline{)18}$

9. $6\overline{)54}$

10. $6\overline{)12}$

Problem Solving

11. There are 30 student desks in Ms. Staples' class. There are 6 student desks in each row. How many rows of student desks are there?

______

12. It takes Dave 6 minutes to run a mile. Dave runs for 18 minutes. How many miles does Dave run?

______

Write About It

13. There are 24 water bottles in a case. How many more bottles would each person receive if 3 people were sharing equally instead of 6 people? Explain your reasoning.

______

______

Name ______________________ Date ______________

LESSON 8-2

Divide by 7

Julia spends 42 days building a model spacecraft. There are 7 days in a week. How many weeks does it take Julia to build the model?

To find the number of weeks, divide: $42 \div 7 = \underline{?}$.

- You can make an array.
  - You want to find how many equal groups.
  - Draw a row of 7 squares.
  - Continue drawing rows of 7 squares until you have 42 squares.
  - Count the number of rows.

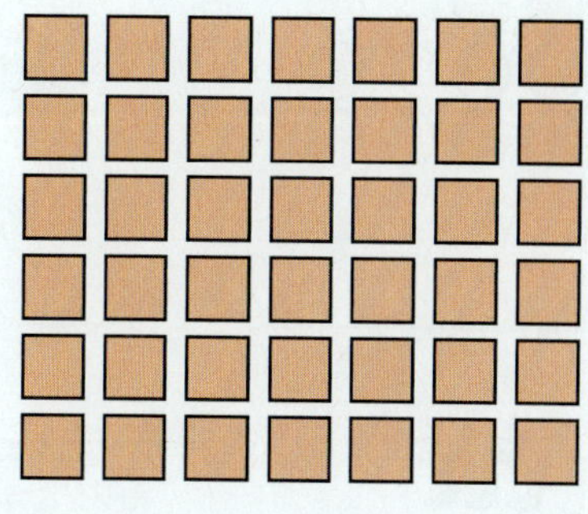

There are 6 rows, so $42 \div 7 = 6$.

- You can also use a related multiplication fact.

Because $6 \times 7 = 42$, you know that $42 \div 7 = 6$.

Think

$\underline{?} \times 7 = 42$

You can write $42 \div 7 = 6$ or $7\overline{)42}$ with quotient 6.

It takes Julia 6 weeks to make the model spacecraft.

MORE PRACTICE

Write a division equation for the model.

1. 

____

2. 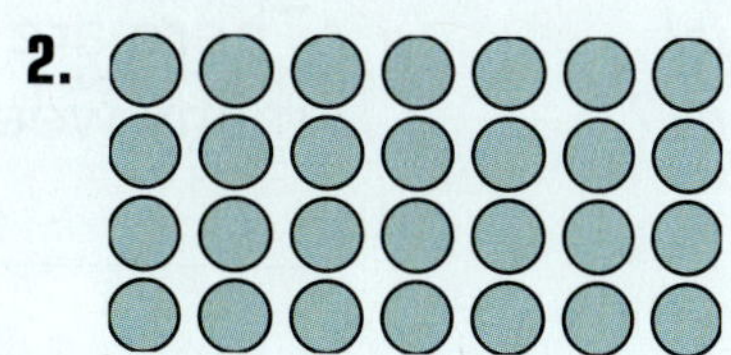

____

3. 

____

4. Explain how to use a related multiplication fact to find $70 \div 7$. Include the quotient in your explanation.

____

HOMEWORK

Write a division equation for the model.

1. ______

2. ______

3. ______

4. 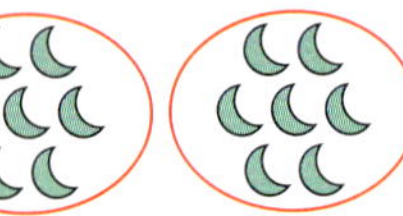

______

5. ______

6. ______

Find the quotient.

7. $63 \div 7 =$ ______

8. $56 \div 7 =$ ______

9. $7\overline{)35}$

10. $7\overline{)21}$

Problem Solving

11. A stack of coins is 21 inches high. If the stack is split into 7 equal stacks, how high is each stack?

______

12. February usually has 28 days. There are 7 days in a week. How many weeks does February have?

______

Write About It

13. Daya has 20 grapes and 15 cherries. She will eat the same number of pieces of fruit each day for 7 days. How many pieces of fruit will she eat each day? Explain your answer.

______

Name ______________________ Date ______________

LESSON 8-3

Divide by 8

George takes 64 photos on his vacation. He takes 8 photos each day. How many days does George's vacation last?

To find the number of days, divide: $64 \div 8 = \underline{?}$.

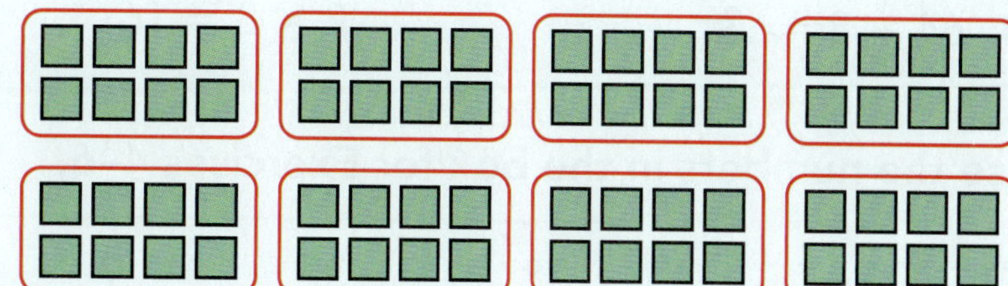

- You can draw a model. Draw 64 squares in groups of 8. There are 8 groups, so $64 \div 8 = 8$.

- You can also use a related multiplication fact: $\underline{?} \times 8 = 64$.

  Because you know $8 \times 8 = 64$, you also know $64 \div 8 = 8$.

  So, $64 \div 8 = 8$ or $8\overline{)64}$ with quotient 8.

George's vacation lasts 8 days.

MORE PRACTICE

Write a division equation for the model.

1.

2.

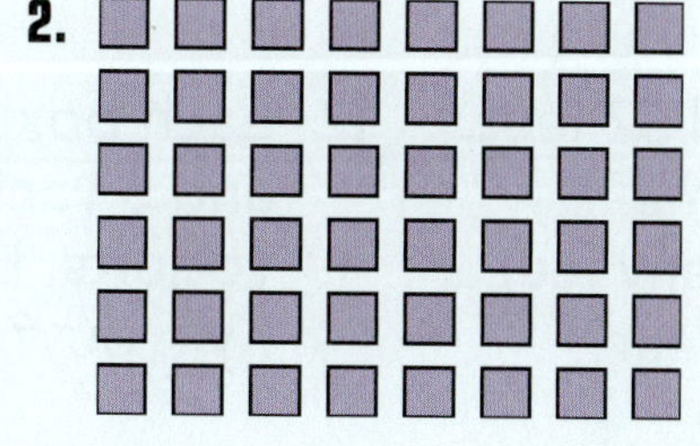

3.

______________ ______________ ______________

4. Explain how to use a related multiplication fact to divide $40 \div 8$. Include the quotient in your explanation.

____

____

HOMEWORK

Match the division fact to its related multiplication fact.

1. $80 \div 8 = \underline{?}$	$8 \times 8 = 64$
	$10 \times 8 = 80$
2. $16 \div 8 = \underline{?}$	$5 \times 8 = 40$
3. $64 \div 8 = \underline{?}$	$2 \times 8 = 16$

Use the numbers in the box for Exercises 4–6.

8	32	9	24

4. If the dividend is 72 and the divisor is 8, what is the quotient? _____

5. If the divisor is 8 and the quotient is 3, what is the dividend? _____

6. If the divisor is 8 and the quotient is 4, what is the dividend? _____

Find the quotient.

7. $40 \div 8 =$ _____ **8.** $56 \div 8 =$ _____ **9.** $8\overline{)48}$ **10.** $8\overline{)16}$

Problem Solving

11. In 8 years, a beach eroded 32 feet. The beach eroded the same amount each year. How many feet did the beach erode last year?

____

12. Each box of yogurt has 5 cherry and 3 vanilla yogurts. Kyle buys 24 yogurts. How many boxes does Kyle buy? Show your work.

____

Write About It

13. Explain how, if you know $48 \div 8 = 6$, you also know that $48 \div 6 = 8$.

____

____

Name ______________________ Date ______________

LESSON **8-4**

Divide by 9

Find 36 ÷ 9.

- You can draw an array. The array shows that 36 squares divided into 9 columns make 4 equal rows. So 36 ÷ 9 = 4.

- You can also use a related multiplication fact.

Think

? × 9 = 36 ⟶ 4 × 9 = 36

So 36 ÷ 9 = 4 or $9\overline{)36}$ with quotient 4.

MORE PRACTICE

Write a division equation for the model.

1.

____

2.

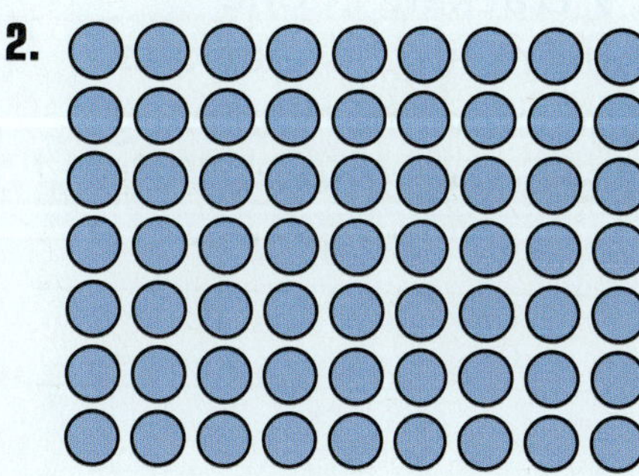

____

3. Explain how to use a related multiplication fact to find 81 ÷ 9. Include the quotient in your explanation.

____

____

____

HOMEWORK

Write a related multiplication fact.

1. $18 \div 9$ ______

2. $90 \div 9$ ______

3. $54 \div 9$ ______

Match the model to the fact it represents.

4.

5.

6.

$45 \div 9 = 5$ $72 \div 9 = 8$ $36 \div 9 = 4$ $18 \div 9 = 2$

Find the quotient.

7. $27 \div 9 =$ ____

8. $81 \div 9 =$ ____

9. $9\overline{)63}$

10. $9\overline{)90}$

Problem Solving

11. There are 9 crackers in one serving. If there are 54 crackers in a package, how many servings are there? Show your work.

______

______

12. Ken and Dan have 36 marbles each. Ken puts his marbles into 9 equal groups. Dan puts his marbles into 4 equal groups. How many more marbles does Dan have than Ken in each of his groups?

______

Write About It

13. If you know $72 \div 9 = 8$, what other facts using 8, 9, and 72 do you know? Explain your answer.

______

______

Name ________________ Date ________

LESSON 8-5

One and Zero in Division

There are 6 eggs in a carton.
Each person will get 1 egg.
How many people will get an egg?

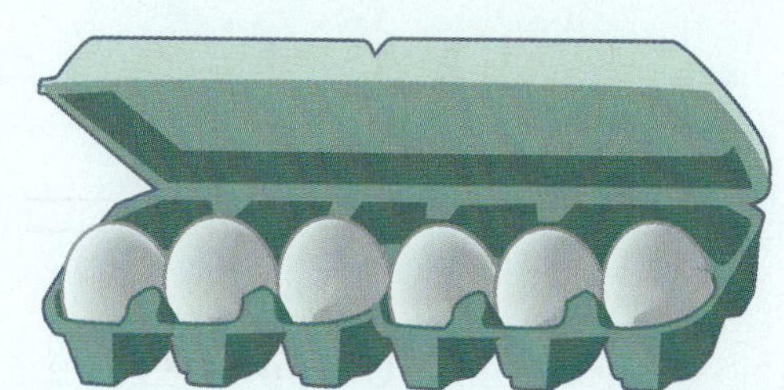

To find the number of people, find $6 \div 1$.

$6 \times 1 = 6$

So $6 \div 1 = 6$.

Six people will receive 1 egg.

When any number is divided by 1, the quotient is that number.

Other Rules

- When any number, except 0, is divided by itself, the quotient is 1. $1 \times 6 = 6$ So $6 \div 6 = 1$.
- When 0 is divided by any number, except 0, the quotient is 0. $0 \times 6 = 0$ So $0 \div 6 = 0$.
- It is not possible to divide by 0. You cannot find $6 \div 0$ because there is no number that makes $\underline{?} \times 0 = 6$ true.

MORE PRACTICE

Divide.

1. $4 \div 1 =$ ______
2. $4 \div 4 =$ ______
3. $0 \div 4 =$ ______
4. $1\overline{)2}$
5. $5\overline{)0}$
6. $1\overline{)7}$

Complete each equation.

7. $8 \times 1 =$ ______
   $8 \div 1 =$ ______
8. $0 \times 2 =$ ______
   $0 \div 2 =$ ______
9. ______ $\times 3 = 3$
   ______ $\div 3 = 1$

HOMEWORK

Write the quotient.

1. $6 \div 1 =$ ______
2. $1 \div 1 =$ ______
3. $0 \div 9 =$ ______
4. $0 \div 8 =$ ______
5. $3 \div 1 =$ ______
6. $2 \div 2 =$ ______
7. $8 \div 1 =$ ______
8. $0 \div 4 =$ ______
9. $9 \div 1 =$ ______
10. $1\overline{)9}$
11. $3\overline{)0}$
12. $7\overline{)7}$
13. $6\overline{)0}$
14. $5\overline{)5}$
15. $2\overline{)2}$
16. $1\overline{)7}$
17. $1\overline{)0}$
18. $4\overline{)4}$

Complete each equation.

19. $5 \times 1 =$ ______
    $5 \div 1 =$ ______
20. $0 \times 9 =$ ______
    $0 \div 9 =$ ______
21. ______ $\times 8 = 8$
    ______ $\div 8 = 1$

Problem Solving

22. Six people share a 6-pack of granola bars equally. How many granola bars does each person receive? Explain your answer.

    ____

    ____

23. Addison is solving a division problem in which the dividend is 0. What is the quotient? How do you know?

    ____

    ____

Write About It

24. Keri says that $0 \div 5 = 0$. Christina says that $5 \div 0 = 0$. Who is correct? Explain your reasoning.

    ____

    ____

Name ______________________ Date ______________

LESSON 8-6

Problem Solving
Work Backward

Nina has 7 more videos on her computer than Addison has on hers. Nina has 15 fewer videos on her computer than Kendall has on hers. Kendall has 42 videos on her computer. How many videos does Addison have?

To solve this problem, work backward. Start with what you know. You know Kendall has 42 videos.

Before you can find the number of videos Addison has, you must first find the number of videos Nina has.

Nina has 15 fewer videos than Kendall.
Subtract 42 − 15 = 27 to find that Nina has 27 videos.

Nina has 7 more videos than Addison.
Subtract 27 − 7 = 20 to find the number of videos for Addison.

Addison has 20 videos on her computer.

MORE PRACTICE

Work backward to solve.

1. Gianna worked on her project for 28 fewer minutes than Danielle. Gianna worked on her project 17 more minutes than Jenna. Jenna worked on her project for 63 minutes. How many minutes did Danielle work on her project?

Jenna worked on her project for ______ minutes.

To find the number of minutes Gianna worked on her project,

____________________.

Gianna worked on her project for ______ minutes.

To find the number of minutes Danielle worked on her

project, ____________________.

Danielle worked on her project for ______ minutes.

MORE PRACTICE

Solve. Show your work.

2. Gavin is thinking of a number. He multiplies it by 4 and then subtracts 8. The result is 20. What number is Gavin thinking of?

3. Alexandra goes apple picking. She keeps 4 apples for herself. Then she divides the rest of her apples equally among her 3 brothers. Each one gets 5 apples. How many apples did Alexandra pick?

4. Elias raises money for the local food bank. Today he collects equal amounts from his 7 neighbors. Then he adds $6 from his own money. Now he has $41. How much did each of Elias's neighbors give?

5. Savannah needs to borrow 30 magnets for a science experiment. Each of 3 friends lends her 7 magnets. How many more magnets does Savannah need?

6. Six children win 2 prizes each at the school fair. Three children win 3 prizes each at the school fair. The school fair only has 9 prizes left. How many prizes did the school fair start the night out with?

Name ______________________ Date __________

Problem Solving
Work Backward

HOMEWORK

Solve.

1. Ryan has shells in 4 equal groups. Tanner has 9 more shells than Ryan. Tanner has 3 fewer shells than Parker. Parker has 48 shells. How many shells are in each of Ryan's groups?

Before you can find how many shells Ryan has, you must find

the number of shells that ________ has.

Parker has ________ shells.

To find the number of shells Tanner has,

________________________.

Tanner has ________ shells.

To find the number of shells Ryan has,

________________________.

Ryan has ________ shells.

To find the number of shells in each of Ryan's groups,

________________________.

Ryan has ________ shells in each group.

2. Sara's paper clip chain has 2-in. paper clips. Sara's chain is 6 in. longer than Lucy's chain. Lucy's paper clip chain is 4 in. longer than Miranda's paper clip chain. Miranda's chain is 8 in. long. How many paper clips are in Sara's chain?

To find the length of Lucy's chain, ________________________.

Lucy's paper clip chain is ________ in. long.

To find the length of Sara's chain, ________________________.

Sara's paper clip chain is ________ in. long.

To find the number of paper clips in Sara's chain,

________________________.

Sara's chain has ________ paper clips.

HOMEWORK

Solve. Show your work.

3. The atomic number for argon is 15 more than the atomic number for lithium. The atomic number for argon is 8 more than the atomic number for neon. The atomic number for neon is 10. What is the atomic number for lithium?

Start at the end and work backward.

4. Molly has her coins in 3 groups. She has 6 more quarters than dimes. She has 9 more nickels than dimes. Molly has 12 nickels. How many coins does Molly have in each group?

5. Write a problem that you can use the work backward strategy to solve.

____

____

____

Write About It

6. Sergio read 7 more pages on Tuesday than on Monday. He read 8 fewer pages on Tuesday than he did on Wednesday. Sergio read 57 pages on Wednesday. How many pages did Sergio read in all? Explain how you found your answer.

____

____

____

____

Name ______________________ Date ______________

Fact Families

Write two multiplication facts and two division facts using the numbers 3, 6, and 18.

A multiplication and division fact family uses the same numbers. Most fact families have two multiplication and two division facts.

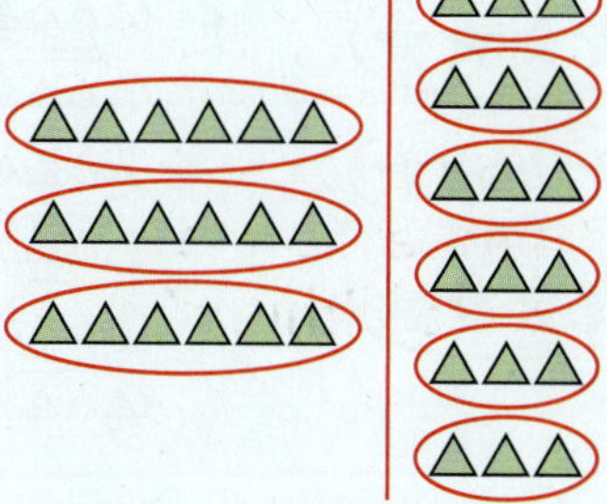

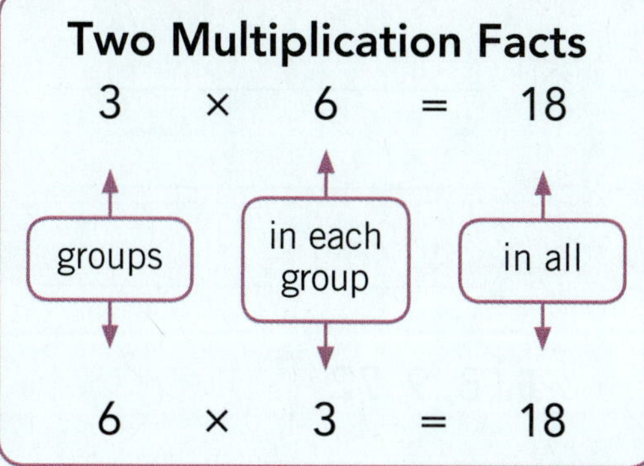

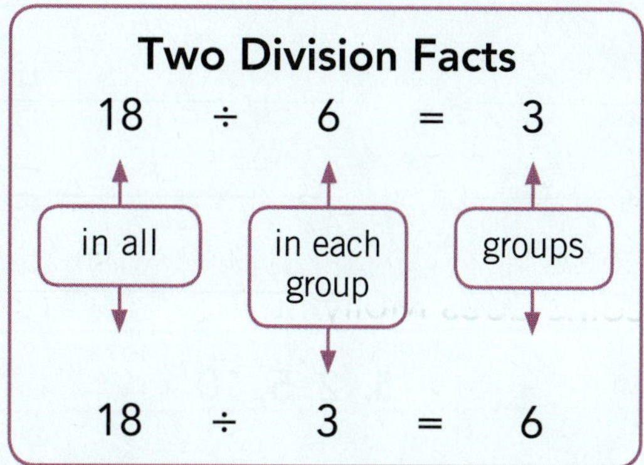

The multiplication and division fact family using 3, 6, and 18 is:

$3 \times 6 = 18$ $\quad 18 \div 6 = 3$

$6 \times 3 = 18$ $\quad 18 \div 3 = 6$

MORE PRACTICE

Write the fact family for each group.

1.

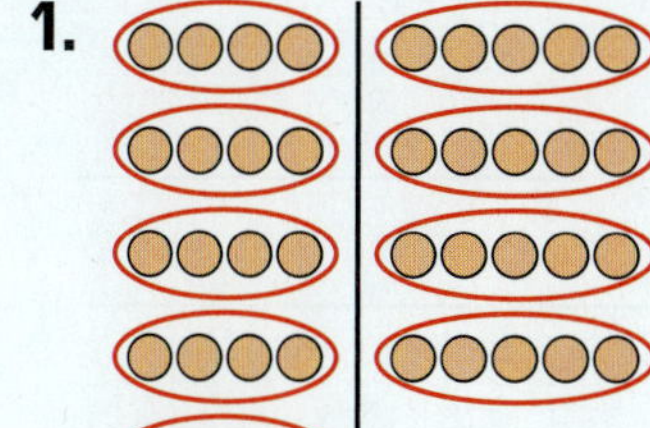

____
____
____
____

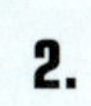

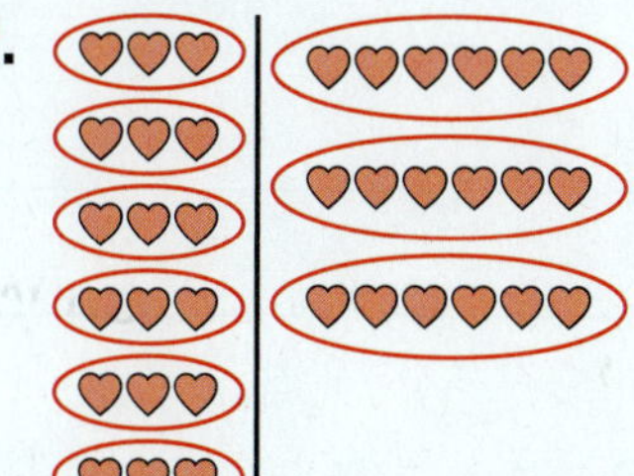

____
____
____
____

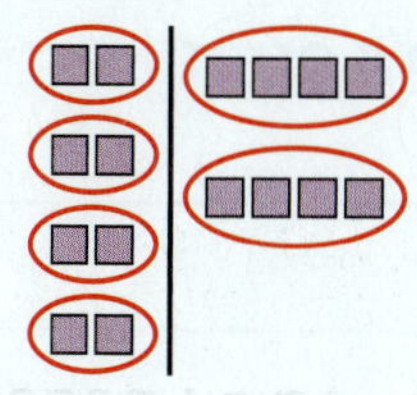

____
____
____
____

HOMEWORK

Write the fact family for the model or given numbers.

1. 

2. 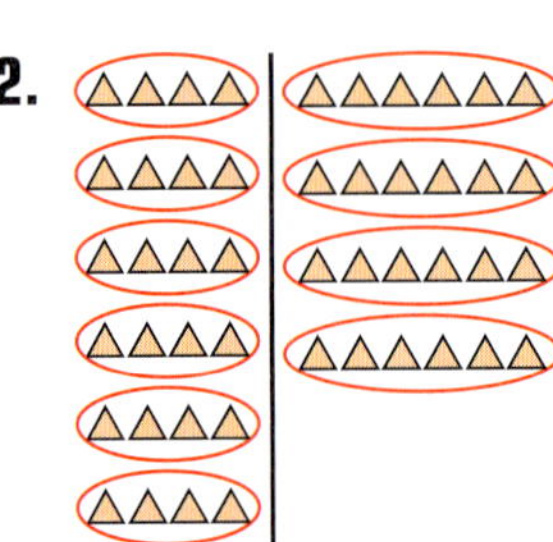

3. 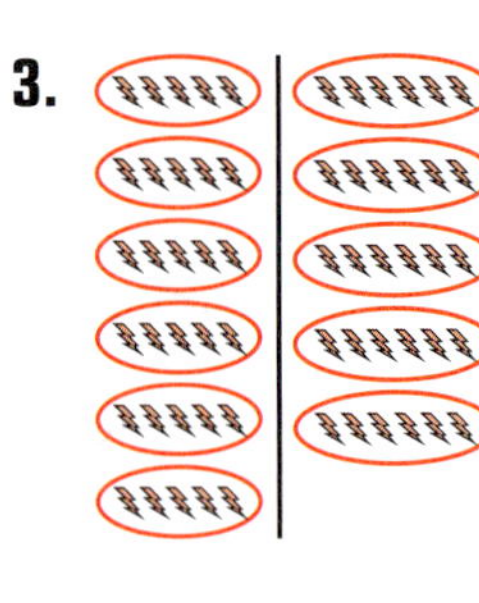

4. 4, 9, 36

5. 2, 5, 10

6. 8, 9, 72

Problem Solving

7. Ramona says the multiplication and division fact family for 2, 2, 4 has 4 facts because 2 + 2 = 4 and 4 − 2 = 2. Explain Ramona's error.

Write About It

8. What is the greatest number of facts an array can show? What is the least number of facts an array can show? Explain.

Name ______________________ Date ____________

LESSON 8-8

Use Facts to Solve Problems

Melissa spends $40 to buy 4 movie tickets. How much does each movie ticket cost?

You can use a division fact or a multiplication fact to solve.

- You can use a division fact.

  $40 ÷ 4 = ?

  $40 ÷ 4 = $10

- You can use a multiplication fact.

  4 × ? = $40

  4 × $10 = $40

Each movie ticket costs $10.

MORE PRACTICE

Write a multiplication fact or division fact to solve the problem.

1. There are 6 baskets with 8 strawberries each. How many strawberries are there in all?

   ____

   ____

2. A store has 56 hats. The same number are on 7 shelves. How many hats are on each shelf?

   ____

   ____

3. There are 40 rose bushes. They are planted in rows of 8. How many rows of rose bushes are there?

   ____

   ____

4. Jillian has 9 nickels that are worth 5¢ each and 4 dimes that are 10¢ each. How much money does Jillian have?

   ____

   ____

5. Fiona has 30 sunflowers planted in rows in one of the fields on her farm. The field has 3 rows. The rows have the same number of sunflowers. How many sunflowers are in each row of the field?

   ____

   ____

6. Cody is in a trivia contest. He gets 10 points for every correct answer. He loses 2 points for an incorrect answer. He gives 6 correct answers and 2 incorrect answers. How many points does Cody score? Show your work.

   ____

   ____

HOMEWORK

Write an equation or equations to solve the problem.

1. A toonie is a Canadian coin that is worth $2. How much money are 8 toonies worth?

____

2. A newspaper stack is 8 inches high. There are 7 stacks piled to form a large stack. What is the height of the large stack?

____

3. Crystal has 4 eggs in her refrigerator. She buys 3 cartons that all have 6 eggs. How many eggs does Crystal have now?

____

Problem Solving

4. Cody uses 54 blocks to make 6 shapes. Derek uses 64 blocks to make 8 shapes. All of Cody's shapes use the same number of blocks. All of Derek's shapes use the same number of blocks. Who uses more blocks per shape? Explain your answer.

____

____

5. Erin has $24 to buy tickets for rides. She can go on rides that cost $3 or $4. If she only goes on $3 rides, how many more rides can she take than if she chose only $4 rides? Explain.

____

____

Write About It

6. Andie bought 4 boxes of pens. Each box has 3 blue pens and 5 black pens. She said she has 60 pens. Explain why Andie is incorrect and correct the error.

____

____

Name ____________________ Date ____________

LESSON 8-9

Use Order of Operations

Adrian has 8 socks in his drawer. He puts 6 pairs of socks into the drawer. How many socks are now in the drawer?

The expression $8 + 2 \times 6$ can be used to represent the number of socks in the drawer now.

When an expression has more than one operation, simplify by using the order of operations.

Order of Operations

- First multiply or divide in order from left to right.
- Then add or subtract in order from left to right.

To find $8 + 2 \times 6$, follow this order:

$8 + 2 \times 6$ — First multiply 2 and 6.

$8 + 12$ — Then add 8 and 12.

20

Adrian now has 20 socks in his drawer.

MORE PRACTICE

Write the operation that should be done first.

1. $12 - 6 + 2$ ____ **2.** $8 \times 4 \div 2$ ____ **3.** $12 - 4 \div 2$ ____

Write the operation symbols in the correct order.

4. $21 \div 3 \times 5$ ________ **5.** $4 + 5 \times 3$ ________ **6.** $24 + 12 \div 6$ ________

Use the order of operations to simplify.

7. $18 - 9 \times 2 =$ ____ **8.** $5 \times 6 \div 3 =$ ________ **9.** $24 \div 3 + 7 =$ ________

10. $6 \times 2 - 3 + 9 =$ ____ **11.** $12 + 15 \div 3 \times 4 =$ ____

HOMEWORK

Write the operation that should be done first.

1. 8 − 2 × 3 ____ **2.** 12 + 6 − 2 ____ **3.** 24 − 12 ÷ 3 ____

Write the operations in the correct order.

4. 6 × 4 ÷ 3 ________ **5.** 7 − 1 × 3 ________ **6.** 16 + 24 ÷ 6 ________

Match the expression to its value.

7. 19 − 3 × 2	4
	5
8. 16 + 12 ÷ 4	6
9. 32 + 8 ÷ 4	10
	13
10. 2 + 6 ÷ 2	19
11. 4 + 2 × 9 ÷ 3	30
	32
12. 15 − 7 + 6 × 4	34

Problem Solving

13. Brody uses the order of operations to write an expression that is equal to 12. Write the operations.

4 ____ 4 ____ 4 = 12

14. Which is greater, 5 + 5 ÷ 5 or 5 + 5 − 5? Explain your answer.

Write About It

15. Why is it important to follow the order of operations? Explain using 2 + 5 × 4.

____

____

____

Name ______________________________ Date ______________

LESSON 9-1

Understand Equal Parts

Reagan wants to share her granola bar with two friends. They will each get an equal part. How many equal parts will Reagan cut her granola bar into? What are the equal parts called?

A whole is all of the parts of one shape.

A whole can be divided into equal parts.
Equal parts must be exactly the same size.

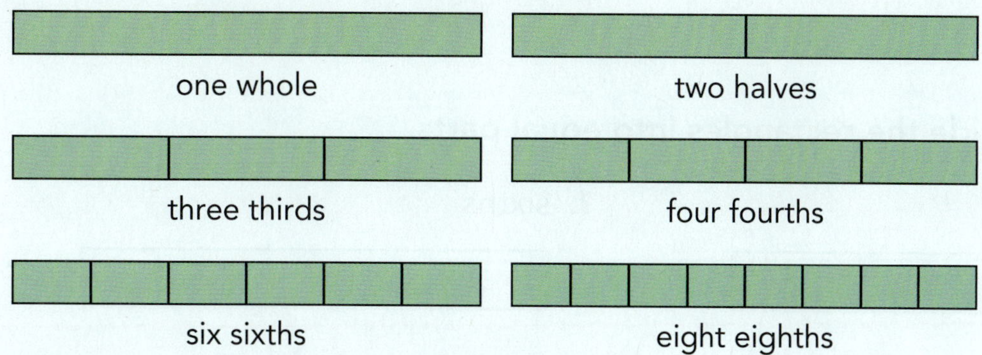

Reagan's granola bar will be cut into 3 equal parts.
The parts are called thirds.

MORE PRACTICE

Circle the shapes that show equal parts. Draw an X through the shapes that show unequal parts. If the shape shows equal parts, write the name of the equal parts on the line.

1. 

____

2. 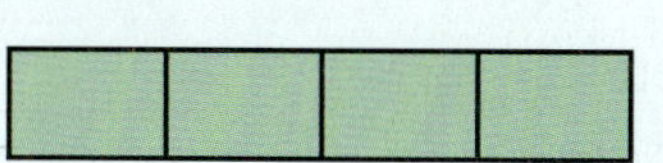

____

3. 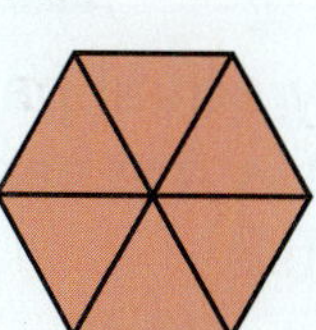

____

4. 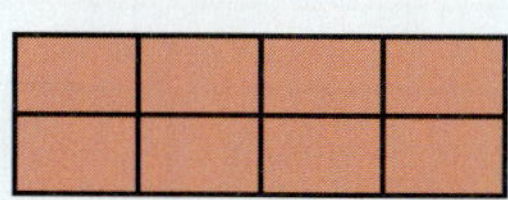

____

5. 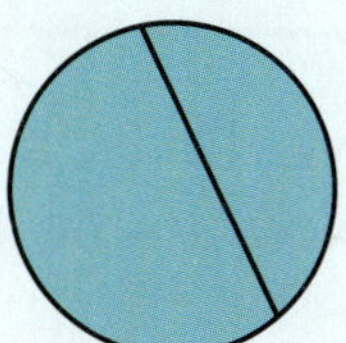

____

6. 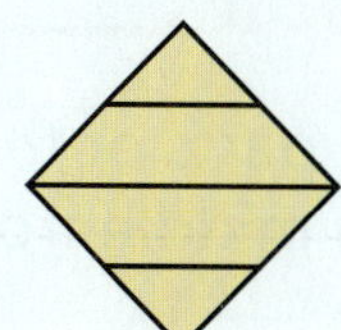

____

HOMEWORK

Use the words in the box to write the number of equal parts.

eighths	fourths	halves	sixths	thirds

1. 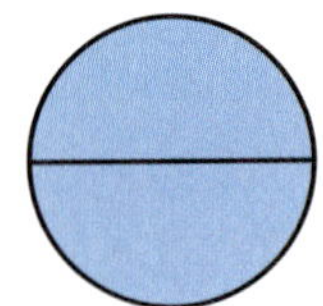 ________

2. 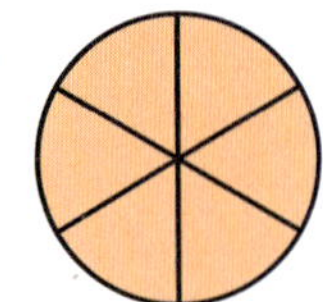 ________

3. 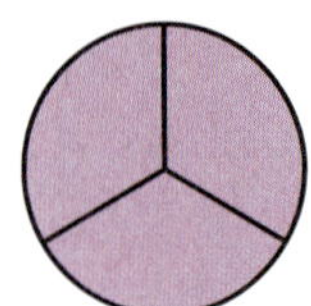 ________

4.  ________

5. 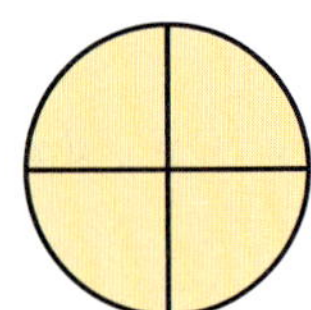 ________

Draw lines to divide the rectangles into equal parts.

6. thirds

7. sixths

8. eighths

9. fourths

Problem Solving

10. Terrence cuts a sandwich into equal parts.

How many equal parts does he cut? What is the name for the equal parts?

____

11. Carrie invents a game that has a playing field with 2 equal parts. She says her field can be shown by two halves. How can she be correct? How can Carrie be incorrect?

____

____

____

Write About It

12. Name the parts of the rectangle shown. Draw a line across the middle from left to right. Now name the parts.

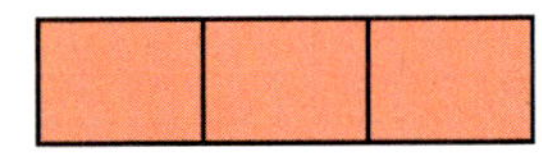

____

Name ______________________________ Date ______________

LESSON 9-2

Name Unit Fractions of a Whole

Jeremy is making note cards. He folds a piece of paper to make 4 equal parts. What fraction of the paper is one equal part?

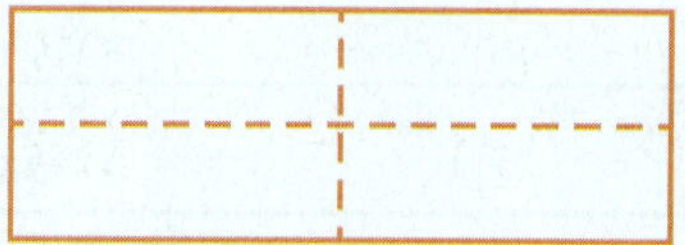

- A fraction is a number that names part of a whole.

The numerator is the number of equal parts being counted. It is the top number of a fraction.

The denominator is the total number of equal parts in the whole. It is the bottom number of a fraction.

number of equal parts being counted ⟶ 1 ⟵ numerator
total number of equal parts ⟶ 4 ⟵ denominator

Word name: one fourth

Write: $\frac{1}{4}$

- A unit fraction is a fraction with a numerator of 1. It names 1 equal part.

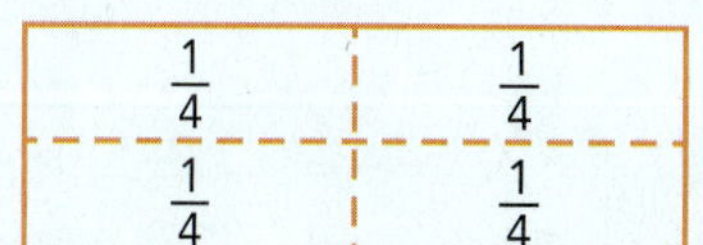

One equal part of Jeremy's paper is $\frac{1}{4}$.

MORE PRACTICE

Write the fraction that names the shaded part.

1. 

____

2. 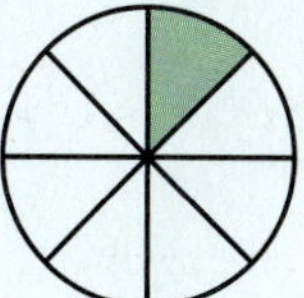

____

3. 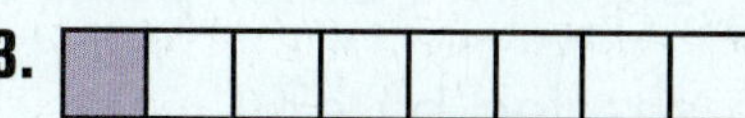

____

4. 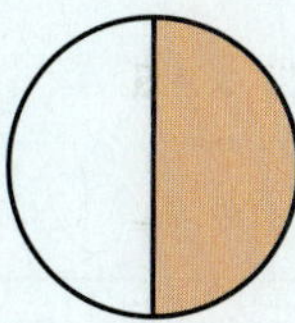

____

5. 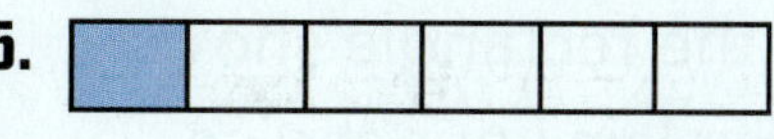

____

6. 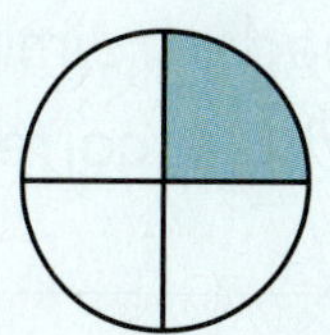

____

HOMEWORK

Divide and shade the rectangle to model each fraction. Then match each fraction to the circle model.

1. $\frac{1}{2}$ 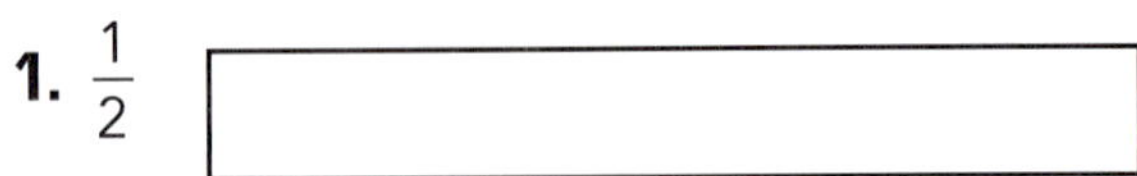

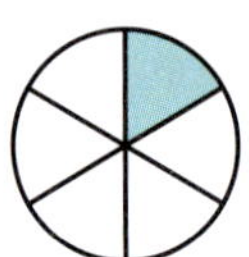

2. $\frac{1}{6}$

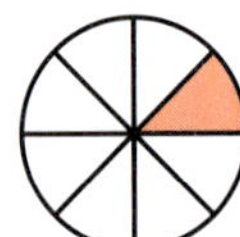

3. $\frac{1}{4}$

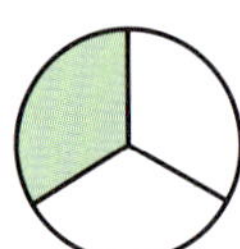

4. $\frac{1}{3}$

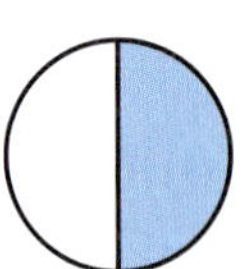

5. $\frac{1}{8}$

Problem Solving

6. Tom slices a melon into 4 equal pieces. He eats one slice.

What fraction of the melon does Tom eat? ________

7. A circle is divided into 3 equal parts. One part is shaded blue. The other parts are shaded red. What fraction is shaded blue? ________

Write About It

8. A rectangle is shown. Dwight says the rectangle shows $\frac{1}{3}$ shaded. Jim says the rectangle shows $\frac{1}{4}$ shaded. Who is correct? Explain your choice.

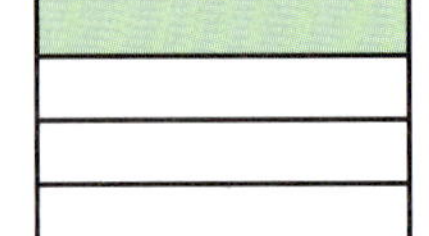

____

____

Name ______________________ Date ______________

LESSON 9-3

Find Unit Fractions on a Number Line

A boardwalk runs along a beach. A snack shack is going to be built $\frac{1}{4}$ of the way from the beach entrance to the lifeguard station. How can you represent the location of the snack shack on a number line?

You can use a number line to show parts of a whole.

- Draw a number line from 0 to 1. This represents one whole.

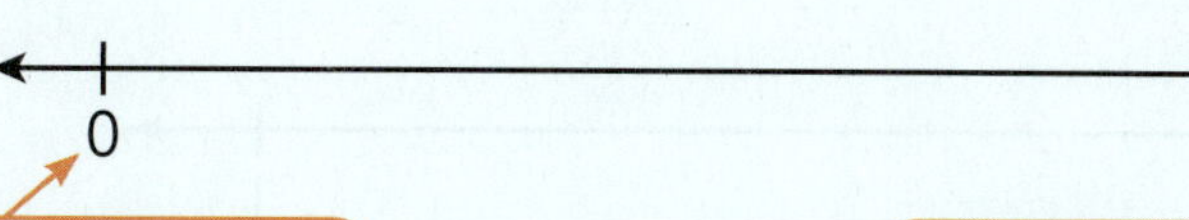

0 represents the entrance.

1 represents the lifeguard station.

- Divide the number line into 4 intervals of equal length, or fourths, because 4 is the denominator of the fraction.

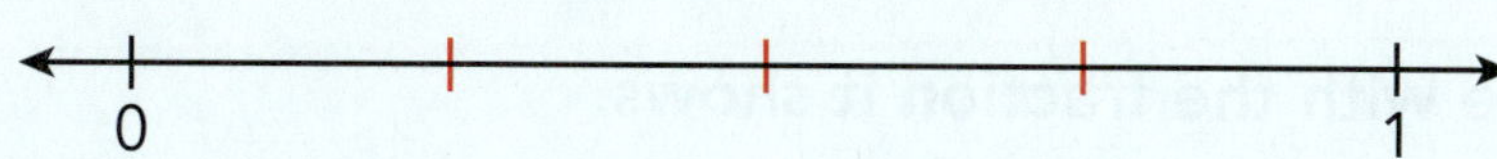

- The first mark represents the point that is $\frac{1}{4}$ the distance from 0 to 1. Plot a point at $\frac{1}{4}$.

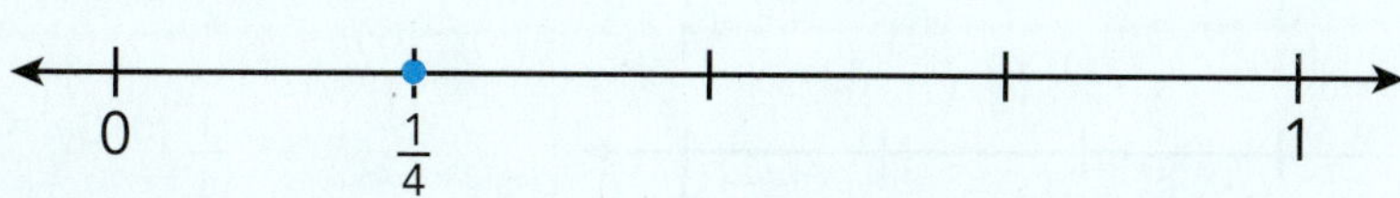

The blue point on the number line represents the location of the snack shack.

MORE PRACTICE

Write the fraction that names each point.

1. 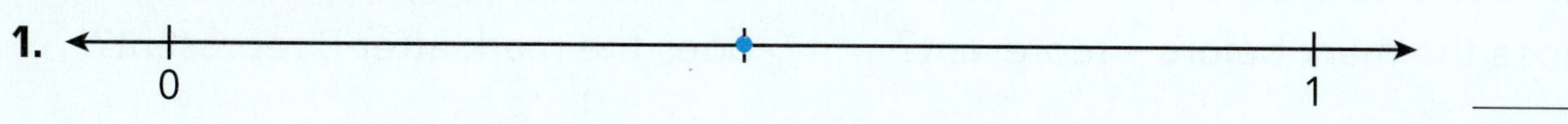

______

2. 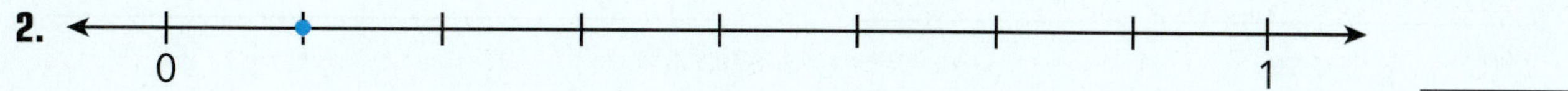

______

3. 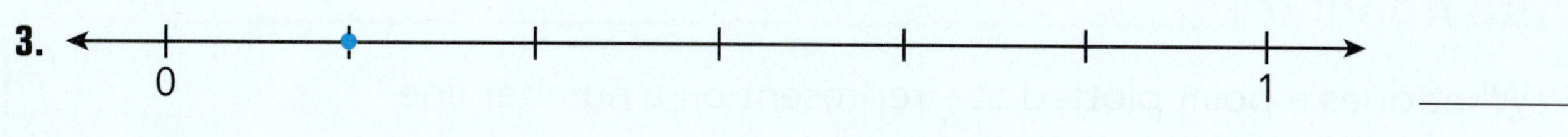

______

4. 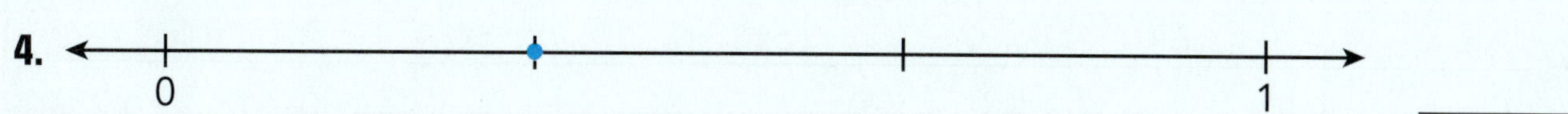

______

HOMEWORK

Complete the number line and plot a point to represent the fraction.

1. $\frac{1}{3}$

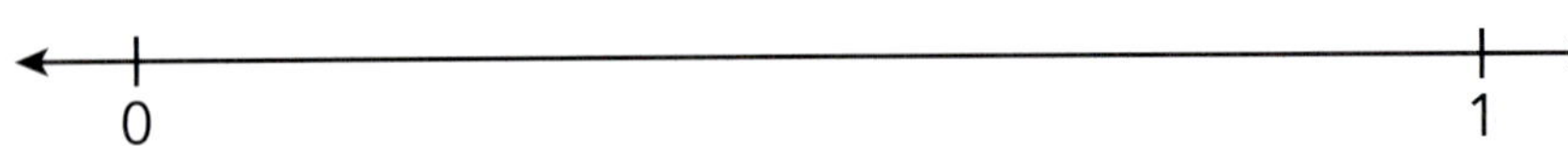

2. $\frac{1}{6}$

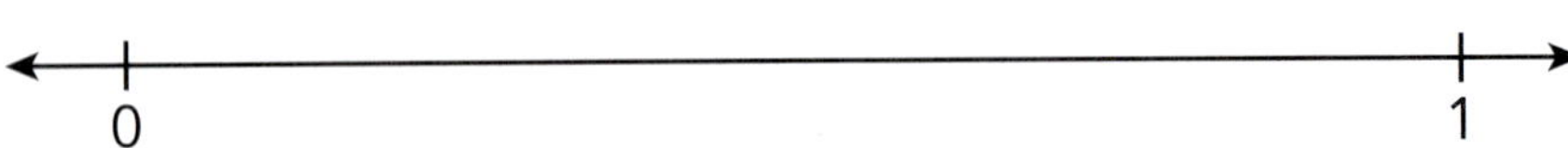

3. $\frac{1}{4}$

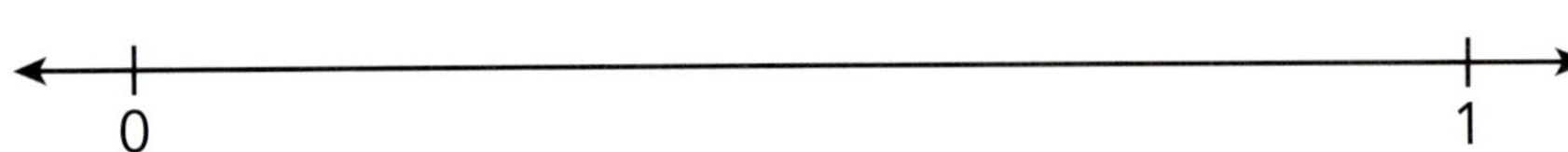

4. $\frac{1}{8}$

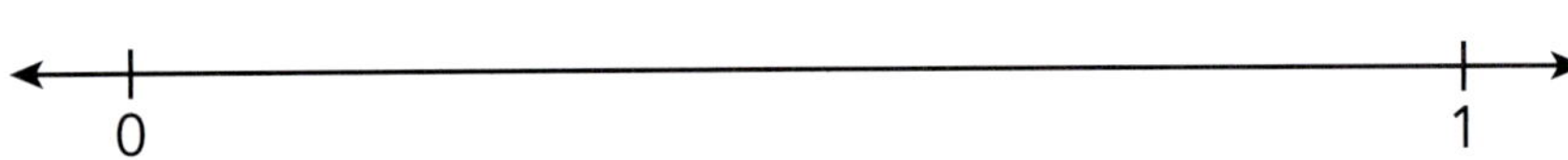

Match each number line with the fraction it shows.

5. 0 1 $\frac{1}{3}$

6. 0 1 $\frac{1}{2}$

7. 0 1 $\frac{1}{4}$

8. 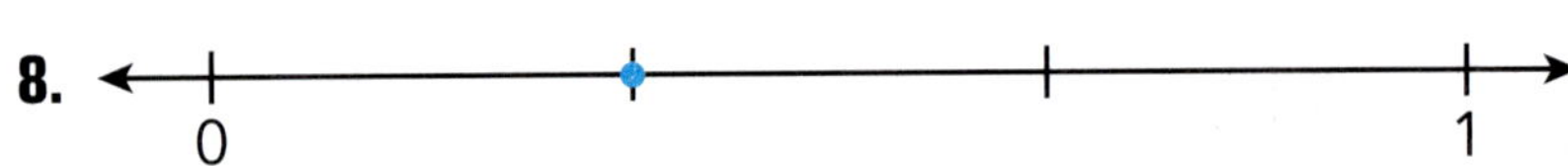 $\frac{1}{6}$

Problem Solving

9. A number line from 0 to 1 is divided into 6 equal parts. What does the mark before $\frac{1}{6}$ represent?

____

10. A number line from 0 to 1 is divided into 8 equal parts. What does the mark after 0 represent?

____

Write About It

11. What does a point plotted at $\frac{1}{6}$ represent on a number line?

____

Name ____________________ Date __________

Name Fractions of a Whole

Autumn is painting a mural that has 4 equal parts. She paints 3 of the parts. What fraction of the mural has Autumn painted?

A fraction can name one or more equal parts of a whole. You can make a fraction by putting copies of unit fractions together.

The mural can be divided into four equal parts that are each $\frac{1}{4}$. There are 3 parts that Autumn has painted.

$\frac{1}{4}$	$\frac{1}{4}$	$\frac{1}{4}$	$\frac{1}{4}$

The entire mural is the whole. It is equal to $\frac{4}{4}$, or 1.

- The numerator names the number of equal parts that are being counted.
- The denominator names the total number of equal parts.

numerator → 3 ← number of equal parts painted
denominator → 4 ← number of equal parts in all

Word name: three fourths
Write: $\frac{3}{4}$

The fraction of the mural that Autumn has painted is $\frac{3}{4}$.

MORE PRACTICE

How many unit fractions make up each fraction?

1. 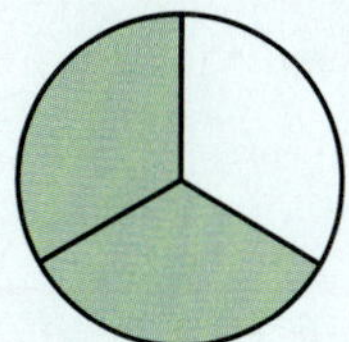

$\frac{2}{3}$ ______

2. 

$\frac{4}{8}$ ______

3.  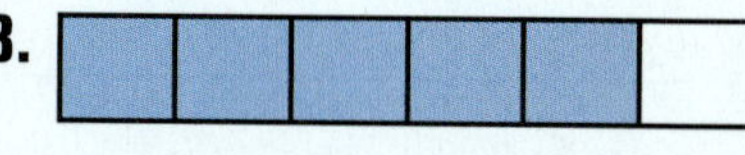

$\frac{5}{6}$ ______

4. If you put together six copies of one eighth together, what fraction do you make? ______

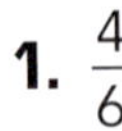

HOMEWORK

Shade each model to show the fraction.

1. $\frac{4}{6}$ 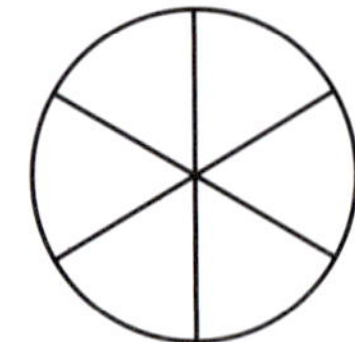

2. $\frac{7}{8}$ 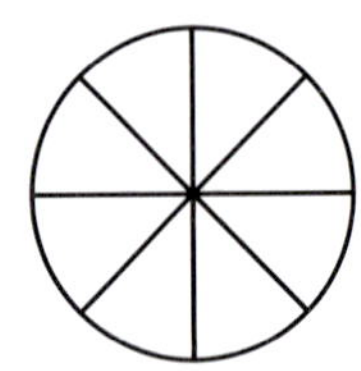

3. $\frac{6}{8}$ 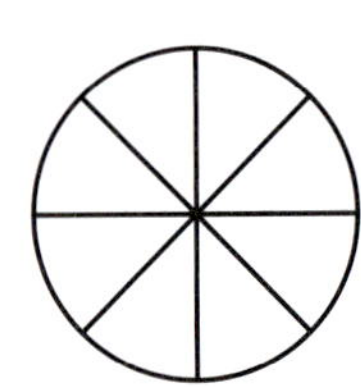

Match each model to the fraction that is shaded.

4. 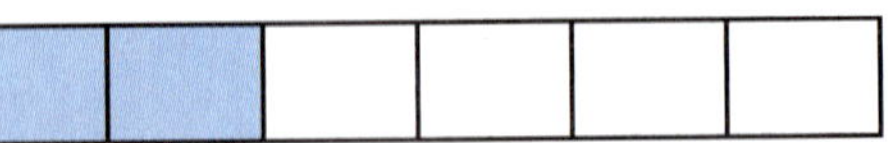 $\frac{2}{6}$

5. 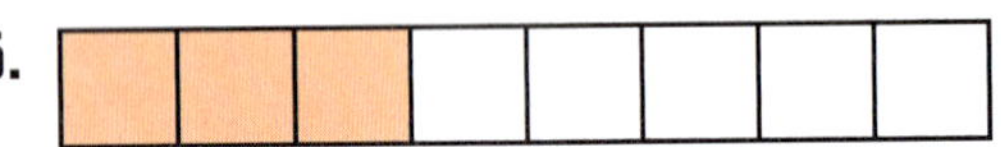 $\frac{2}{8}$

6. 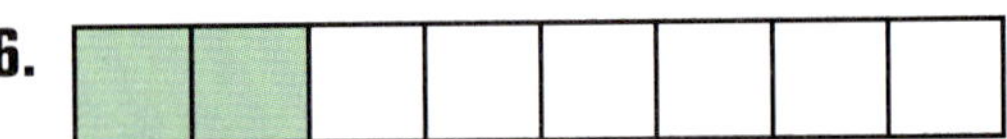 $\frac{3}{6}$

7. 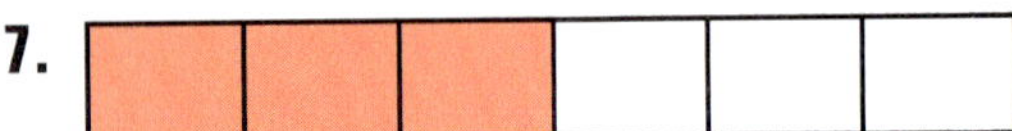 $\frac{3}{8}$

Divide each model and shade to show the fraction.

8. $\frac{2}{4}$

9. $\frac{5}{8}$

10. $\frac{2}{3}$

Problem Solving

11. A garden is divided into 8 equal parts. Four of the parts are planted with daisies. What fraction of the garden has daisies?

____

12. A mango is cut into 3 equal pieces. Craig eats 2 pieces. What fraction of the mango does Craig eat?

____

Write About It

13. What fraction do you get from putting together 8 copies of the unit fraction $\frac{1}{2}$? Explain how you found the numerator.

____

____

Name ______________________ Date ____________

LESSON 9-5

Find Fractions on a Number Line

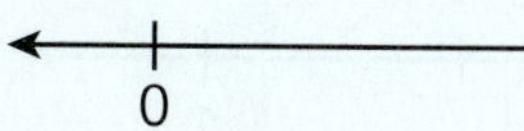

Where does $\frac{5}{6}$ belong on a number line?

- Draw a number line from 0 to 1.

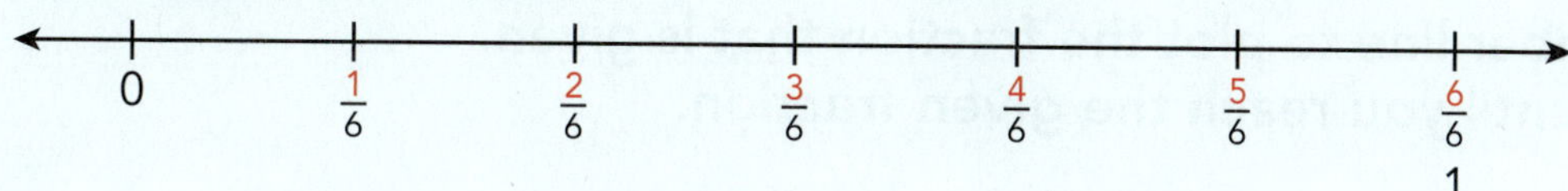

- The denominator tells you how many equal parts to divide the whole into. Divide the number line into 6 intervals of equal length. Each length is $\frac{1}{6}$ of the whole. Each numerator is equal to the number of lengths of $\frac{1}{6}$ the tick mark is from 0.

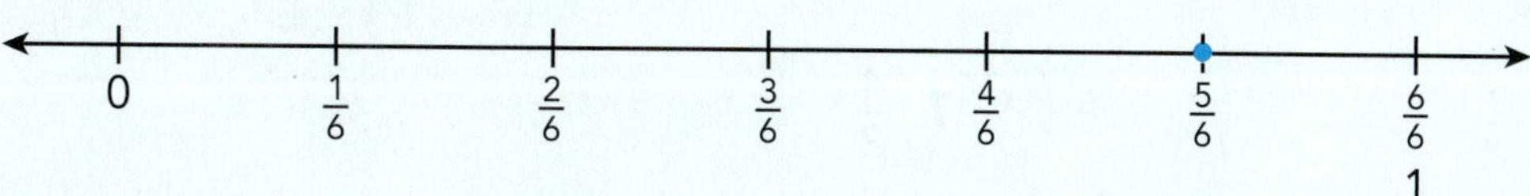

- Count 5 lengths of $\frac{1}{6}$ from 0 to make the distance $\frac{5}{6}$. Plot a point at $\frac{5}{6}$.

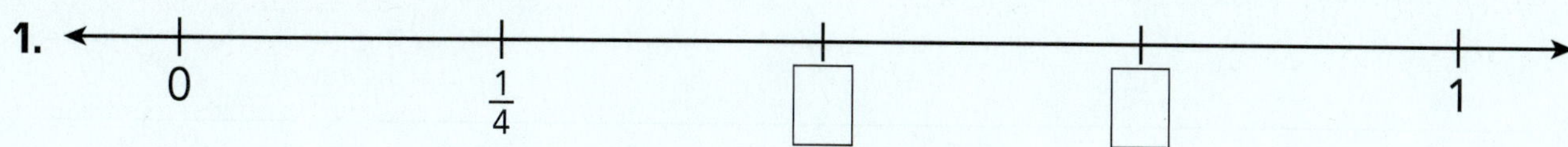

So the blue point on the number line represents $\frac{5}{6}$.

MORE PRACTICE

Complete each number line.

1.

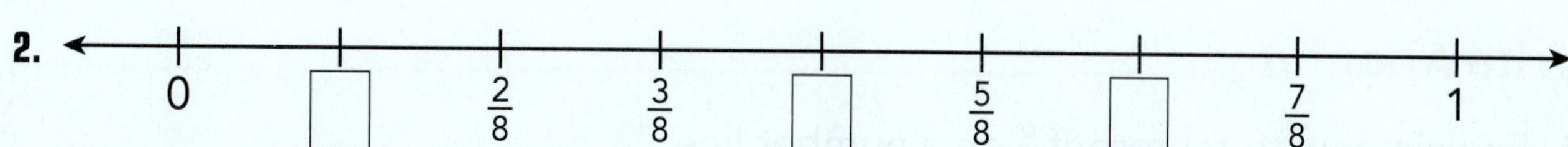

2.

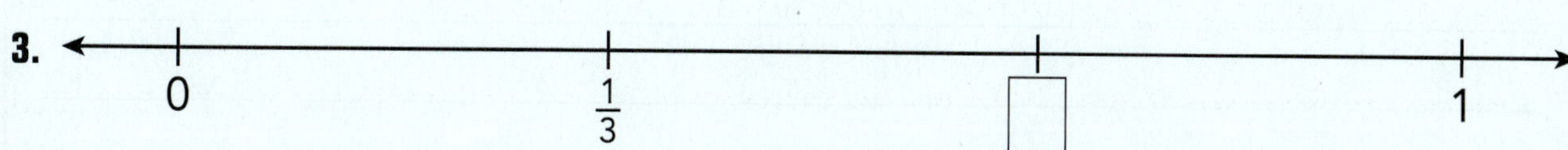

3.

0 — $\frac{1}{3}$ — ☐ — 1

HOMEWORK

Complete each number line.

1. 0, $\frac{1}{6}$, ☐, $\frac{3}{6}$, $\frac{4}{6}$, ☐, 1

2. 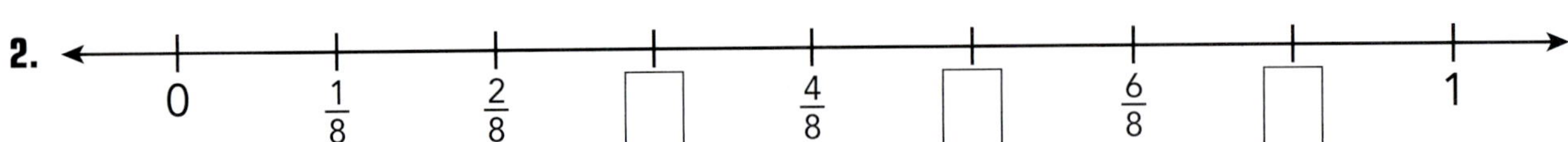

3. 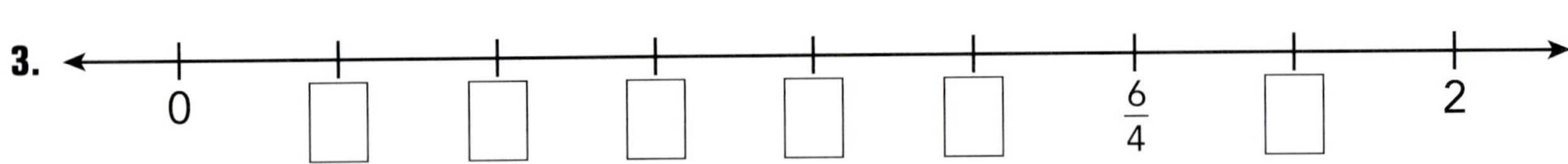

Partition each number line to plot the fraction that is given. Name each mark until you reach the given fraction.

4. $\frac{5}{6}$

0, 1

5. $\frac{3}{8}$

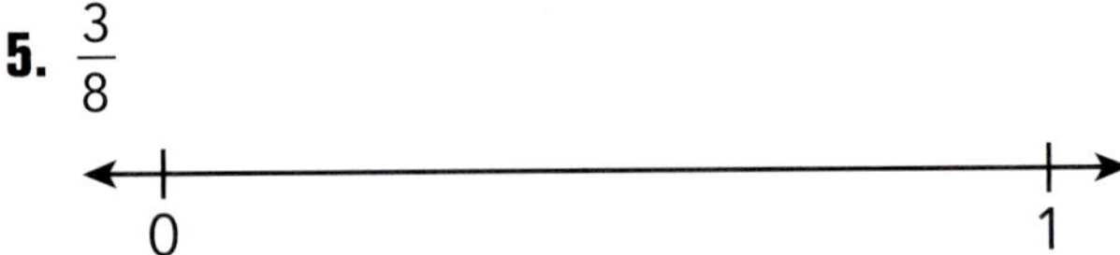

6. $\frac{3}{4}$

0, 1

7. $\frac{4}{3}$

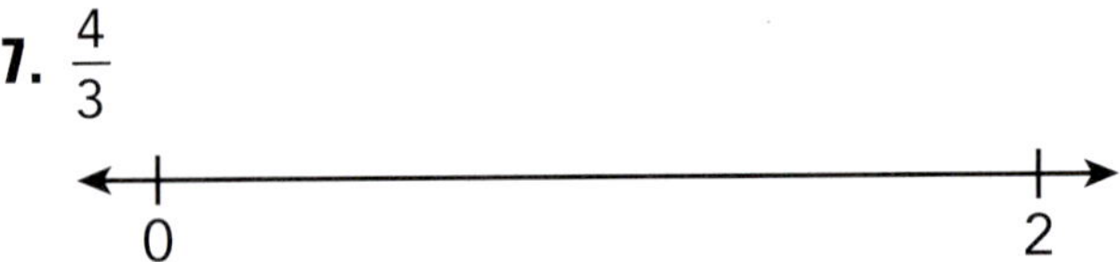

Problem Solving

8. Matt said the fraction that represents point *A* is $\frac{8}{6}$. Is Matt correct? Explain your answer.

A, 0, 1

____

____

Write About It

9. Explain how to represent $\frac{6}{4}$ on a number line.

____

____

____

Name ______________________ Date ______________

LESSON 9-6

Use a Fraction to Find the Whole

This is $\frac{1}{6}$ of a drinking straw. What does the whole straw look like?

You can use a fractional part to find the whole.

Each piece is $\frac{1}{6}$ of the whole straw.

$\frac{1}{6}$ $\frac{1}{6}$ $\frac{1}{6}$ $\frac{1}{6}$ $\frac{1}{6}$ $\frac{1}{6}$

If you put the 6 equal pieces together, they will form 1 whole straw.

The whole straw looks like this:

6 copies of $\frac{1}{6}$ make $\frac{6}{6}$, or 1 whole.

MORE PRACTICE

Complete the drawing to show a whole. Then write the fraction represented by the whole.

1. ______

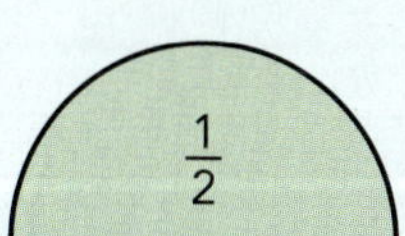

2. ______

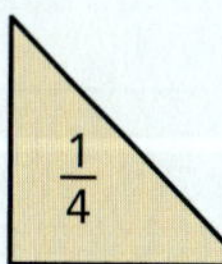

3. ______

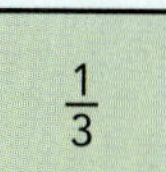

4. ______

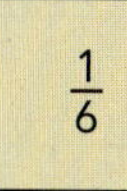

HOMEWORK

Match each part of a whole to its whole.

1. 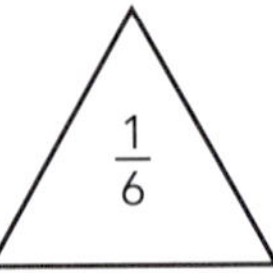

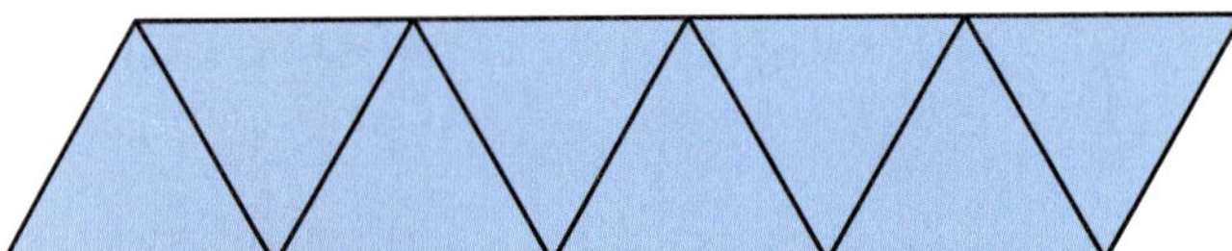

2. 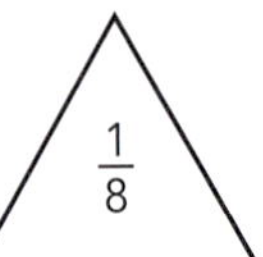

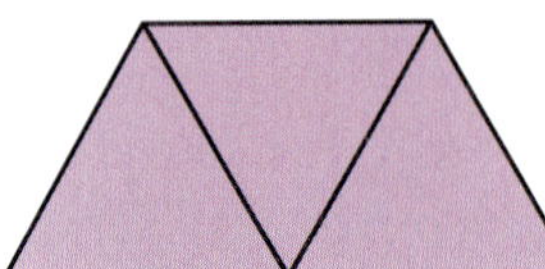

3. 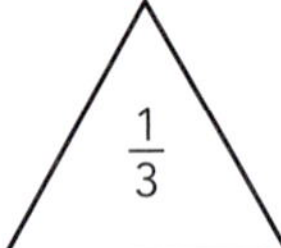

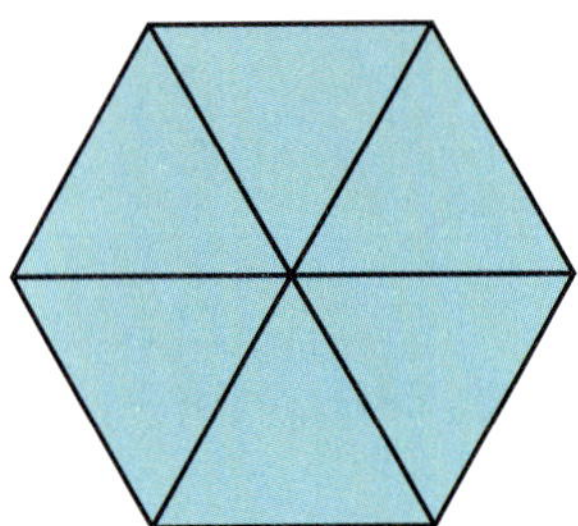

Problem Solving

4. Each line represents $\frac{1}{4}$ of a whole. Will the whole be greater for the blue line or the red line? Explain your reasoning.

____

____

Write About It

5. Ron and Seth each used [blue square] to represent $\frac{1}{6}$ of a rectangle. Who drew a whole correctly? Explain your answer.

____

____

____

____

Ron

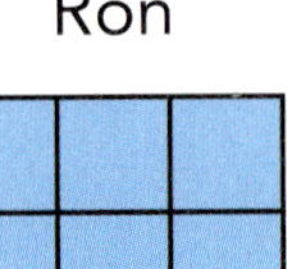

Seth

Name ______________________ Date ____________

LESSON 9-7

Problem Solving
Use a Model

A piece of wood is cut into 6 equal parts. Five of the parts are needed for a project. Molly says that she needs $\frac{5}{6}$ of the wood. Is Molly correct?

To find if Molly is correct, you can make a fraction model.

- The wood was cut into 6 equal parts. Draw a regular hexagon because it has 6 sides.

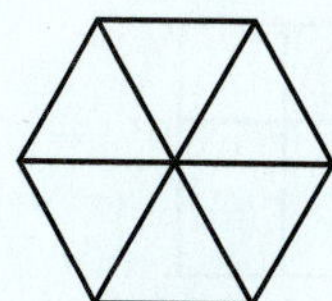

- Because 5 of the equal parts of the wood are needed, shade 5 of the parts a color.

  The hexagon is $\frac{5}{6}$ shaded.

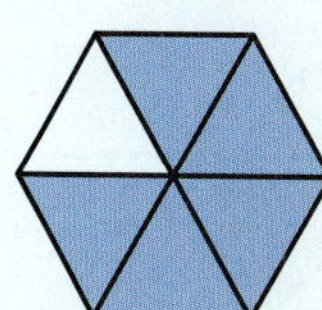

The fraction of the wood that is needed is $\frac{5}{6}$. Molly is correct.

MORE PRACTICE

1. Clara lives 1 mile from school. Clara rides $\frac{3}{4}$ of the way to school. How many miles from school is she? Use a model to explain your reasoning.

____

____

____

2. The model represents $\frac{2}{6}$. Write a story about what the shaded part of the model represents.

____

____

____

____

MORE PRACTICE

3. Jonas lives 1 mile from school. Pablo lives between Jonas and the school. The distance to Pablo's house is shown on the number line as point P.

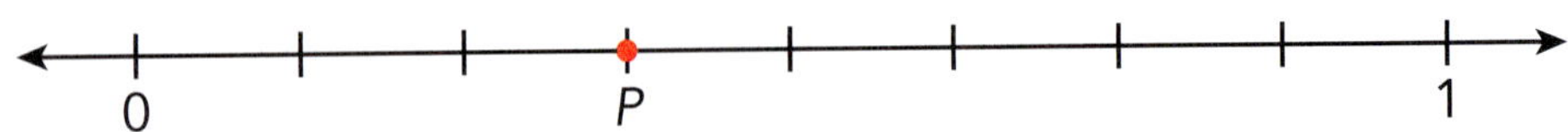

Which other models can be used to represent the distance from Jonas's house to Pablo's house? Circle all that apply.

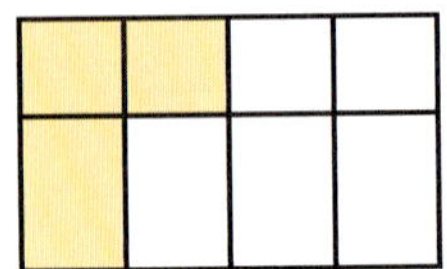
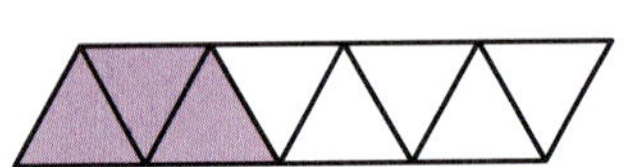
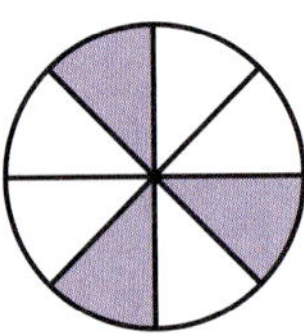
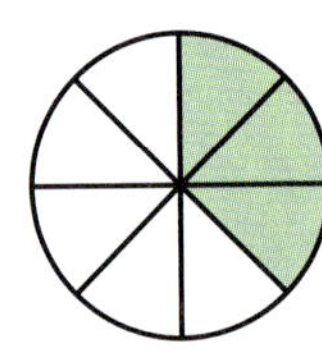
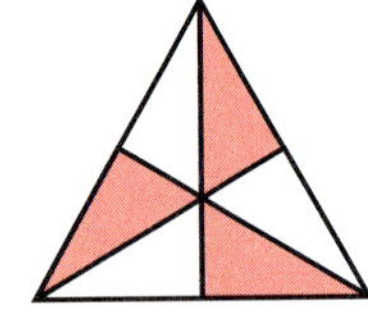

How many miles does Pablo live from Jonas? ______

4. Tucker divides his whiteboard into 6 equal parts. Tucker fills 4 of the parts with his drawings. What fraction of the whiteboard is empty? Divide the rectangle to help you. ______

5. Andrea answered $\frac{1}{8}$ of the questions on a quiz incorrectly. What fraction did she answer correctly? Shade the model and use it to explain your reasoning.

____

____

6. Write a story to represent the part of the model that is shaded.

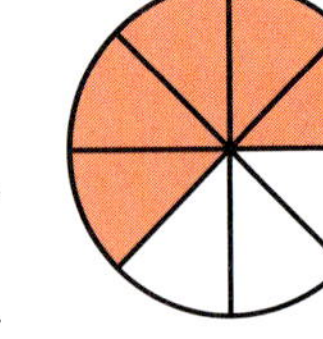

____

____

Name ______________________ Date ____________

Problem Solving
Use a Model

HOMEWORK

1. The wall coming up the stairs is $\frac{5}{6}$ covered with family photos. What fraction of the wall is not covered with family photos? Shade the model and use it to explain your reasoning.

____

____

____

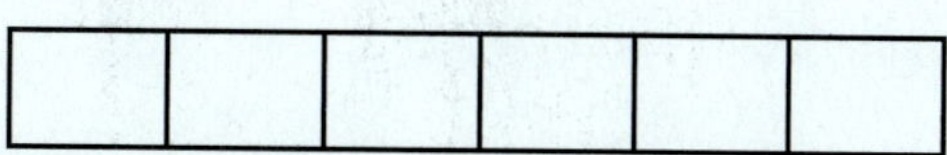

Use this model for Exercises 2–3.

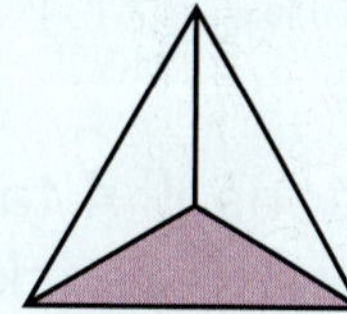

2. Write a story to represent the part of the model that is shaded.

____

____

____

____

3. Write a different story to represent the part of the model that is not shaded.

____

____

____

4. A pizza is cut into 8 equal slices. The model shows the fraction of the pizza for one slice.

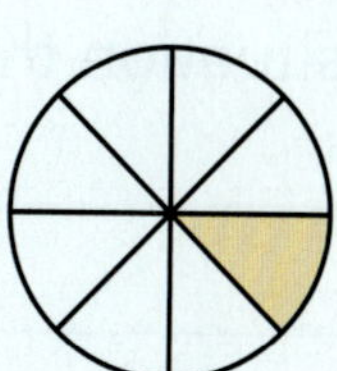

Divide the rectangle and shade it to show a different model of the fraction for one slice of the pizza.

HOMEWORK

5. Yaretzi and her mom drive $\frac{2}{8}$ of the distance to school when they see Nora walking. Her mother picks up Nora. Draw a number line to show the distance that Yaretzi and her mother drive before picking up Nora. Place a point at the correct part of the distance.

6. A stick of butter is shown.

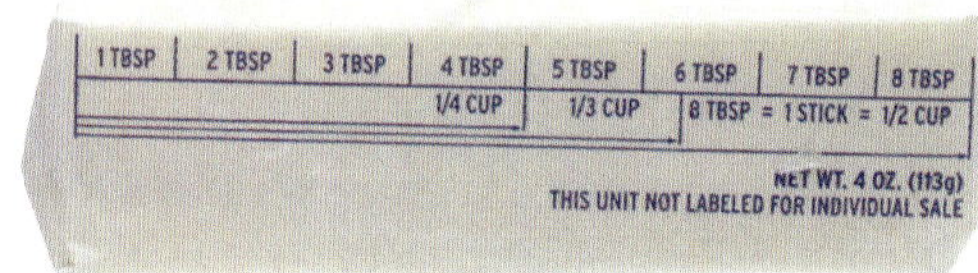

The stick is equal to 8 tablespoons. If 4 tablespoons of butter have been used, what fraction of the stick is left? Shade the rectangle to help you find the fraction. ______

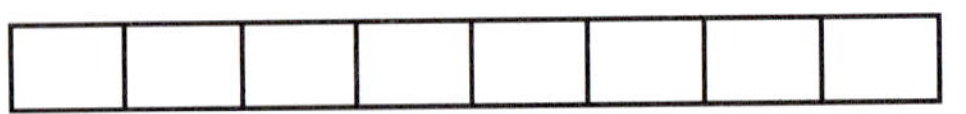

7. A meatloaf is cut into 8 equal parts. Six of the pieces are eaten. Vishal says that $\frac{2}{8}$ of the original meatloaf is still there. Dakota says that $\frac{6}{8}$ of the original meatloaf is still there. Who is correct? Explain. Use the model to help you.

____

Write About It

8. How can the shape chosen for the model help to explain the situation the model represents? Give an example.

____

____

____

____

Name ______________________ Date ______________

LESSON 10-1

Whole Numbers and Fractions

What are some ways Natalia can write 2 as a fraction?

- You can write a whole number as a fraction. Write the whole number as the numerator and 1 as the denominator.

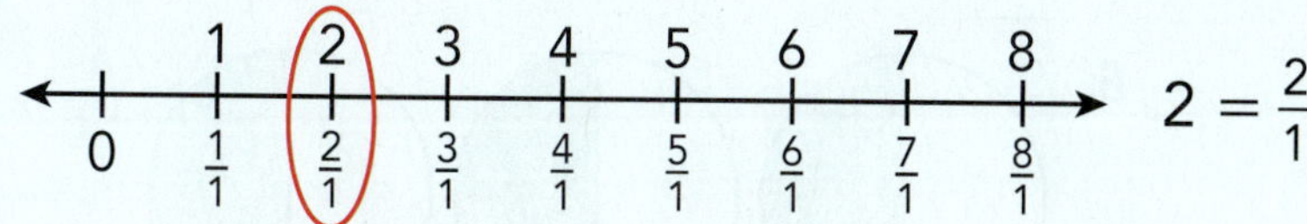

$2 = \frac{2}{1}$

- You can also write other fractions that are equivalent to whole numbers.

  If two numbers are at the same point on a number line, they are equivalent.

  - To write equivalent fractions for 2, draw two number lines from 0 to 2.
  - Partition the first number line into halves.

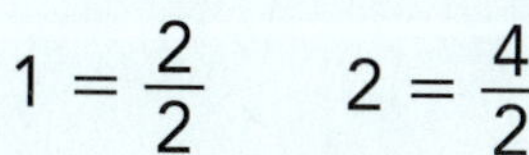

$1 = \frac{2}{2}$ $\quad 2 = \frac{4}{2}$

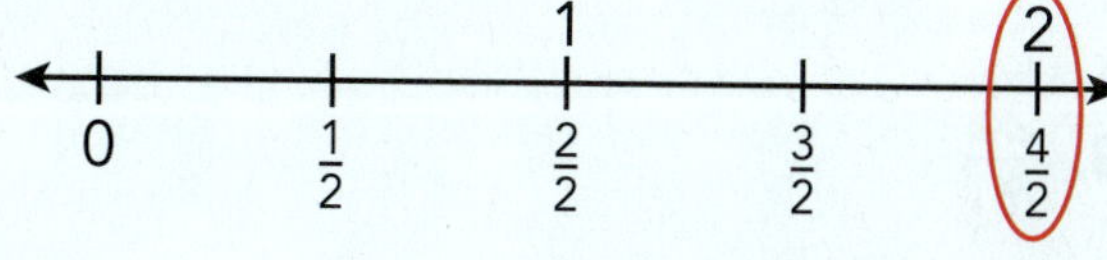

  - Partition the second number line into fourths.

$1 = \frac{4}{4}$ $\quad 2 = \frac{8}{4}$

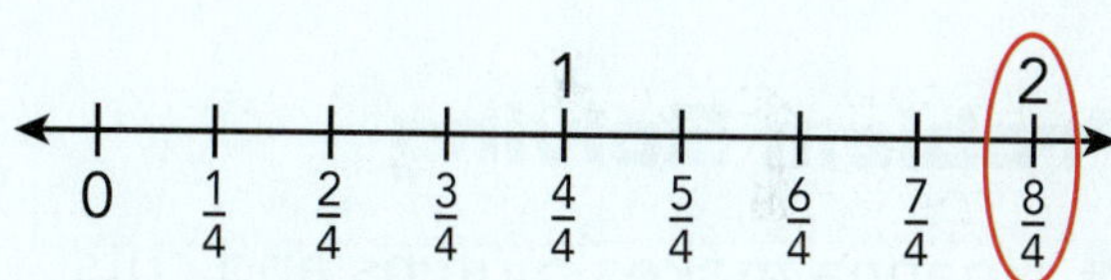

Some ways Natalia can write 2 as a fraction are $\frac{2}{1}$, $\frac{4}{2}$, and $\frac{8}{4}$.

MORE PRACTICE

Write the whole number for each fraction. Draw a number line to help you.

1. $\frac{8}{8}$ ______ **2.** $\frac{8}{1}$ ______ **3.** $\frac{8}{2}$ ______ **4.** $\frac{12}{4}$ ______

Complete the fraction for each whole number.

5. $6 = \frac{6}{\square}$ **6.** $7 = \frac{21}{\square}$ **7.** $10 = \frac{20}{\square}$ **8.** $5 = \frac{\square}{8}$

HOMEWORK

Complete the fraction for each whole number.

1. $2 = \frac{\square}{8}$ 2. $1 = \frac{\square}{6}$ 3. $5 = \frac{\square}{2}$ 4. $3 = \frac{\square}{3}$

Each shape is 1 whole. Write a fraction and whole number for the shaded parts.

5. 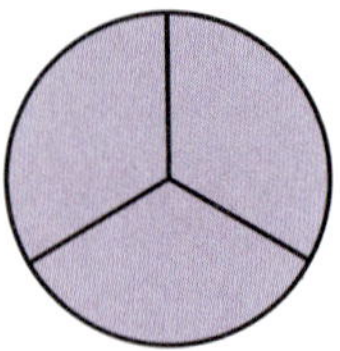

____

6. 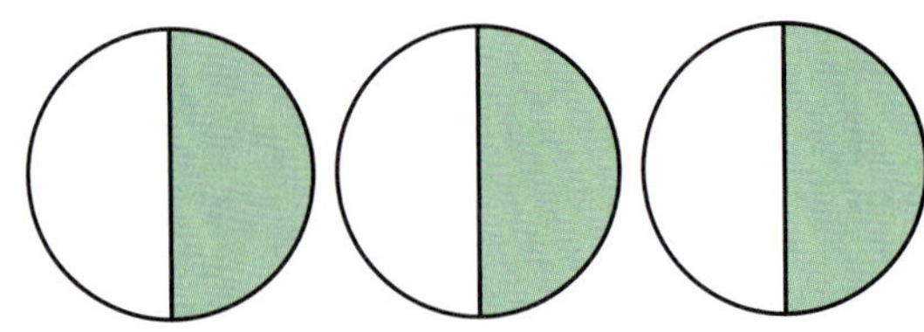

____

Draw a model to represent each fraction.

7. $\frac{12}{4}$

8. $\frac{24}{6}$

Problem Solving

9. Joanna makes muffins and cuts them into thirds. A total of $\frac{15}{3}$ muffin parts are eaten. How many whole muffins are eaten?

______

10. Two bulletin boards are divided into 4 equal sections. Write a fraction to represent the parts of the bulletin boards that can be filled. ______

Write About It

11. Explain how to find the whole number that is equivalent to $\frac{12}{2}$ by using a number line.

____

____

____

Name ______________________________ Date ______________

LESSON **10-2**

Find Equivalent Fractions

Amanda has painted $\frac{1}{2}$ of a wall. What are two other fractions that name the part of the wall Amanda has painted?

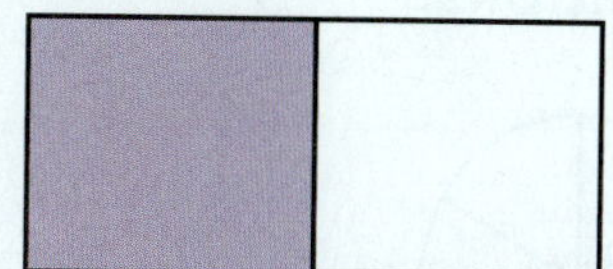

Different fractions can name the same amount of the same whole. Fractions that name the same amount are called equivalent fractions.

You can use fraction strips to find fractions equivalent to $\frac{1}{2}$.

1							
$\frac{1}{2}$							
$\frac{1}{4}$		$\frac{1}{4}$					
$\frac{1}{8}$	$\frac{1}{8}$	$\frac{1}{8}$	$\frac{1}{8}$				

The strips are the same length.

1 of 2 equal parts $= \frac{1}{2}$

2 of 4 equal parts $= \frac{2}{4}$

4 of 8 equal parts $= \frac{4}{8}$

$\frac{1}{2} = \frac{2}{4} = \frac{4}{8}$ These are equivalent fractions.

Amanda has painted $\frac{1}{2}$, $\frac{2}{4}$, or $\frac{4}{8}$ of the wall.

MORE PRACTICE

Shade the model on the right to show equivalent fractions. Then write the fractions.

1. 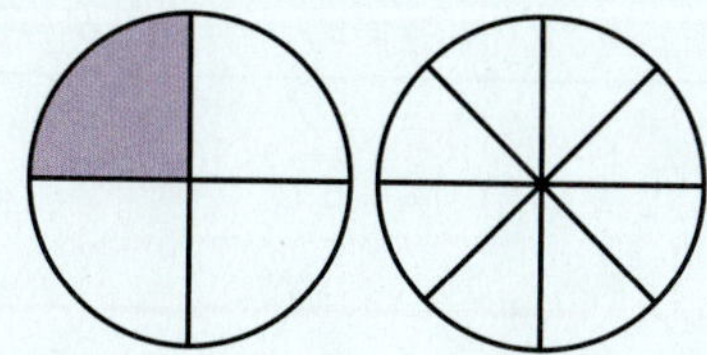

____

2. 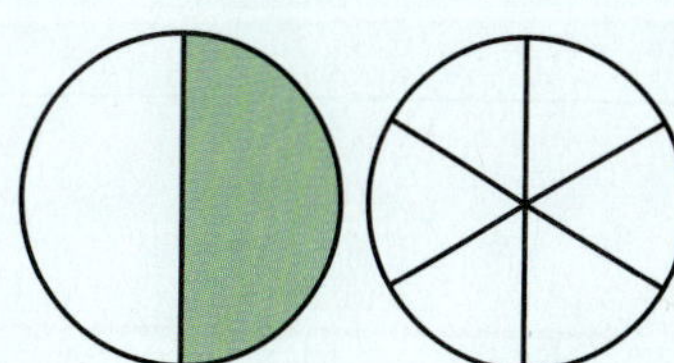

____

3. 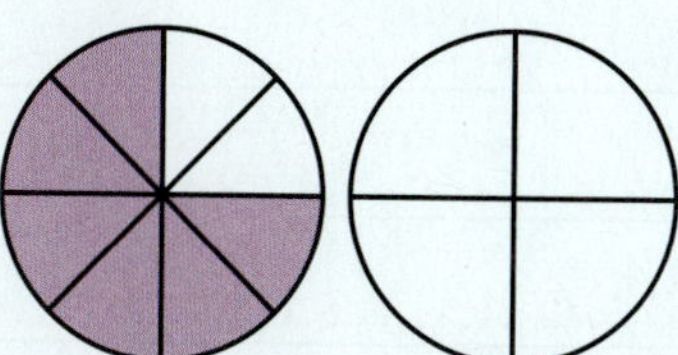

____

4. 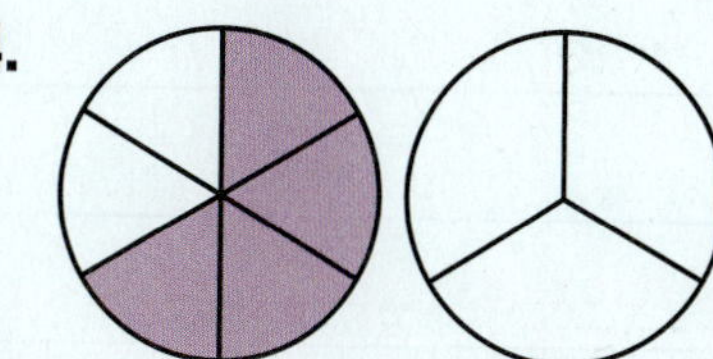

____

HOMEWORK

Shade each model on the right to show equivalent fractions. Then write the fractions.

1. 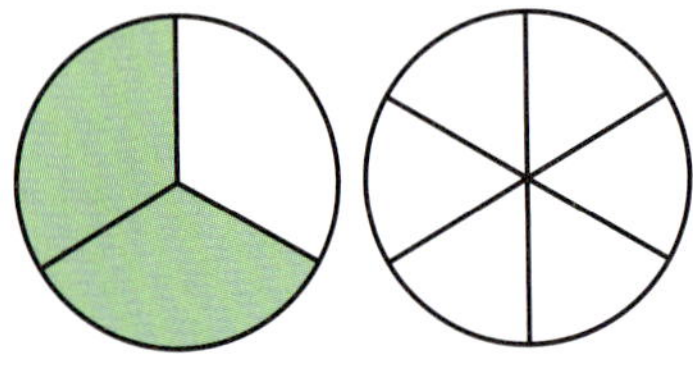

____

2. 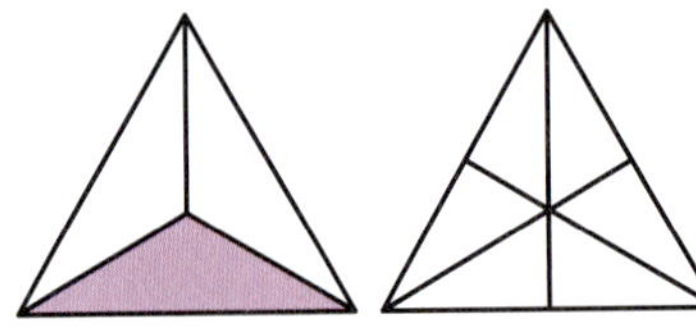

____

3. 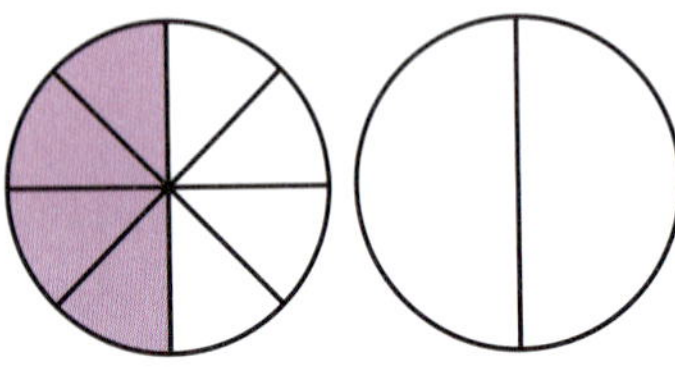

____

4. 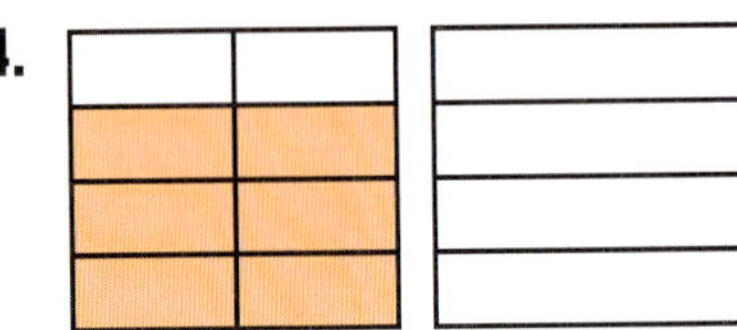

____

Problem Solving

5. Sage has two apple pies that are the same size. He cuts the first pie into 4 pieces, and the second pie into 8 pieces. How many pieces of the second pie are equivalent to 2 pieces of the first pie? ______________

6. Randy is planting a garden. He plants flowers in $\frac{1}{3}$ of the garden. He plants vegetables in $\frac{2}{6}$ of the garden. Does Randy plant more flowers or vegetables?

____

Write About It

7. Anh needs to find an equivalent fraction for $\frac{1}{3}$. How can Anh use only one rectangle to help her find the fraction?

____

____

____

____

Name ______________________ Date ______________

LESSON **10-3**

Find Equivalent Fractions on a Number Line

Haley has knitted $\frac{1}{3}$ of a scarf. How much of the scarf has Haley knitted in sixths?

You can use a number line to find an equivalent fraction for $\frac{1}{3}$ with a denominator of 6.

- Draw a number line from 0 to 1 by thirds. Then draw a second number line from 0 to 1 by sixths.

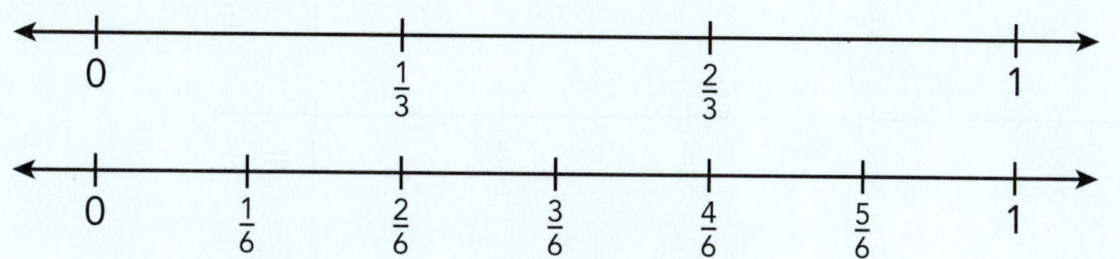

Align the number lines on the 0 mark. Make sure the distances between 0 and 1 are the same.

- Look at the point that aligns with $\frac{1}{3}$.

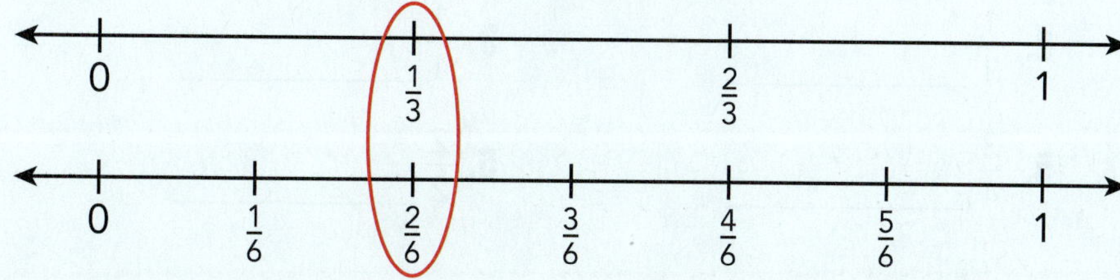

That point is $\frac{2}{6}$. So $\frac{1}{3}$ and $\frac{2}{6}$ are equivalent fractions.

Haley has knitted $\frac{2}{6}$ of the scarf.

MORE PRACTICE

Partition the second number line to find an equivalent fraction with the given denominator. Write the equivalent fraction.

1. fourths

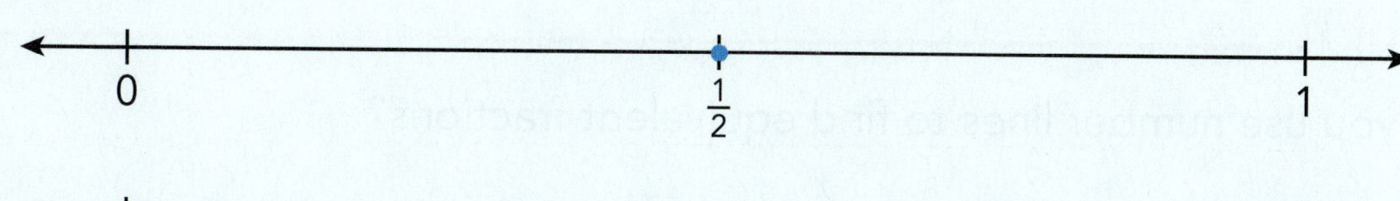

$\frac{1}{2}$ = ______

HOMEWORK

Write all the equivalent fractions that are shown on the number lines for each given fraction.

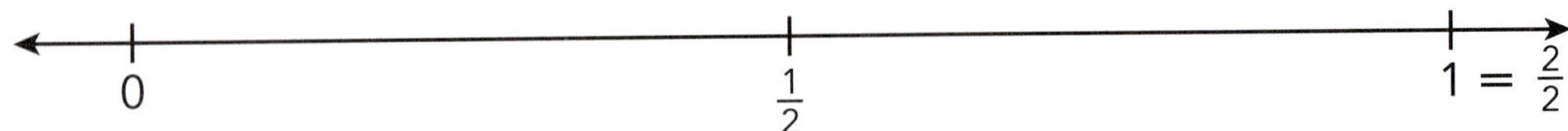

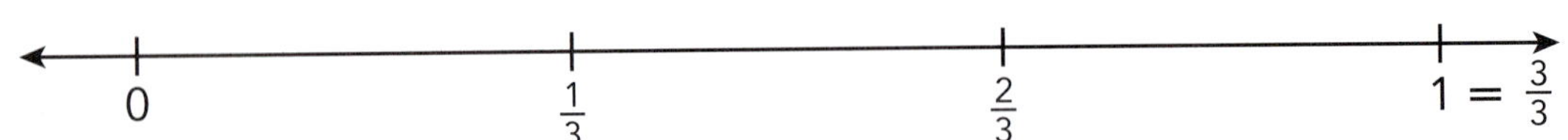

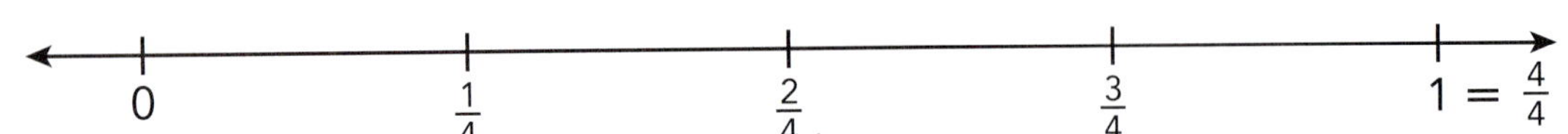

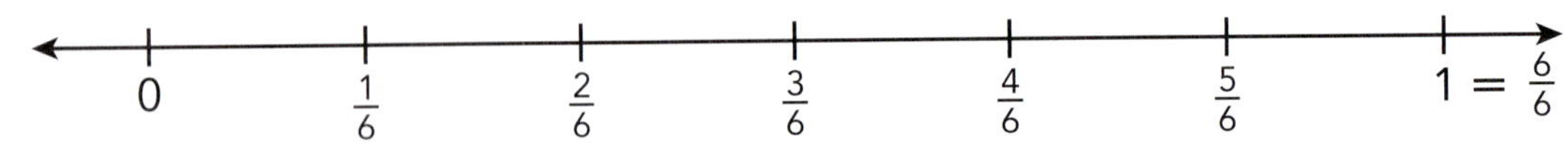

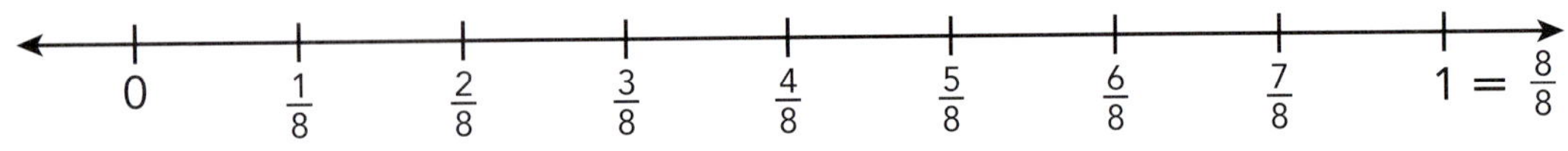

1. $\frac{1}{2}$ ______ **2.** $\frac{1}{3}$ ______ **3.** $\frac{1}{4}$ ______

4. $\frac{2}{3}$ ______ **5.** $\frac{3}{4}$ ______ **6.** $\frac{2}{2}$ ______

Problem Solving

7. A box is $\frac{4}{6}$ filled with books. Name an equivalent fraction for the part of the box that is filled. ______

8. Use number lines to find if $\frac{5}{6}$ and $\frac{7}{8}$ are equivalent. Explain why or why not.

______

______

Write About It

9. Why can you use number lines to find equivalent fractions?

______

______

______

Name ______________________ Date ______________

LESSON 10-4

Compare Fractions with the Same Denominator

Which fraction is greater, $\frac{2}{4}$ or $\frac{3}{4}$?

- You can use a number line to compare fractions with the same denominator.

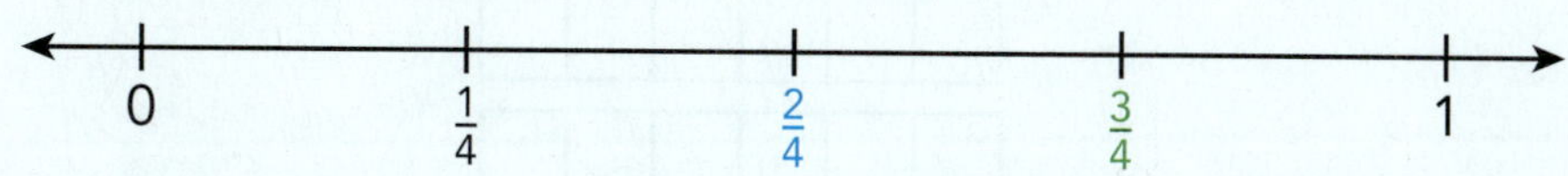

  - Just like with whole numbers, the fraction to the right is the greater fraction. Write $\frac{3}{4} > \frac{2}{4}$.
  - The fraction to the left is the lesser fraction. Write $\frac{2}{4} < \frac{3}{4}$.

- You can also use fraction strips to compare fractions with the same denominators.
  - Compare the lengths.
  - The strip showing $\frac{3}{4}$ is longer than the strip showing $\frac{2}{4}$.
  - The strip showing $\frac{2}{4}$ is shorter than the strip showing $\frac{3}{4}$.

1			
$\frac{1}{4}$	$\frac{1}{4}$		
$\frac{1}{4}$	$\frac{1}{4}$	$\frac{1}{4}$	

When fractions have the same denominator, the fraction with the greater numerator is the greater fraction.

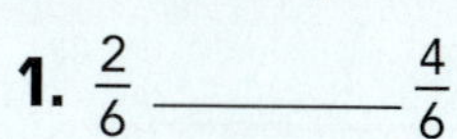
So $\frac{3}{4} > \frac{2}{4}$ and $\frac{2}{4} < \frac{3}{4}$.

MORE PRACTICE

Plot each point on the number line. Then compare. Use > or <.

1. $\frac{2}{6}$ ______ $\frac{4}{6}$

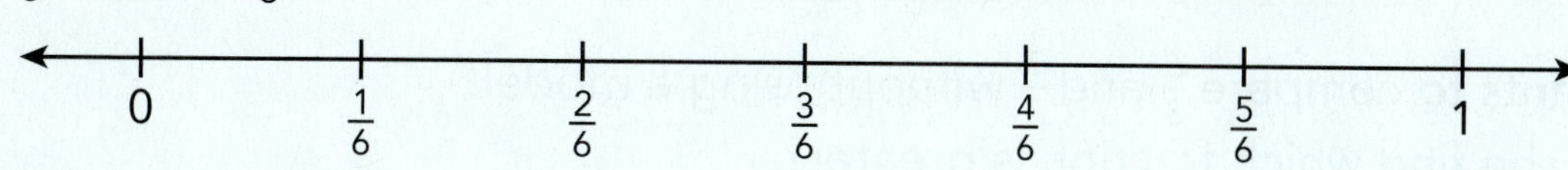

2. $\frac{5}{8}$ ______ $\frac{3}{8}$

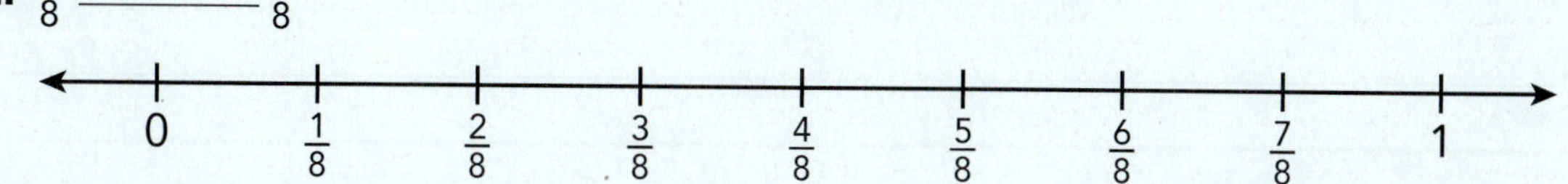

Shade the models to represent each fraction. Then compare. Use > or <.

1. $\frac{3}{4}$ ______ $\frac{2}{4}$

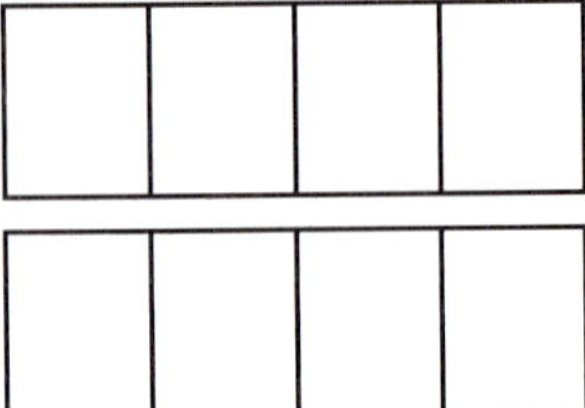

2. $\frac{3}{6}$ ______ $\frac{4}{6}$

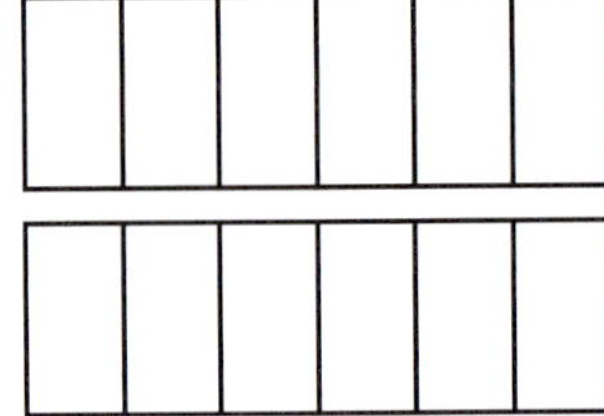

Circle a fraction that is greater than the given fraction. Draw a square around a fraction that is less than the given fraction.

3. $\frac{4}{6}$

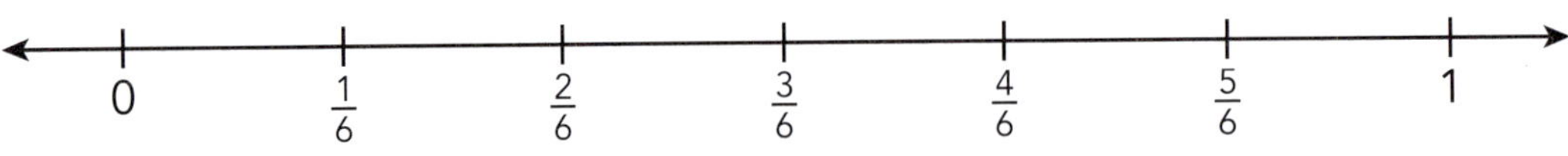

4. $\frac{5}{8}$

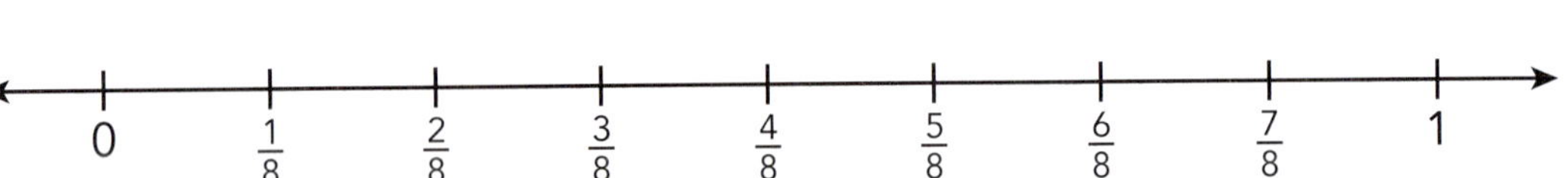

Problem Solving

5. Roberto reads $\frac{1}{4}$ of the number of pages in a book. Manny reads $\frac{1}{4}$ of the number of pages in a different book. Roberto says that Manny and he read the same number of pages because $\frac{1}{4} = \frac{1}{4}$. Is Roberto correct? Explain.

______

______

______

Write About It

6. Teresa wants to compare $\frac{6}{8}$ and $\frac{7}{8}$ without using a model. How can she find which fraction is greater?

______

______

Name ______________________ Date ____________

LESSON 10-5

Compare Fractions with the Same Numerator

Compare $\frac{2}{3}$ and $\frac{2}{4}$.

- You can use models to compare fractions with the same numerators.

- Draw two rectangles.

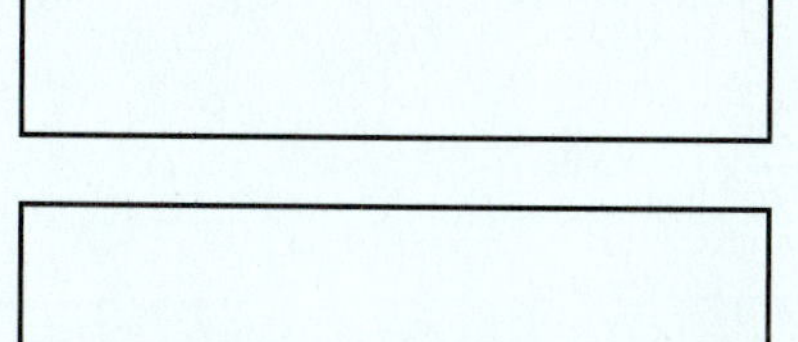

- Partition one rectangle into thirds and the other into fourths. Shade two parts of each.

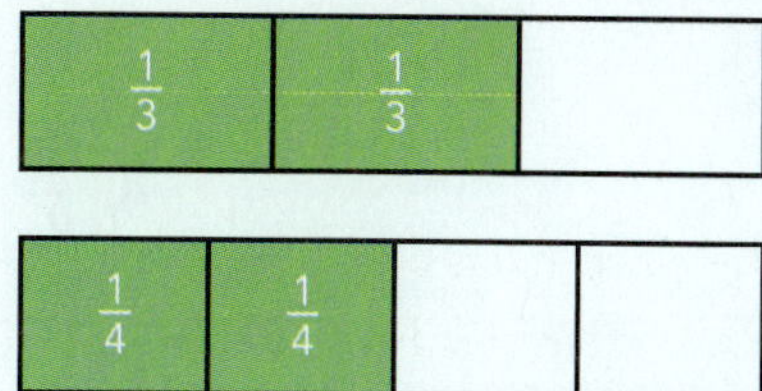

- Compare the models. $\frac{2}{3} > \frac{2}{4}$.

- You can also use number lines.

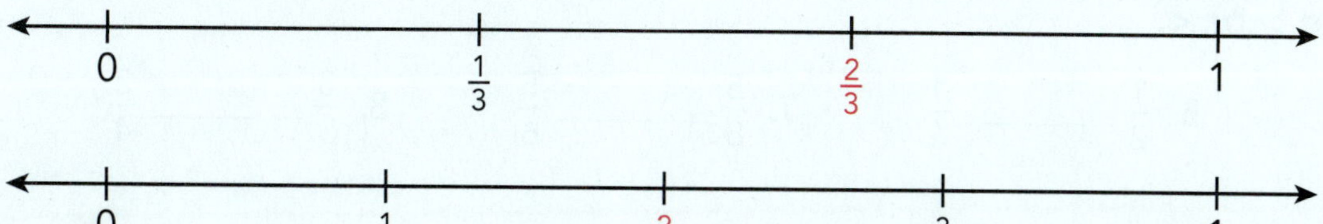

Find $\frac{2}{3}$ and $\frac{2}{4}$ on the number lines. $\frac{2}{4}$ is to the left of $\frac{2}{3}$. So $\frac{2}{4} < \frac{2}{3}$.

So $\frac{2}{3} > \frac{2}{4}$ and $\frac{2}{4} < \frac{2}{3}$.

MORE PRACTICE

Shade the models. Then compare the fractions. Write > or <.

1. $\frac{2}{8}$ ______ $\frac{2}{6}$

1							
$\frac{1}{8}$	$\frac{1}{8}$	$\frac{1}{8}$	$\frac{1}{8}$	$\frac{1}{8}$	$\frac{1}{8}$	$\frac{1}{8}$	$\frac{1}{8}$
$\frac{1}{6}$	$\frac{1}{6}$	$\frac{1}{6}$	$\frac{1}{6}$	$\frac{1}{6}$	$\frac{1}{6}$		

2. $\frac{1}{4}$ ______ $\frac{1}{6}$

1					
$\frac{1}{4}$	$\frac{1}{4}$	$\frac{1}{4}$	$\frac{1}{4}$		
$\frac{1}{6}$	$\frac{1}{6}$	$\frac{1}{6}$	$\frac{1}{6}$	$\frac{1}{6}$	$\frac{1}{6}$

HOMEWORK

Shade the models. Then compare the fractions. Use > or <.

1. $\frac{3}{4}$ ______ $\frac{3}{6}$

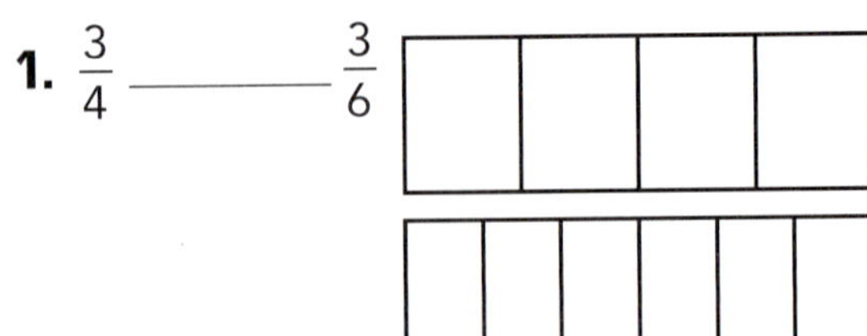

2. $\frac{4}{8}$ ______ $\frac{4}{6}$

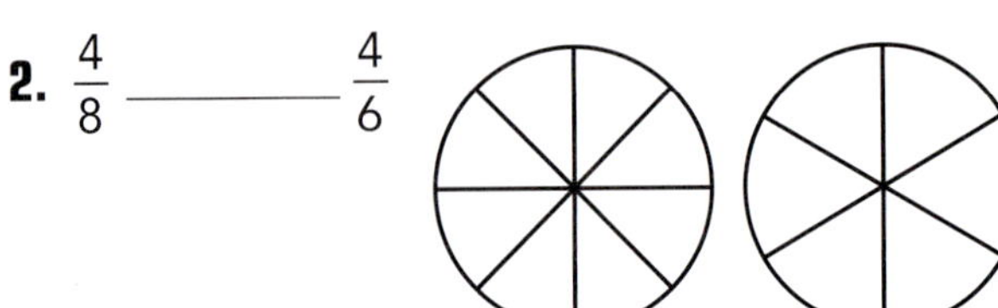

Draw a model to represent each fraction. Then compare the fractions. Use > or <.

3. $\frac{1}{3}$ ______ $\frac{1}{8}$

4. $\frac{2}{6}$ ______ $\frac{2}{3}$

Compare. Write > or <.

5. $\frac{3}{8}$ ______ $\frac{3}{4}$

6. $\frac{1}{2}$ ______ $\frac{1}{6}$

7. $\frac{5}{8}$ ______ $\frac{5}{6}$

8. $\frac{3}{3}$ ______ $\frac{3}{4}$

Problem Solving

9. Ken paints $\frac{1}{4}$ of a wall in the office. Leo paints $\frac{1}{3}$ of a wall in the cafeteria. Can you tell who paints more? Explain.

____

____

Write About It

10. How is comparing fractions with the same numerator different from comparing fractions with the same denominator?

____

____

____

Name ______________________ Date ______________

LESSON 10-6

Order Fractions

Order the fractions $\frac{3}{4}$, $\frac{3}{8}$, and $\frac{1}{2}$ from greatest to least.

- If two fractions have the same numerator, the fraction with the lesser denominator is the greater fraction. So $\frac{3}{4} > \frac{3}{8}$.

- Use fraction strips to find equivalent fractions for $\frac{1}{2}$ that have 4 and 8 in the denominator.

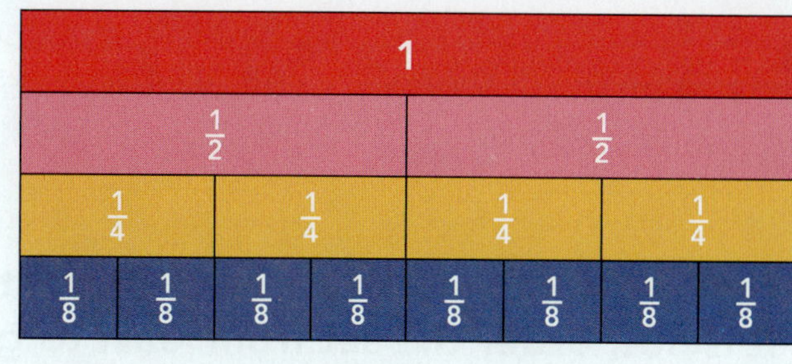

  - The models show that $\frac{1}{2} = \frac{2}{4} = \frac{4}{8}$. So you can compare $\frac{2}{4}$ to $\frac{3}{4}$ or $\frac{4}{8}$ to $\frac{3}{8}$.
  - If two fractions have the same denominator, the fraction with the greater numerator is the greater fraction. So $\frac{2}{4} < \frac{3}{4}$ and $\frac{4}{8} > \frac{3}{8}$. This means that $\frac{1}{2} < \frac{3}{4}$ and $\frac{1}{2} > \frac{3}{8}$.

The order from greatest to least is $\frac{3}{4}$, $\frac{1}{2}$, and $\frac{3}{8}$.

MORE PRACTICE

Use fraction strips to order the fractions from greatest to least.

1. $\frac{4}{8}$ $\frac{6}{8}$ $\frac{3}{8}$ ______

2. $\frac{1}{8}$ $\frac{3}{4}$ $\frac{1}{2}$ ______

3. $\frac{5}{8}$ $\frac{3}{4}$ $\frac{1}{2}$ ______

4. $\frac{3}{8}$ $\frac{3}{4}$ $\frac{1}{3}$ ______

5. $\frac{1}{6}$ $\frac{1}{3}$ $\frac{3}{4}$ ______

6. $\frac{5}{6}$ $\frac{7}{8}$ $\frac{2}{3}$ ______

Use fraction strips to order the fractions from least to greatest.

7. $\frac{1}{2}$ $\frac{3}{4}$ $\frac{7}{8}$ ______

8. $\frac{1}{3}$ $\frac{1}{6}$ $\frac{3}{6}$ ______

9. $\frac{5}{8}$ $\frac{1}{4}$ $\frac{1}{2}$ ______

HOMEWORK

Write the fractions in order from least to greatest. Use the fraction strips to help you.

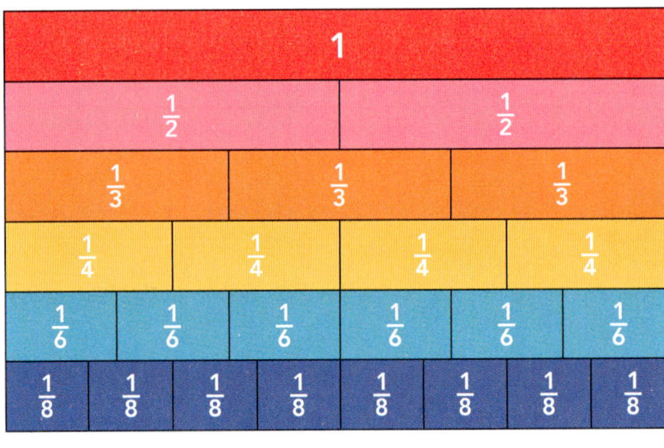

1. $\frac{3}{6}$ $\frac{2}{6}$ $\frac{5}{6}$ ______

2. $\frac{3}{4}$ $\frac{2}{3}$ $\frac{3}{8}$ ______

3. $\frac{4}{6}$ $\frac{1}{3}$ $\frac{2}{4}$ ______

4. $\frac{5}{8}$ $\frac{2}{4}$ $\frac{3}{4}$ ______

If the set is ordered from least to greatest, write *Yes*. If it is not, order the set from least to greatest.

5. $\frac{5}{8}, \frac{6}{8}, \frac{7}{8}$ ______

6. $\frac{3}{8}, \frac{3}{6}, \frac{2}{3}$ ______

7. $\frac{1}{2}, \frac{3}{4}, \frac{5}{8}$ ______

If the set is ordered from greatest to least, write *Yes*. If it is not, order the set from greatest to least.

8. $\frac{3}{8}, \frac{3}{6}, \frac{3}{4}$ ______

9. $\frac{4}{6}, \frac{4}{8}, \frac{1}{4}$ ______

10. $\frac{5}{6}, \frac{2}{3}, \frac{1}{2}$ ______

Problem Solving

11. It took Sheryl $\frac{1}{2}$ hour to complete her math homework, $\frac{3}{4}$ hour to complete her science homework, and $\frac{1}{4}$ hour to study for a spelling quiz. Order the subjects by greatest to least time spent. ______

Write About It

12. Explain how using fraction strips helps to order fractions with different denominators.

______

______

Name ______________________ Date ______________

LESSON 10-7

Problem Solving
Act It Out

Two pies are the same size. The cherry pie has $\frac{2}{3}$ left and the blueberry pie has $\frac{5}{6}$ left. Which pie has more left?

To find out which pie has more left, take two sheets of paper.

- Fold both sheets of paper in thirds.

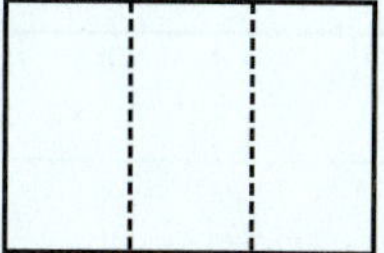
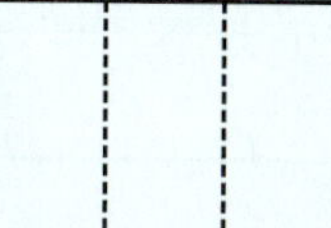

- Fold one of the sheets of paper in half in the other direction.

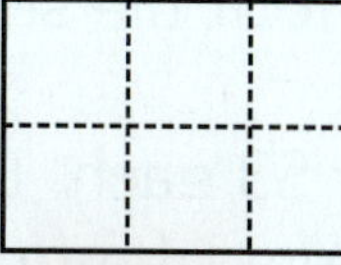

- Shade to represent the fractions. Then place one sheet above the other.

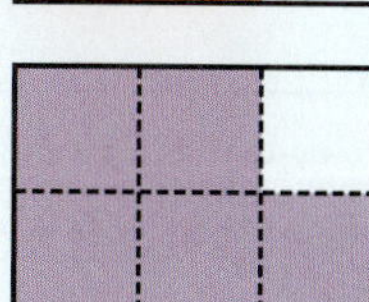

Because $\frac{2}{3} < \frac{5}{6}$, there is more blueberry pie left.

MORE PRACTICE

A pitcher of water is $\frac{7}{8}$ full. A pitcher that is the same size as the pitcher of water is $\frac{3}{4}$ filled with lemonade. Use this information for Exercises 1–2.

1. Explain how to use two sheets of paper that are the same size to find which pitcher has more liquid in it.

____

____

____

____

2. Which pitcher has more liquid in it? ______________

MORE PRACTICE

Molly sees two types of square bathroom tiles. One has sides $\frac{2}{3}$-foot long and the other has sides $\frac{1}{2}$-foot long. She wants to purchase the smaller tile. Use this information for Exercises 3–4.

3. Explain how to use fraction strips to find which tile is shorter.

____

____

____

4. Is the $\frac{2}{3}$-foot tile or the $\frac{1}{2}$-foot tile shorter? _______________

5. Yemi sells 6 fruit tarts for $3 each. Explain how you can act it out to find the total amount of money Yemi earns from fruit tart sales. Include the answer in your explanation.

____

____

6. Mia bought 5 avocados for $10. Each avocado cost the same amount. Explain how you can act it out to find the cost of each avocado. Include the answer in your explanation.

____

____

____

Alyssa is filling two containers that are the same size. One container is $\frac{1}{2}$ full of sand. The other container is $\frac{3}{8}$ full of mulch. Use this information for Exercises 7–8.

7. Explain how to use two sheets of paper that are the same size to find which container has more in it.

____

____

____

8. Which container has more in it? _______________

Name ______________________________ Date ______________

Problem Solving
Act It Out

HOMEWORK

Holly eats $\frac{1}{2}$ of a papaya on Monday. She eats $\frac{3}{8}$ of the same papaya on Tuesday. Use this information for Exercises 1–2.

1. Explain how to use two sheets of paper to find if Holly eats more of the papaya on Monday or Tuesday.

____

____

____

____

2. On which day did Holly eat more of the papaya? ______________

Caleb shoots 20 free throws. He makes 12 of the free throws. Caleb will use counters to find if he makes or misses more free throws. Use this information for Exercises 3–4.

3. Explain how to use the counters to tell if Caleb makes or misses more free throws.

____

____

____

4. Did Caleb make or miss more free throws? How many more?

____

Joelle cut a watermelon into 8 equal slices. Joelle and each of her friends eat 2 slices of watermelon and there is none left. Use this information for Exercises 5–6.

5. Explain how to use pencils to find how many friends share the watermelon with Joelle.

____

____

6. How many friends share the watermelon with Joelle? ______________

HOMEWORK

Maryanne needs fabric for a project. She sees one piece of fabric that is $\frac{3}{4}$ of a yard, another that is $\frac{5}{6}$ of a yard, and a last one that is $\frac{2}{3}$ of a yard. She wants to buy the longest piece. Use this information for Exercises 7–8.

7. Explain how you can use fraction strips to find which piece of fabric is the longest.

____

____

____

____

8. Which piece of fabric should Maryanne buy? ____________

Joe and Tom plant part of a garden. Joe plants $\frac{1}{4}$ of the garden and Tom plants $\frac{3}{8}$ of the garden. Use this information for Exercises 9–10.

9. Explain how to use this model to find who planted more of the garden.

____

____

____

10. Who plants more? Explain.

____

Write About It

11. How is acting it out to solve a problem helpful?

____

____

____

Name ______________________ Date ______________

LESSON 11-1

Measure Length

What is the length of this key to the nearest quarter inch?

You can use a ruler to measure length. Look at the markings on the ruler.

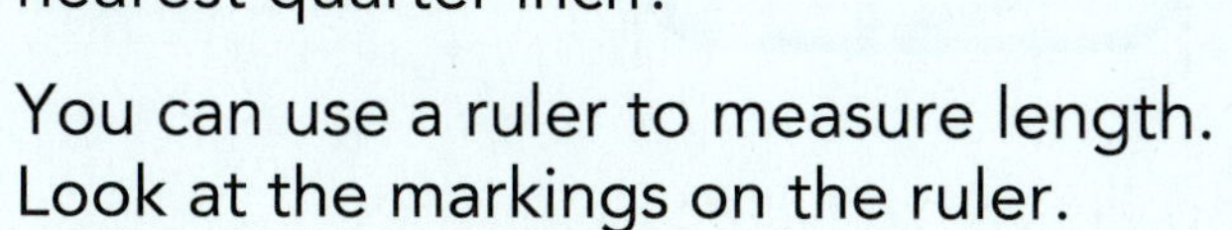

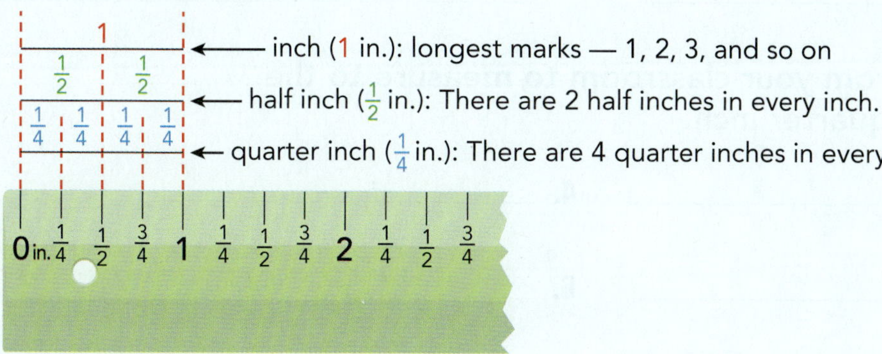

Line up the left end of the key with the 0 mark on the ruler.

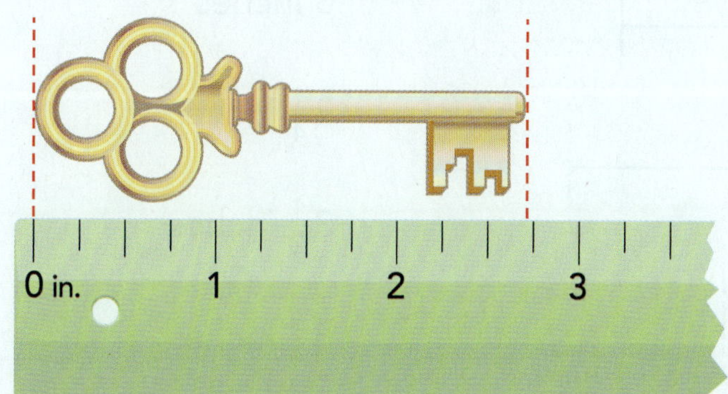

When a measure is halfway between two measures, round up to the greater measure.

Round lengths between two marks to the closer mark. The right end of the key is closer to the third mark after 2 in. That is $2\frac{3}{4}$ in.

To the nearest quarter inch, the key is $2\frac{3}{4}$ inches long.

MORE PRACTICE

Draw a line with the length shown.

1. $1\frac{1}{2}$ inches

2. $2\frac{3}{4}$ inches

HOMEWORK

Measure each length to the nearest half inch and quarter inch.

1.

2.

Choose four objects from your classroom to measure to the nearest half inch and quarter inch.

3. ______

4. ______

5. ______

6. ______

Match each line to its length.

7.

8.

9.

3 inches

$3\frac{1}{4}$ inches

$3\frac{1}{2}$ inches

$3\frac{3}{4}$ inches

Problem Solving

10. An arrow is $2\frac{1}{2}$ inches long to the nearest $\frac{1}{2}$ inch and the nearest $\frac{1}{4}$ inch. What is the shortest the arrow can be?

Write About It

11. Explain how to use a ruler to draw a line that is $5\frac{1}{2}$ in. long.

Name ______________________ Date ____________

Estimate and Measure Liquid Volume

Look at the jar and cup. How can you use a 1-liter beaker to find how much water each object can hold?

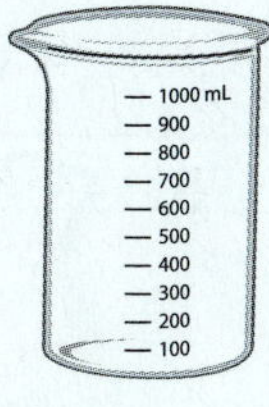

Two metric measures of liquid volume or capacity are the liter (L) and the milliliter (mL).

1 liter = 1000 milliliters

Use liters to measure large amounts of liquid. A liter is about 4 juice glasses. Use milliliters to measure small amounts of liquid. There are about 20 drops of water in 1 milliliter.

- Fill the 1-liter beaker and pour it into the jar. It takes three times to fill the jar. So, the jar holds 3 liters.

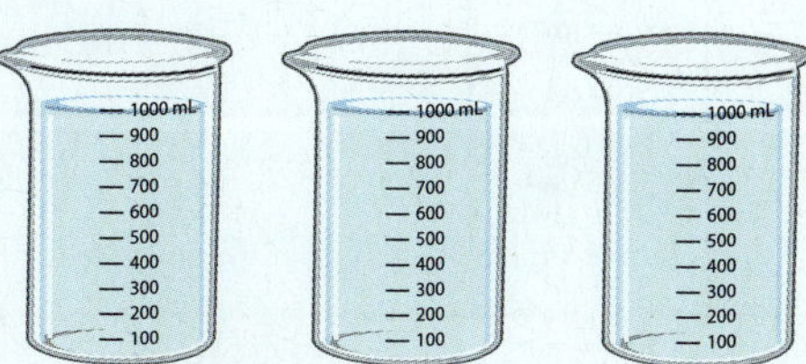

- Fill the cup and pour the water into the 1-liter beaker. Find the line where the water stops. Read the number on the line. The water stops at 600 mL. So, the cup holds 600 milliliters.

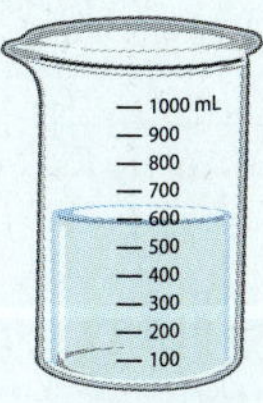

MORE PRACTICE

Write *less than 1 liter, about 1 liter,* or *more than 1 liter* for the amount of liquid each container holds.

1. 

____

2. 

____

3. 

____

HOMEWORK

Draw a circle around the objects you should measure in liters. Underline the objects you should measure in milliliters.

2. 

3. 

4. 

5. 

6. 

Write the amount of liquid in each beaker.

7. 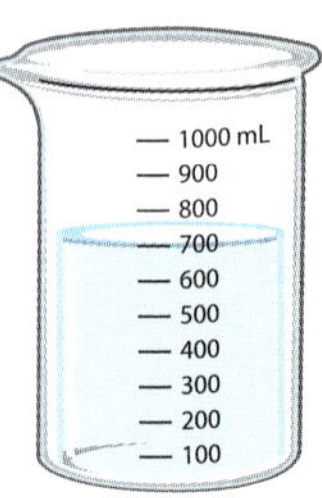

____

8. 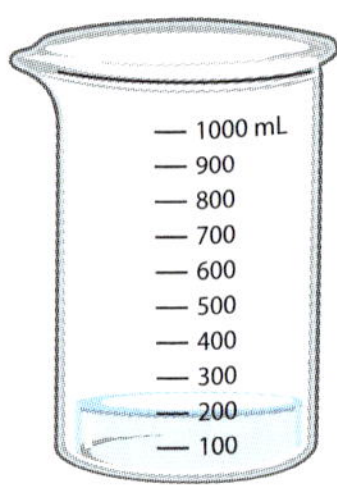

____

9. 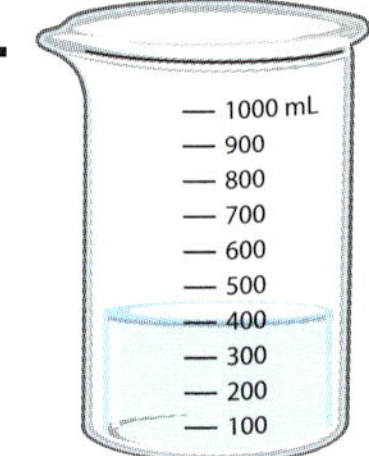

____

Problem Solving

10. Forty drops of water are in a dropper. Are there 2 mL or 2 L in the dropper?

____

11. A 500-mL beaker contains 300 mL of water. How many milliliters of water can still be added?

____

Write About It

12. Ana says a pitcher holds 2 liters. Erica says the pitcher holds 200 milliliters. Who is correct? Why?

____

____

Name ________________________ Date ______________

LESSON 11-3

Operations with Liquid Volume

Donovan has a fish tank that holds 15 liters of water. He uses a pitcher that holds 3 liters to fill the tank. How many times does Donovan fill the pitcher?

- The liquid volume of the tank is 15 liters.
- The liquid volume of the pitcher is 3 liters.

◆ You can make a table.

Number of Pitchers	1	2	3	4	5
Number of Liters	3	6	9	12	15

Find 15 liters in the table. It takes 5 pitchers.

◆ You can also use a bar model. The bar model shows that $15\text{ L} \div 3\text{ L} = 5$.

15 L				
3 L	3 L	3 L	3 L	3 L

Donovan fills the pitcher 5 times.

MORE PRACTICE

Solve.

1. A pool holds 245 liters of water when another 180 liters are added. How much water is now in the pool?

Make a bar model. ________

2. Each test tube contains 100 milliliters of a liquid. There are 6 such test tubes on a stand. How much liquid in all is in the test tubes? Use the beaker. ________

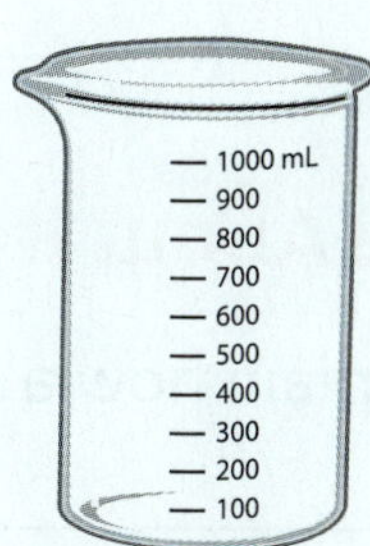

HOMEWORK

Use the table to solve Exercises 1–3.

Drinks Sold	
Drink	**Volume in Liters**
Bottled Water	128
Fruit Punch	54
Iced Tea	81
Lemonade	64

1. Each pack of fruit punch contains 6 liters. How many packs of fruit punch are sold?

   ____

2. How much more bottled water than iced tea is sold? ______

3. How much iced tea and lemonade is sold in all? Complete the bar model. ______

4. Jorge tries to drink 3 liters of water each day. How much water does Jorge try to drink in 7 days? Complete the table. ______

Number of Days							
Number of Liters							

Problem Solving

1 L = 1000 mL

5. A bottle contains 90 milliliters of water. Do 8 bottles contain more than or less than 1 liter of water? Explain.

   ____

6. Graham plans to drink 14 liters of water this week. He drinks 6 liters in the first 3 days of the week. How many liters does he have left to drink this week? Explain your answer.

   ____

   ____

Write About It

7. Explain how a model helps you solve liquid volume problems.

   ____

   ____

Name ______________________ Date ______________

LESSON 11-4

Estimate and Measure Mass

Clark has a new phone. Does Clark's phone have a mass that is greater than 1 kilogram, about 1 kilogram, or less than 1 kilogram?

Mass is the amount of matter an object contains. Two measures of mass are the gram (g) and the kilogram (kg).

You can use benchmarks to estimate and compare mass.

Grams are often used to measure light objects.

A paper clip has a mass of about 1 gram.

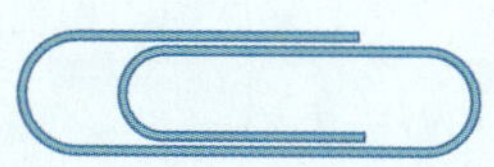

Kilograms are often used to measure heavy objects.

A baseball bat for an adult has a mass of about 1 kilogram.

To find if Clark's phone has a mass of more than 1 kilogram, about 1 kilogram, or less than 1 kilogram, compare its mass to the mass of the baseball bat.

1 kilogram = 1000 grams

The phone has less mass than the baseball bat.

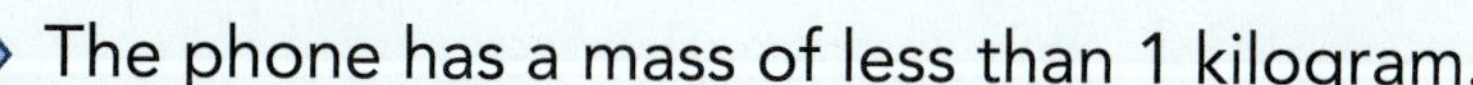

The phone has a mass of less than 1 kilogram.

MORE PRACTICE

Write *less than 1 kilogram, about 1 kilogram,* or *more than 1 kilogram* for the mass of each object.

1. 

____

2. 

____

3. 

____

HOMEWORK

Draw a circle around the objects you should measure in kg.
Draw a line below the objects you should measure in g.

1. 

2. 

3. 

4. 

5. 

6. 

Match each object with the best estimate of its mass.

7. 

400 g

8. 

10 kg

9. 

50 kg

Problem Solving

10. A book has a mass of 820 grams. Does the book have a mass that is greater than or less than 1 kilogram? ______________

11. Tate said the mass of a flying disc is 175. He forgot to include the unit of measure. Did Tate mean grams or kilograms? ______________

Write About It

12. Which better describes the mass of a dumbbell that an athlete might use, 5 g or 5 kg? Explain your reasoning.

____

____

Name ______________________ Date ______________

LESSON

11-5

Operations with Mass

A restaurant has a 20-kilogram bag of rice. After dinner, 17 kilograms of rice remain in the bag. How many kilograms of rice were used for dinner?

- What information have you been given from the problem?

  The mass of the bag was 20 kilograms before dinner.

  After dinner, the mass was 17 kilograms.

- Make a bar model to represent the problem.

20 kg	
17 kg	? kg

- To find the number of kilograms of rice that were used, write an equation. Let *d* represent the number of kilograms that were used: $20 - 17 = d$.

- Solve $20 - 17 = d$. $d = 3$

There were 3 kilograms of rice used for dinner.

MORE PRACTICE

Henry's model airplane has a mass of 235 grams. He has a model car that has a mass of 360 grams. Use this information to answer Exercises 1–3.

1. Write an equation you can use to find the difference between the mass of the car and the mass of the airplane.

____

2. How much more mass does the car have than the airplane? Complete the bar model and solve your equation. ______________

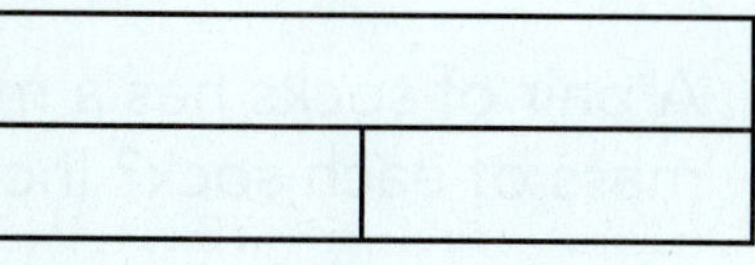

3. What is the total mass of the two models? Complete the bar model. ______________

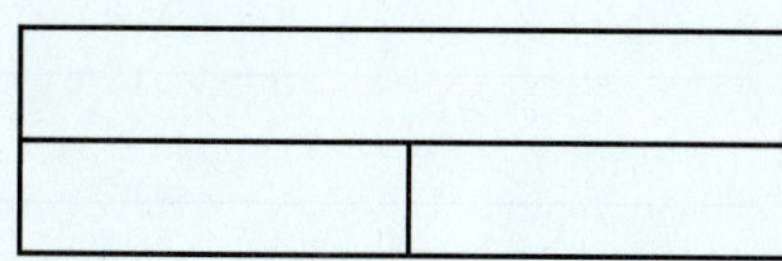

HOMEWORK

Use the table for Exercises 1–4.

Mass of Fruit	
Fruit	**Mass in Grams**
Apple	90
Mango	200
Orange	160
Papaya	280
Pear	140

1. What is the mass of 5 apples? Complete the bar model. ______

2. What is the difference between the mass of an orange and the mass of an apple? ______

3. Cara cuts an apple into 3 equal slices. What is the mass of each slice? Complete the bar model. ______

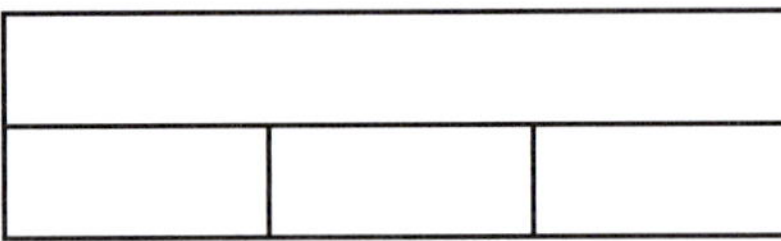

4. Quan has eaten two papayas this week. What is the mass of the papayas that Quan has eaten? ______

Problem Solving

5. A bag contains 32 grams of marbles. Each marble has a mass of 4 grams. How many marbles are in the bag?

______

6. Marvin has 20 markers in a box. Each marker has a mass of 8 grams. What is the mass of the markers inside the box?

______

Write About It

7. A pair of socks has a mass of 60 g. How would you find the mass of each sock? Include the mass in your explanation.

______

______

______

Name ______________________ Date ______________

LESSON 11-6

Problem Solving
Write an Equation

The total mass of two books in Alondra's backpack is 840 grams. One of the books has a mass of 355 grams. What is the mass of the second book?

Read and Understand

What information have you been given in the problem?

- The total mass of two books is 840 grams.
- One book has a mass of 355 grams.

Represent the Situation

- Make a bar model.
- Some are being taken away from a whole. To help find the number of grams of the second book, write an equation.
- Let *b* represent the number of grams that are left: $840 - 355 = b$.

840 grams	
355 grams	?

Make and Use a Plan

- Solve $840 - 355 = b$.
- $485 = b$

Look Back

You can check your answer by adding: $485 + 355 = 840$.

The mass of the second book is 485 grams.

MORE PRACTICE

1. A sports cooler is filled with 40 liters of water before each soccer game. The Comets have played 8 games. How many liters of water have been in the sports cooler this season?

   Write an equation. ______________

   Solve your equation. ______________

MORE PRACTICE

2. Angel has 36 photos in an album. Each page of the album has 4 photos. How many pages of the album are filled?

   Write an equation. ____________________

   Solve your equation. ____________________

3. One pile of shingles has a mass of 28 kilograms. The other has a mass of 16 kilograms. What is the total mass of the shingles?

   ____

Use the table for Exercises 4–8. Write an equation to represent the situation and solve.

Volume of Drinks	
Drink	**Volume (Liters)**
Bottled Water	80
Iced Tea	28
Juice Box	8
Lemonade	24

4. Each iced tea bottle holds 4 liters. How many bottles of iced tea are there?

   ____

5. How many more liters of bottled water are there than iced tea?

   ____

6. It takes 5 juice boxes to make 1 liter. How many juice boxes are there?

   ____

7. How many liters of iced tea and lemonade are there in all?

   ____

8. Each lemonade bottle holds 3 liters. How many bottles of lemonade are there?

   ____

9. Daniela bowls 136. Jen bowls 174. Daniela wants to use an addition equation to find how many more points Jen scored. Jen wants to use a subtraction equation. Who is correct? Why?

   ____

   ____

Name ______________________ Date ____________

Problem Solving
Write an Equation

HOMEWORK

Write an equation to represent the situation. Then solve your equation.

1. Jeremy puts 4 boxes in the trunk of his mother's car. Each box has a mass of 20 kilograms. What is the total mass of the boxes that Jeremy puts in his mother's car?

   Write an equation. ______________________

   Solve your equation. ______________________

2. In Melanie's hometown, 30 inches of snow fell in January and February combined. In January, 18 inches of snow fell. How many inches of snow fell in February?

   Write an equation. ______________________

   Solve your equation. ______________________

3. Veronica scored 62 points on the first part of her test. She scored 29 points on the second part. How many points did Veronica score in all?

   Write an equation. ______________________

   Solve your equation. ______________________

4. For sushi night, Martin pours 24 milliliters of soy sauce from packets into a dish. Each packet contains 6 milliliters of soy sauce. How many packets of soy sauce does Martin use?

   ____

5. Sandy buys a printer for her computer for $129. She had $200 to spend on the printer. How much money does Sandy have left?

   ____

6. Jordan drinks 350 milliliters of water in the morning and 575 milliliters of water in the afternoon. How many milliliters of water does Jordan drink in all?

   ____

HOMEWORK

The first book Manny read was 364 pages long. The second book was 248 pages long. Use this information for Exercises 7–8. Write and solve an equation.

7. How many pages longer is the first book that Manny read than the second book?

____

8. How many pages did Manny read in all?

____

Use the table for Exercises 9–11. Write an equation to represent the situation and solve.

Masses of Office Supplies	
Object	**Mass (grams)**
Pencil Sharpener	250
Ruler	20
Stapler	240
Tape Dispenser	300

9. What is the mass of 3 rulers?

____

10. What is the total mass of a pencil sharpener and a stapler?

____

11. How much more mass does a tape dispenser have than a stapler?

____

12. Howie bikes for 25 minutes riding laps at a constant rate. He bikes 5 laps. How many minutes did each lap take?

____

Write About It

13. Petra's vacation lasted 35 days. Lisa wants to write a multiplication equation to find the number of weeks Petra's vacation lasted. Ha wants to find the number of weeks by writing a division equation. Who is correct? Why?

____

____

Name ______________________ Date ______________

LESSON
12-1

Read Picture Graphs

Mrs. Call takes a poll on favorite type of pizza. The results are shown in the picture graph. How many votes were there for cheese pizza?

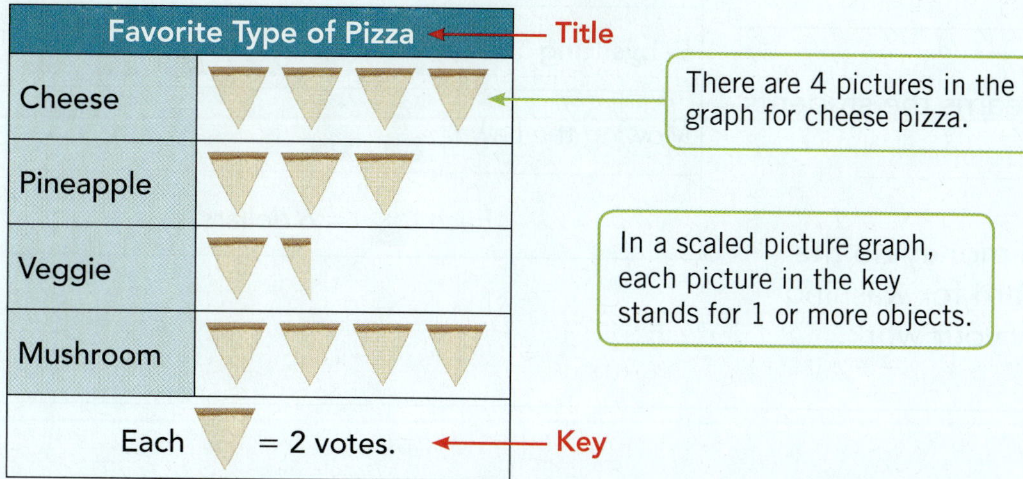

There are 4 pictures in the graph for cheese pizza.

In a scaled picture graph, each picture in the key stands for 1 or more objects.

You can use the scaled picture graph to help answer this question.

Multiply to find how many votes for cheese pizza: $4 \times 2 = 8$ votes.

So, there were 8 votes for cheese pizza.

MORE PRACTICE

Use the "Favorite Type of Pizza" picture graph.

1. Which type of pizza was chosen the least? ____________

2. Suppose 5 more students voted for veggie pizza. How many pizza slices would there be in the veggie row? Explain.

____

3. For which type of pizza can you use the equation $3 \times 2 = 6$ to find how many votes there were?

____

4. Use skip counting to find the total number of students who voted for cheese or pineapple pizza.

____

HOMEWORK

Use the picture graph to answer Exercises 1–3.

Money Earned from Summer Jobs	
Cleaning	$ $ $ $
Washing Cars	$ $ $
Babysitting	$ $ $ $ $ $
Mowing the Lawn	$ $
Each $ = 6 dollars.	

1. What does half a money-bag symbol represent?

____

2. Which job earns the students $24? _______________

3. How much money do the students earn for washing cars? Show your work.

____

Problem Solving

Scouts are collecting food. Use the picture graph for Exercises 4–6.

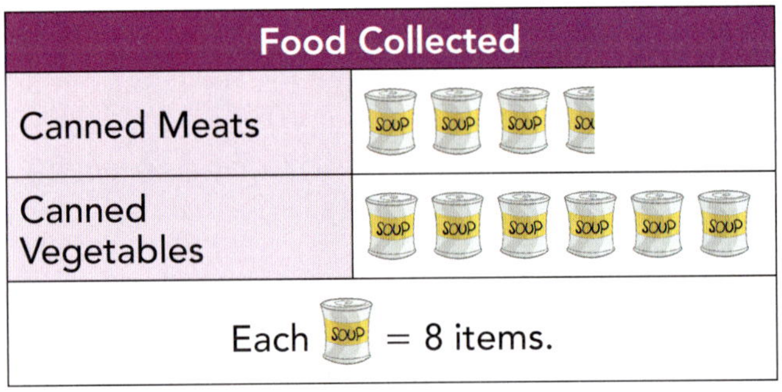

Food Collected	
Canned Meats	SOUP SOUP SOUP SO
Canned Vegetables	SOUP SOUP SOUP SOUP SOUP SOUP
Each SOUP = 8 items.	

4. The scouts collect 40 cans of fruit. How many can symbols should they add to a "Canned Fruit" row in the picture graph? Explain.

____

____

5. The scouts add a row to the graph for canned soup. They use 4 can symbols. How many cans of soup have they collected?

____

Write About It

6. How can you use multiplication to find out how many cans of vegetables the scouts have collected?

____

____

Name ______________________ Date ______________

LESSON 12-2

Make Picture Graphs

The tally chart shows the bears Andrew sighted on his trip to Alaska. How can Andrew make a scaled picture graph to show how many bears he saw each day?

Bear Sightings by Day	
Day 1	𝍸 III
Day 2	𝍸 𝍸 II
Day 3	𝍸 𝍸
Day 4	𝍸 𝍸 𝍸 I

To make a scaled picture graph, follow these steps:

- Select a title for your graph, such as "Bear Sightings by Day".
- Choose a symbol for your graph, like 🧸.
- Decide how many of each item the symbol will represent.

  🧸 can represent 4 bears. Half 🧸 will represent 2 bears.
- Make a graph with a title, two columns, a row for each day, and a key.
- Find the number of symbols per row, and complete the graph.

Andrew's picture graph is shown.

Bear Sightings by Day	
Day 1	🧸 🧸
Day 2	🧸 🧸 🧸
Day 3	🧸 🧸 half 🧸
Day 4	🧸 🧸 🧸 🧸
Each 🧸 = 4 bears.	

MORE PRACTICE

Use the picture graph "Bear Sightings by Day" to answer Exercise 1.

1. On Day 5, Andrew saw 6 bears. How many bear symbols would he need to add it to his graph?

____

HOMEWORK

1. Libby made a tally chart for the number of birds she saw on a trip. Use it to complete the picture graph.

Birds Seen on Trip	
Cardinal	卌 I
Robin	卌 卌 II
Bluebird	III
Blackbird	卌 IIII

______________________	
Cardinal	
Robin	
Bluebird	
________	
Each ________ = ________	

2. Shauna listed the servings of foods that she ate last week. Use the tally chart to complete Shauna's picture graph.

Food Eaten Last Week	
Fruit	卌 卌
Vegetables	卌 卌 IIII
Meat	卌 I
Dairy	卌 卌 卌 卌

______________________	
________	
________	
________	
________	
Each ________ = ________	

Problem Solving

3. Choose a symbol to represent 3 hours of Jared's homework. How many would Jared draw in the row for Week 3 in a picture graph?

____

____

Hours of Homework	
Week 1	卌 IIII
Week 2	卌 I
Week 3	卌 IIII
Week 4	III

Write About It

4. Why is it important to include a key for any picture graph?

____

____

Name ______________________ Date ______________

LESSON 12-3

Read Bar Graphs

How many hours did the cheerleading team practice in Week 4?

A scaled bar graph uses bars to show and compare different information. The bars can be displayed vertically or horizontally.

The vertical scaled bar graph shows a scale of hours on the left side of the graph. The horizontal scaled bar graph shows a scale of hours at the bottom of the graph.

The height or length of each bar shows the number of hours of practice that week.

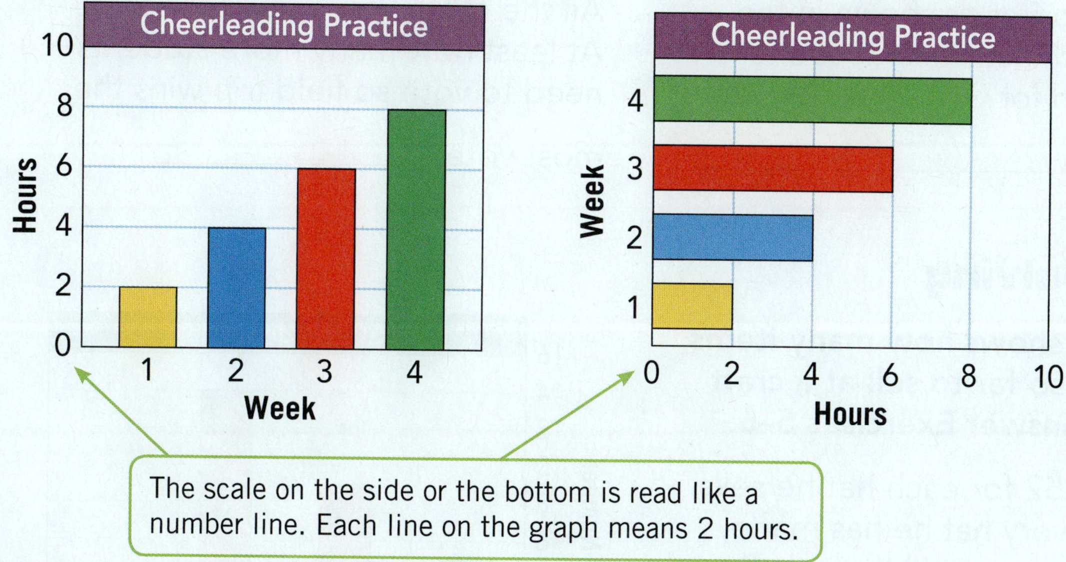

Look at Week 4 on either graph. The bar ends at 8, or 8 hours.

The cheerleading team practiced 8 hours in week 4.

MORE PRACTICE

Use "Cheerleading Practice" bar graphs for Exercises 1–3.

1. In which week did the team practice the most? ______________

2. In which week did the team practice the least? ______________

3. What do you notice from Week 1 to Week 4? ______________________

HOMEWORK

Mrs. Davis recorded her students' favorite activity in the bar graph. Use it for Exercises 1–4.

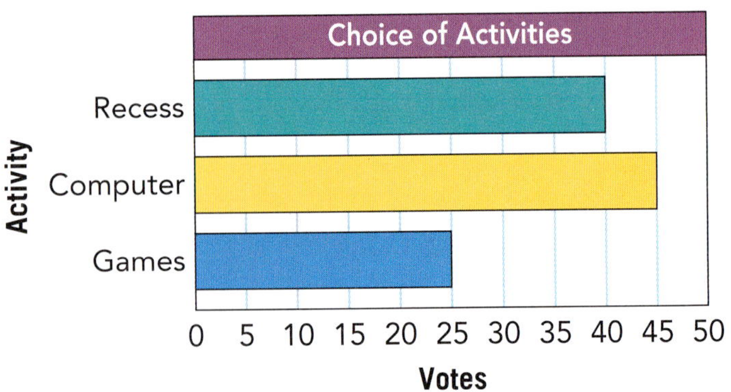

1. How many votes were there for computer? ______

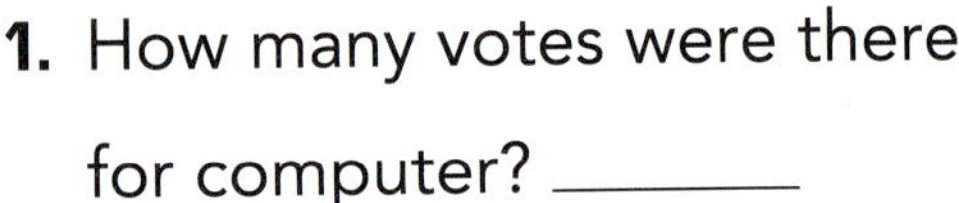

2. How many students voted in all?

______

3. Mrs. Davis needs to plan for the top two favorites as shown in the graph. Which activities does she need to plan for?

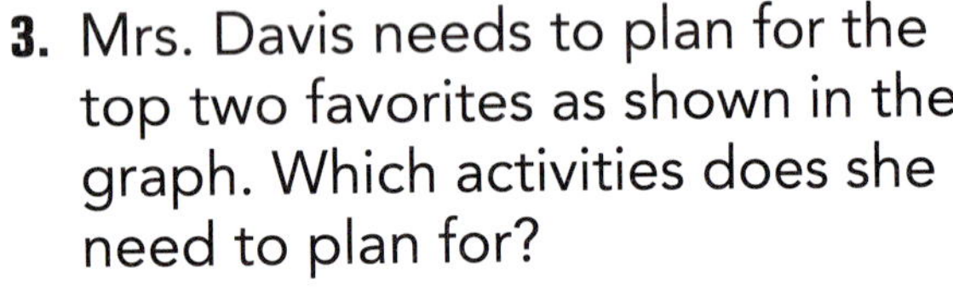

______

4. "Field trip" is added as an activity. All the other votes stay the same. At least how many more students need to vote so field trip wins the most votes? ______

Problem Solving

The bar graph shows how many items Ben has made so far to sell at a craft fair. Use it to answer Exercises 5–6.

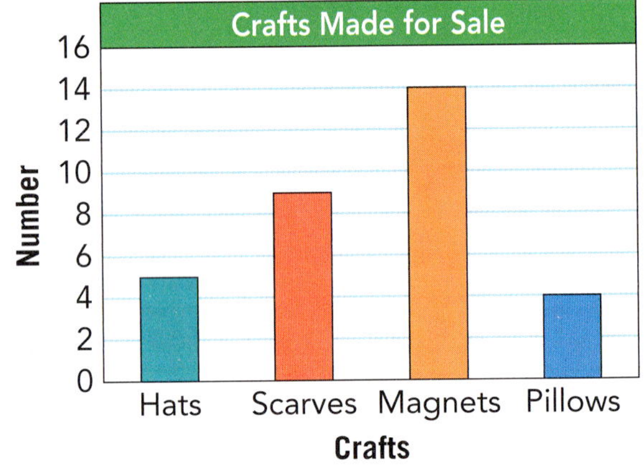

5. Ben makes $2 for each hat he sells. If he sells every hat he has made, how much money will he make?

______

6. Ben started out with enough supplies for making 30 magnets. How many more magnets can Ben make?

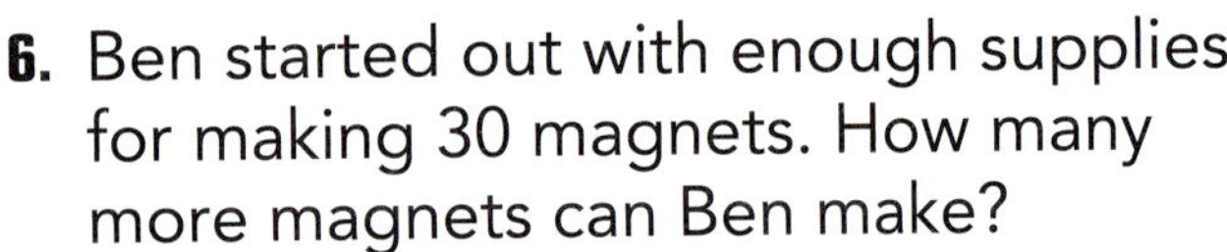

______

Write About It

7. Compare horizontal and vertical bar graphs by explaining one way they are alike and one way they are different.

______

______

Name ______________________________ Date ______________

LESSON 12-4

Make Bar Graphs

Ryan surveyed his classmates on their favorite type of movie. He recorded his results in this tally chart. How can Ryan use the data to make a scaled bar graph?

Type of Movie	
Action	𝍷𝍷𝍷𝍷
Comedy	𝍸 𝍸
Animation	𝍸 𝍷
Drama	𝍷𝍷𝍷

- Give the bar graph a title. Ryan chooses "Favorite Type of Movie."
- List each type of movie at the bottom.
- Use the data from the tally chart to create a scale. The greatest number of votes for any movie type is 10. Ryan picks a scale from 0 to 12. Most of the movie types have an even number of votes. So Ryan labels the graph by 2s.
- Draw and shade bars to represent the number of students who selected each movie type.

Ryan's bar graph is shown.

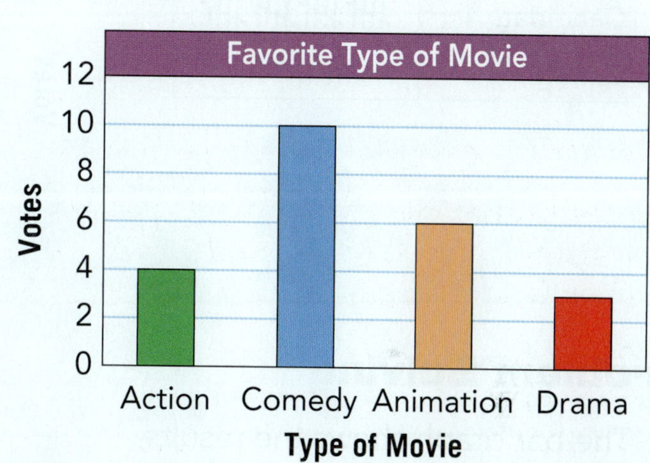

MORE PRACTICE

A camp counselor surveyed campers about their favorite activities. The results are in the tally chart shown. She wants to make a vertical bar graph.

Activity	
Crafts	𝍸 𝍸 𝍷𝍷
Kayaking	𝍸 𝍸 𝍸 𝍷𝍷𝍷
Hiking	𝍸 𝍸 𝍸

1. What is the height of the bar for crafts? ________

2. What is the height of the bar for kayaking? ________

3. What is the height of the bar for hiking? ________

4. What scale would you use for this data?

____

HOMEWORK

Use the data in each tally chart to complete the bar graph. Include the scale in your answer.

1.

Favorite Game	
Game 1	𝍸 |||
Game 2	𝍸 𝍸 ||||
Game 3	||||
Game 4	𝍸 𝍸

2.

Votes for Each Candidate	
Candidate 1	𝍸 𝍸 𝍸 𝍸
Candidate 2	𝍸 𝍸 ||||

Votes for Each Candidate

Votes

Candidate 1 Candidate 2

Candidates

Problem Solving

3. The bar graph shows the results of a survey of 100 people about their favorite music. Draw the bar for classical music. How many people chose classical as their favorite?

____

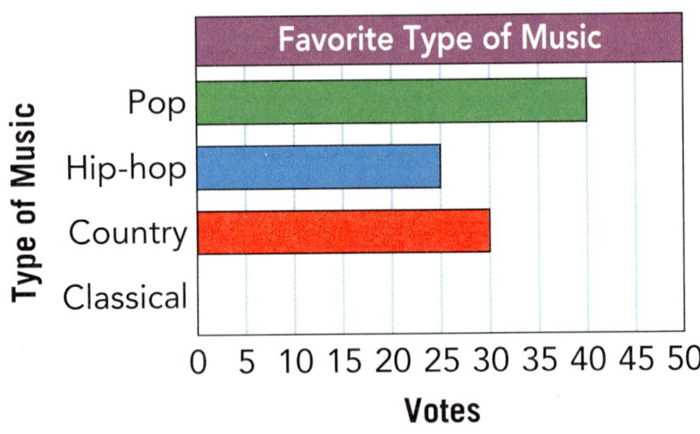

Write About It

4. How do you choose a scale when making a bar graph?

____

____

____

Name ______________________ Date ____________

LESSON 12-5

Data and Two-Step Problems

How many more hours does Elizabeth practice than Tammy and Sandra combined?

- Find and add the numbers of hours Tammy and Sandra practice: $6 + 4 = 10$.
- Find the number of hours Elizabeth practices: 18.
- Find the difference of 18 and 10: $18 - 10 = 8$.

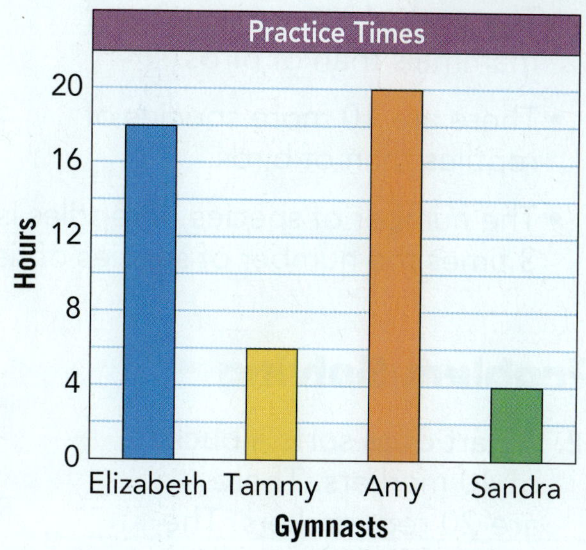

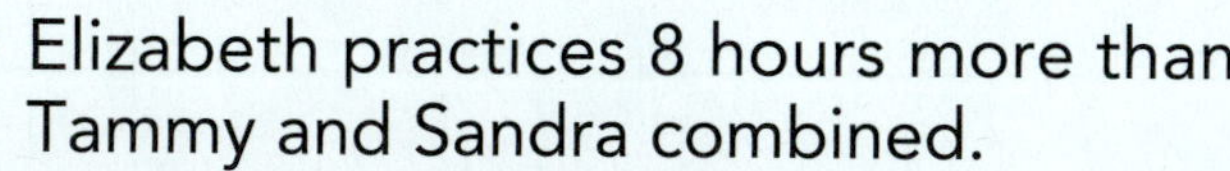

Elizabeth practices 8 hours more than Tammy and Sandra combined.

MORE PRACTICE

The bar graph shows the hours of practice so far this season. Use the graph for Exercises 1–4.

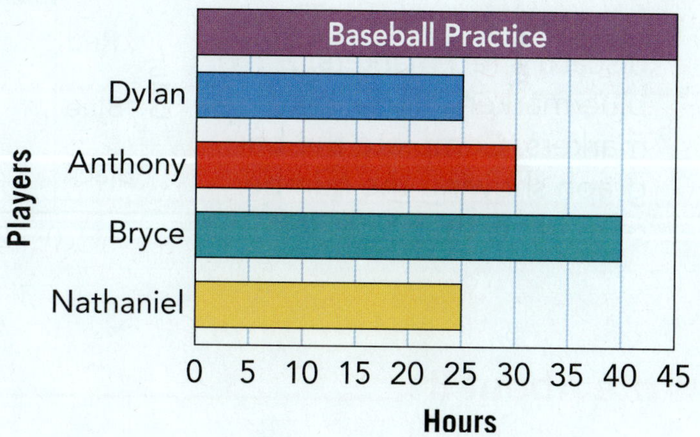

1. Are the total hours of practice for the four players more or less than 125 hours? How many hours more or less?

____

2. Nathaniel practices for 1 hour every school day each week. How many weeks did he practice?

____

3. William practices 5 more hours than the player shown on the graph who practices the most. How many hours does William practice?

____

4. How many fewer hours does Bryce practice than Dylan and Anthony combined?

____

HOMEWORK

1. Complete the bar graph using the graph and clues.
   - There are 40 more species of mammals than of birds.
   - There are 10 more species of reptiles than of birds.
   - The number of species of reptiles is 3 times the number of species of fish.

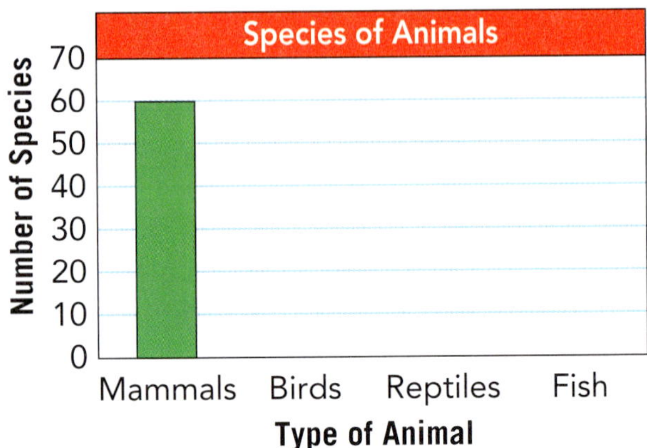

Problem Solving

2. An art class sorts a bucket of 40 markers. There are 20 red markers. The numbers of blue and black markers are equal. Complete the bar graph.

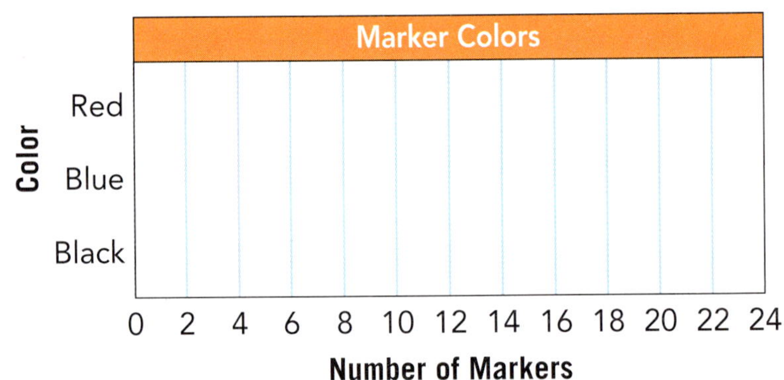

3. After sorting, the class tests for working markers. They discard 4 red markers, 2 blue markers, and 2 black markers. Complete the bar graph showing the number of markers they have left.

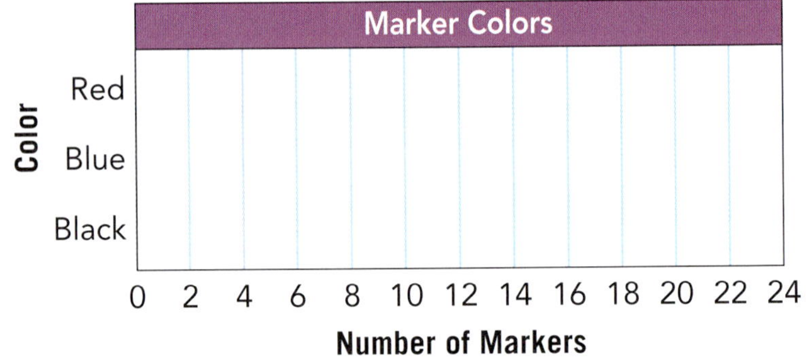

Write About It

4. In the election, 20 students voted. Alex got 6 votes. Riley got 2 more votes than Sam. Complete the bar graph. Who won? Explain.

____

____

____

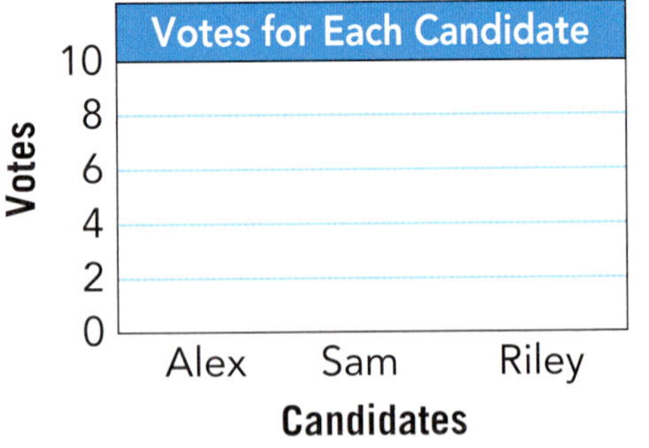

Name ______________________ Date __________

LESSON 12-6

Problem Solving
Use a Model

Eva's family is driving home from the state fair. Eva makes a tally chart of the different state license plates she sees. What model should Eva use for the data?

State Plates	
CT	||||/ ||||/ ||||/ ||||/
MA	||||/ ||||/ ||||/	
RI	||||/ |||
NY	||||/ ||||/ ||

Eva can make different kinds of graphs to model her data.

♦ Eva can make a bar graph.

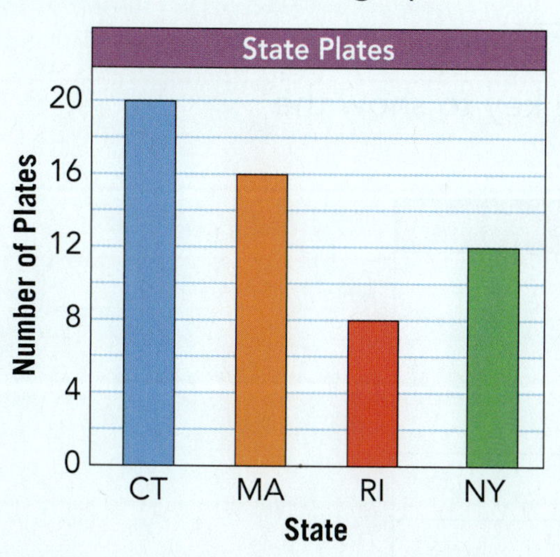

♦ Eva can make a picture graph.

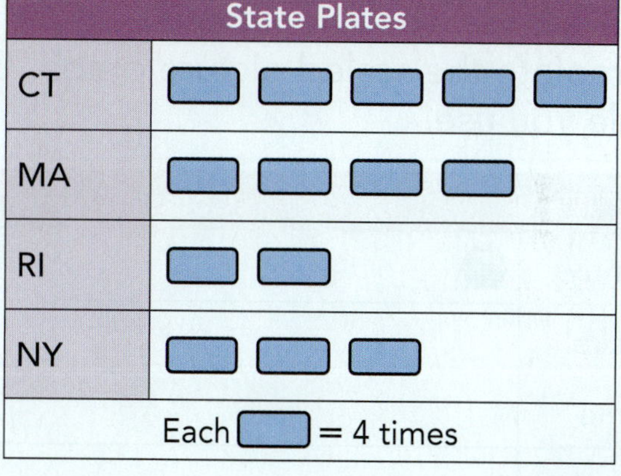

The bar graph makes it easy to see the total numbers of different state plates. The picture graph gives a visual image of how the numbers compare.

Eva could use either graph.

MORE PRACTICE

Use the data for state license plates Eva sees.

1. How many more CT plates than RI plates does she see?

____

2. Circle the state you think Eva lives in. Explain your reasoning.

CT MA RI NY

____

MORE PRACTICE

Mark makes a tally chart of his coins. To show his parents how much money he saves, he wants to display the number of coins. Use this information for Exercises 3–6.

3. Complete the tally chart.

Coin	Tally	Number
Penny	卌 卌 卌 卌 IIII	
Nickel	卌 卌 卌 卌 卌 卌 卌 I	
Dime	卌 卌 II	
Quarter	卌 I	

4. Complete the scaled picture graph. Use the key to show the scale you use.

Coins	
Penny	●
Nickel	
Dime	
Quarter	
Each ● = _______ coins.	

5. Is the amount of money in Mark's bank more or less than $2? Explain how you know.

____

____

____

____

6. Do you agree that a picture graph is the best way for Mark to display the coins in his bank? Explain why or why not.

____

____

____

Name ______________________________ Date ____________

Problem Solving
Use a Model

HOMEWORK

Russell collects stamps. He has 45 Saudi Arabian stamps, 27 German stamps, 54 United States stamps, and 36 Canadian stamps. He wants to compare how well a bar model and a bar graph work for recording the numbers of his stamps. Use this information for Exercises 1–4.

1. Complete the bar model of Russell's stamps.

___ stamps in all

___ Saudi Arabian	___ German	___ United States	___ Canadian

2. Complete the bar graph of Russell's stamps.

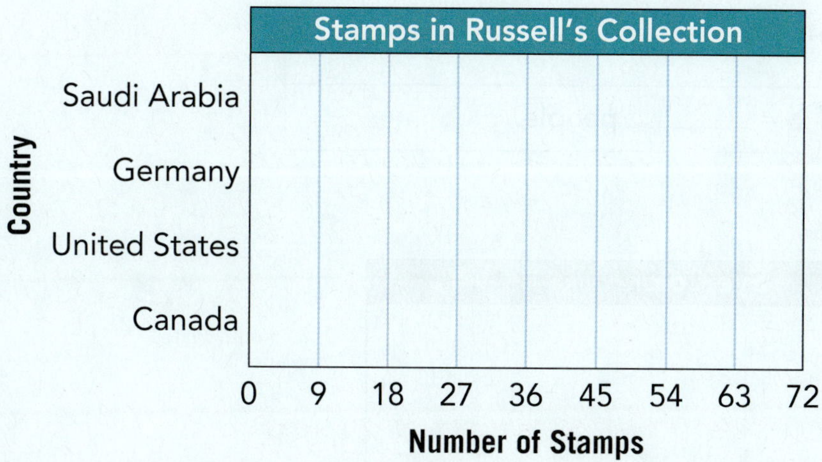

3. Which model better represents Russell's stamps? Why?

____

____

____

4. How can Russell change the models if he gets more stamps?

____

____

____

HOMEWORK

Carry out a survey on eye color. Use it for Exercises 5–7.

5. Collect and record your data.

Eye Color	Tally	Number
Blue		
Brown		
Green		
Hazel		

6. Make a picture graph.

Eye Color	
Blue	
Brown	
Green	
Hazel	
Each 👁 = ______ people.	

7. Make a bar graph.

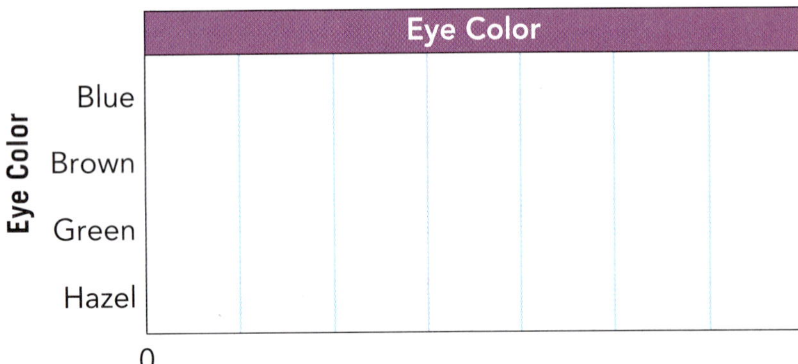

Write About It

8. You have to display data for a project on how plants grow. What models do you want to use? Why?

____

____

____

Name ______________________ Date ____________

LESSON **12-7**

Read Line Plots

Attacus atlas caterpillars can grow up to 5 inches long. A biologist is studying the caterpillars and measures all of the caterpillars in her lab to the nearest quarter inch.

A line plot uses Xs above a number line to represent data.

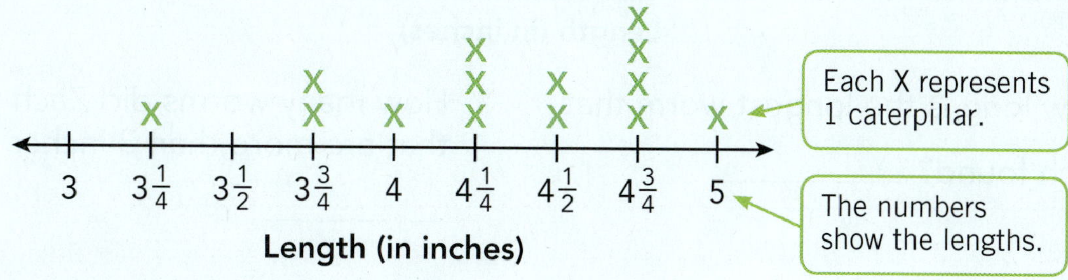

There are 3 Xs above the number $4\frac{1}{4}$.

This means that 3 caterpillars are $4\frac{1}{4}$ inches long.

MORE PRACTICE

The line plot shows each student's longest jump to the nearest foot. Use it for Exercises 1–4.

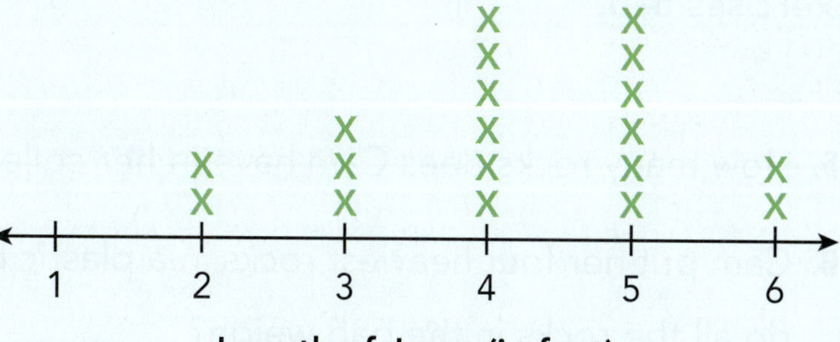

1. What is the distance that the most students jumped?

____

2. What is the shortest distance that any student jumped?

____

3. Did more students jump 3 feet or 6 feet?

____

4. How many students jumped 4 feet?

____

HOMEWORK

Zach found 8 worms. He made a line plot to show the length of each worm. Use the data to answer Exercises 1–4.

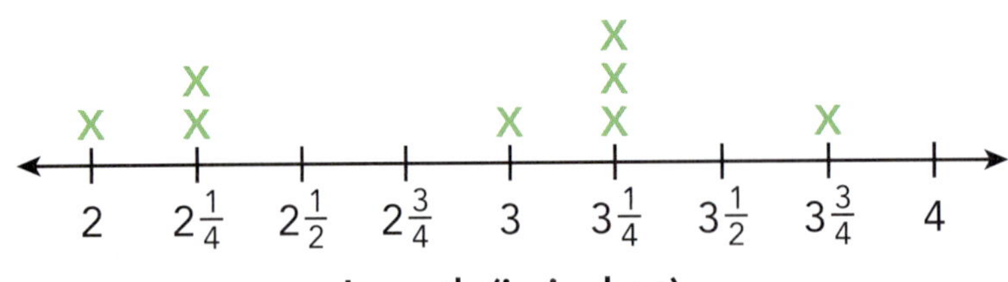

1. How long is the longest worm that Zach found? ________

2. How many worms did Zach find that are more than 3 inches long? ________

3. Three worms are the same length. How long are they? ________

4. How many worms are 4 inches long? ________

Problem Solving

Cam made a line plot to show the weights of her rocks to the nearest ounce. Use the line plot to answer Exercises 5–6.

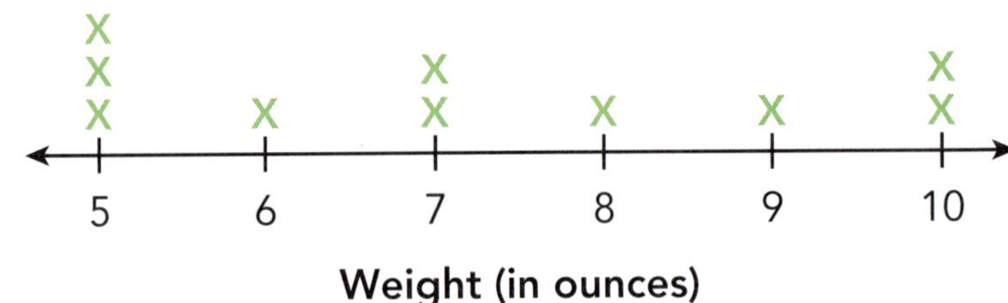

5. How many rocks does Cam have in her collection? ________

6. Cam put her four heaviest rocks in a plastic bag. How much do all the rocks in the bag weigh? ________

Write About It

7. Aiden made a line plot to show the lengths of each of his toy cars. Aiden has 3 cars that are 2 in. long, so he put 2 Xs above the number 3 in his line plot. Is Aiden correct? Explain.

____

____

Name ______________________________ Date ______________

LESSON 12-8

Make Line Plots

Caroline records the length of each carrot she grows to the nearest inch in the tally chart. How can she use the data to make a line plot?

Length of Carrot (in inches)	
4	IIII
5	~~IIII~~
6	
7	III
8	I

- Draw a number line.
- Label the number line. The shortest carrot is 4 inches long. The longest carrot is 8 inches long. So the numbers on the number line show a range of 4–8.
- Draw an X above each length for each tally. Each X represents one carrot.
- Give the line plot a title.

Caroline's line plot is shown.

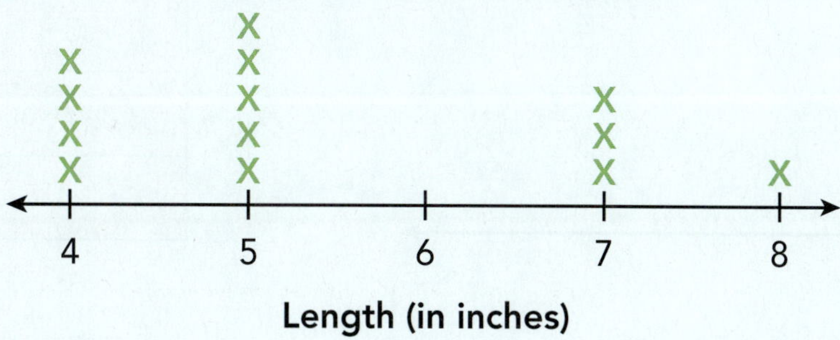

MORE PRACTICE

William measured the length of each nail to the nearest quarter inch and recorded the data in a tally chart.

1. Create a line plot to show the data.

Nail Length (in inches)	
$\frac{1}{2}$	IIII
1	~~IIII~~ I
$1\frac{1}{4}$	III
$1\frac{1}{2}$	II
2	I

HOMEWORK

Mr. Anderson's class recorded the length of each frog in the tally chart.

1. Complete the line plot to show the frog size data.

Frog Lengths (in.)	
2	III
$2\frac{1}{4}$	II
$2\frac{1}{2}$	~~IIII~~
3	I
$3\frac{1}{2}$	IIII

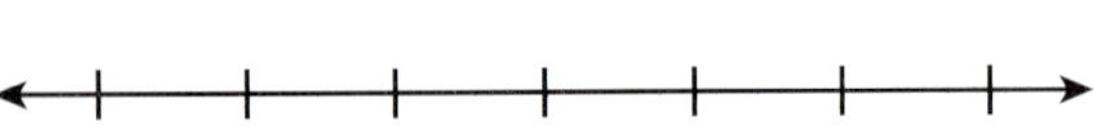

Carly measured the height of each seedling and recorded the data in a tally chart.

2. Create a line plot to show the seedling height data.

Seedling Heights (in.)	
$2\frac{1}{2}$	II
3	I
$3\frac{1}{4}$	III
$3\frac{3}{4}$	~~IIII~~ I
4	IIII

Problem Solving

Use the line plots you made to answer the questions.

3. What is the combined length of the 3 shortest frogs?

____

4. How many seedlings are $3\frac{1}{2}$ in. tall? How can you tell?

____

____

Write About It

5. How are a line plot and a ruler similar? How are they different?

____

____

Name ______________________ Date ______________

LESSON 13-1

Tell Time to the Minute

Stella sets her alarm clock for the time shown on the clock. What time is it?

The shorter hand tells the hour. The hour hand is past 6 but not yet at 7. This means the hour is 6.

The longer hand tells the minutes.

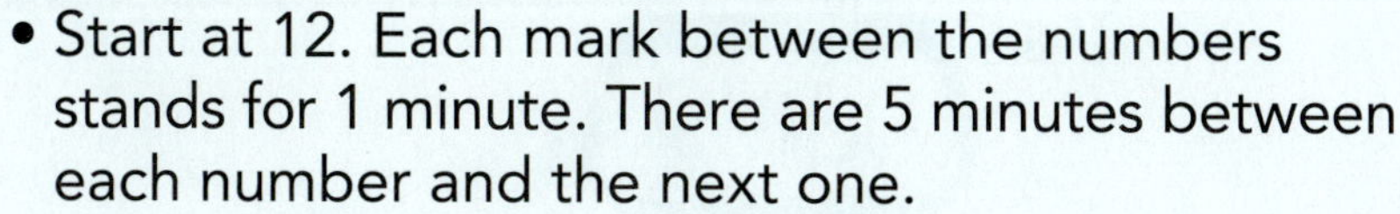

- Start at 12. Each mark between the numbers stands for 1 minute. There are 5 minutes between each number and the next one.

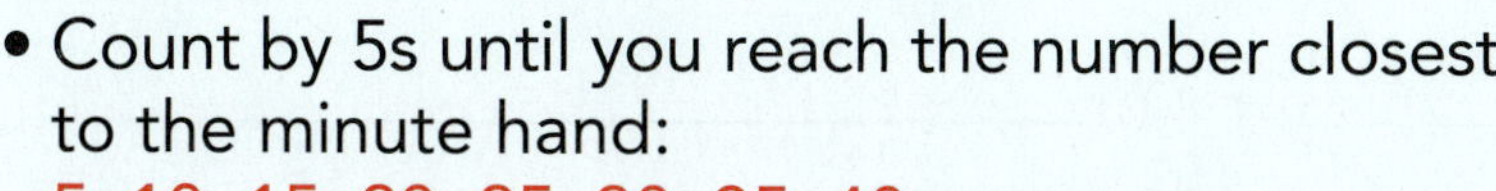

- Count by 5s until you reach the number closest to the minute hand:
  5, 10, 15, 20, 25, 30, 35, 40.

- Count by 1s from 40 until you reach the minute hand:
  41, 42.

Write: 6:42.

Read: six forty-two, eighteen minutes before seven, or forty-two minutes after six.

1 hour = 60 minutes
1 half hour = 30 minutes
1 quarter hour = 15 minutes

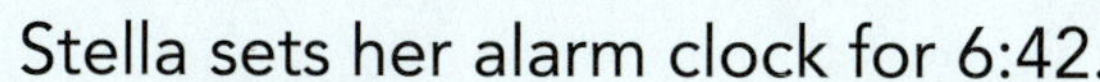

Stella sets her alarm clock for 6:42.

MORE PRACTICE

Draw the hands on the clock to show the time given. Then write the time in two ways.

1. 7:25

____

____

2. 1:33

____

____

3. 11:59

____

____

HOMEWORK

Write the time in standard form.

1. 38 minutes before six ________
2. six minutes past five ________
3. a quarter to three ________
4. half past four ________

Write the time in words, in as many ways as you can.

5. 

____

____

6. 

____

____

Draw the hands on the clock to show the time.

7. 4:12

8. 12:24

9. 2:43

10. 10:57

Problem Solving

11. Robotics Club begins at twenty-five minutes before eight. Write this time in standard form. ________

12. The school bus arrives at sixteen minutes after eight. Write this time in standard form. ________

Write About It

13. Raina says the time shown can be written as twelve minutes before eight. Nia says the time is forty-two minutes after seven. Who is correct? What mistake did the other girl make?

____

____

Name ______________________________ Date ______________

LESSON 13-2

Measure Elapsed Time

What is the elapsed time in one afternoon shown by the clocks?

Elapsed time is the amount of time between two given times.

- Use the clocks to find the elapsed time.

  - Start at 4:15. Count the hours to 6:15.

    From 4:15 to 6:15 is 2 hours.

  - Count the minutes from 6:15 to 6:25.

    From 6:15 to 6:25 is 10 minutes.

Add: 2 hours + 10 minutes = 2 hours 10 minutes

- You can use a number line to find elapsed time. The number line breaks the elapsed time into hours and minutes.

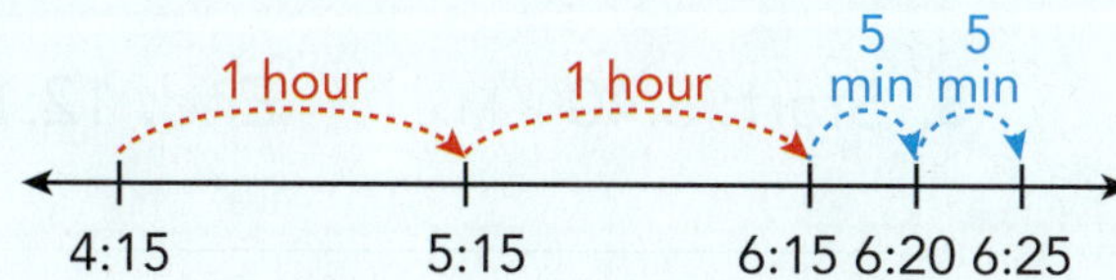

1 hour = 60 minutes

1 hour + 1 hour + 5 minutes + 5 minutes = 2 hours 10 minutes

The elapsed time is 2 hours 10 minutes.

MORE PRACTICE

Find the elapsed time.

1.

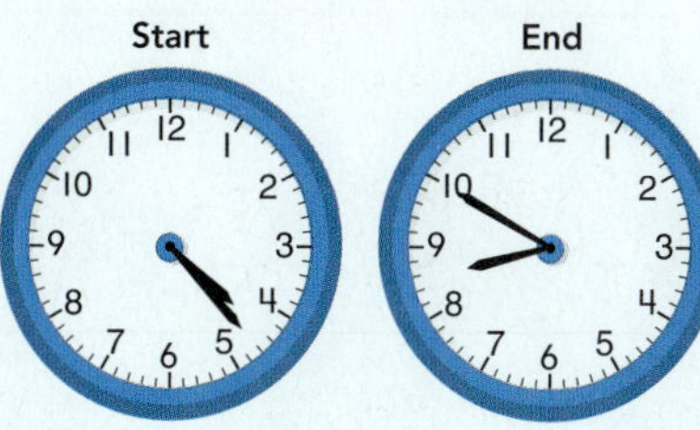

______ hours ______ minutes

2.

______ hours ______ minutes

HOMEWORK

Find the elapsed time using the number line.

1. Start: 8:27 A.M. End: 8:56 A.M. _______ minutes

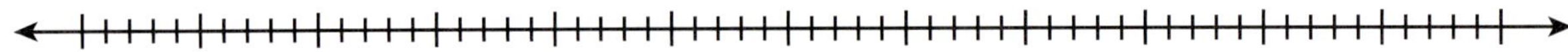

Find the elapsed time in hours and minutes.

2. Start  End 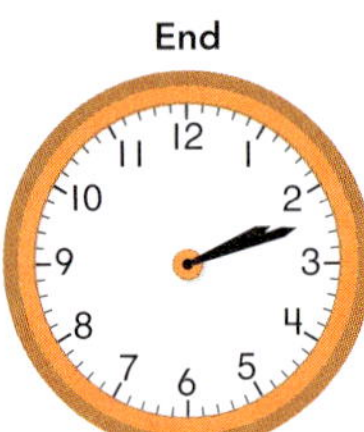

_______ hours _______ minutes

3. Start  End 

_______ hours _______ minutes

Write the elapsed time.

4. Start: 3:25 P.M. End: 7:10 P.M.

____

5. Start: 8:40 P.M. End: 12:15 A.M.

____

Problem Solving

6. The early movie begins at 10:45 A.M. and ends at 1:03 P.M. What is the length of the movie?

____

7. A train ride lasted from 6:15 A.M. to 7:40 P.M. How long did the train ride last?

____

Write About It

8. Explain how to find the elapsed time from 7:45 A.M. to 1:30 P.M. Give the elapsed time in your explanation.

____

____

____

Name ______________________________ Date ______________

LESSON 13-3

Find Start and End Times

What time will it be 35 minutes after the time shown on the clock?

- Draw a number line.

Start the number line at 5:35. The elapsed time is less than 1 hour. So, make the number line go to 6:35.

- You can use a clock to find a start or end time. From 5:35 to 6:00 is 25 minutes. Keep counting 10 minutes more for a total of 35 minutes.

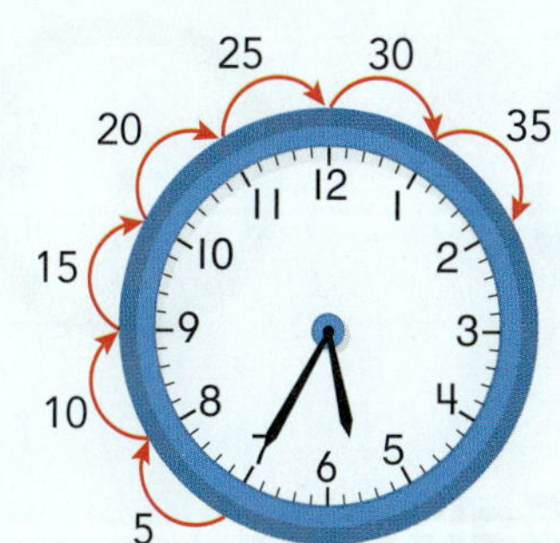

The time will be 6:10.

What is 40 minutes before 6:35 A.M.?

End the number line at 6:35. The elapsed time is less than 1 hour. So, make the start of the number line at 5:35.

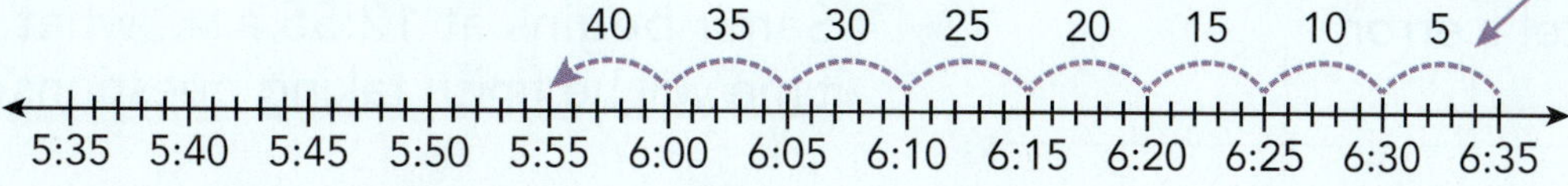

The time is 5:55 A.M.

MORE PRACTICE

Write the time 25 minutes after the time shown.

1.  ______________

2.  ______________

3.  ______________

4.  ______________

HOMEWORK

Draw the hands on the clock to show 36 minutes later.

1. 2:12

2. 4:08

3. 7:30

4. 12:46

Draw the hands on the clock to show 42 minutes earlier.

5. 3:55

6. 6:50

7. 9:15

8. 1:21

Problem Solving

9. A video is 18 minutes long. The video ends at 3:10 P.M. Hazel said the video started at 3:28 P.M. Correct Hazel's error.

____

____

10. Samir's presentation will last 22 minutes. Then the audience has 15 minutes to ask questions. If Samir begins at 12:55 P.M., what time will he finish taking questions?

____

Write About It

11. Act 1 of a play is 25 minutes long. After Act 1 is a 10-minute intermission. Act 2 is 20 minutes long. The play starts at 11:30 A.M. What time does the play finish? Explain how you could use a clock to find your answer.

____

____

____

____

Name ______________________ Date ______________

LESSON 13-4

Operations with Time

Doug wakes up at the time shown on the clock. It takes him 24 minutes to get ready for school. It then takes him 17 minutes to walk to school.

How many minutes, from the time he wakes up, does Doug take to arrive at school? When does Doug arrive at school?

- Use a bar model to find how much time it takes.

? min	
24 min	17 min

The bar model shows that 24 + 17 = __?__.

24 + 17 = 41 minutes

From the time he wakes up, Doug takes 41 minutes to arrive at school.

- Use the elapsed time to find the time Doug arrives at school.
  - Count by 5s until you get to 40, then count one more minute.
  - 41 minutes after 6:45 A.M. is 7:26 A.M.

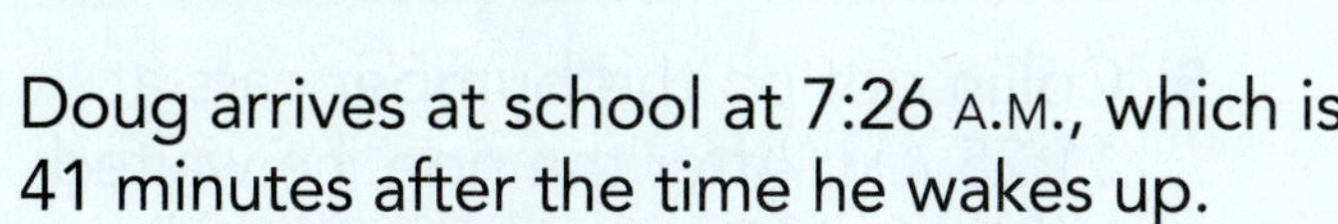

Doug arrives at school at 7:26 A.M., which is 41 minutes after the time he wakes up.

MORE PRACTICE

Solve. Show your work in the space below.

1. Milo starts reading at 8:36 A.M. He reads for 25 minutes and then makes a phone call that lasts for 18 minutes. At what time did Milo's phone call end?

____

2. Ling puts her fishing pole into the water at 7:42 A.M. She catches her second fish at 8:17 A.M. It takes her 16 minutes to catch her first fish. How many minutes does it take her to catch her second fish?

____

HOMEWORK

Solve. Explain your reasoning.

1. A train leaves Springfield at 2:46 P.M. It takes 12 minutes to arrive at the first stop and let passengers on and off. It then takes 25 minutes to arrive at the second stop.

   When does the train arrive at the second stop? ________

2. A town picnic ended at 4:25 P.M. The Elktons were there for 38 minutes. They left 9 minutes before the end of the picnic.

   When did the Elktons arrive at the picnic? ________

3. Hyun started exercising at 6:45 A.M. He finished at 7:24 A.M. Hyun jogged for 22 minutes and walked the rest of the time.

   How many minutes did Hyun walk? ________

4. A race began at 10:15 A.M. and ended at 11:10 A.M. The first runner finished 28 minutes before the race ended.

   How many minutes did the first runner take? ________

Problem Solving

5. Whitney planned on spending 53 minutes to paint a picture. She finished it 15 minutes early at 10:12 A.M. At what time did Whitney start painting the picture? ________

6. Collin got on the bumper cars at 11:25 A.M. After the ride, he waited in line for 10 minutes, and rode them again. He finished at 11:47 A.M. How long does each ride on the bumper cars last? ________

Write About It

7. Explain why it is not important to know the exact times of each event to answer Exercise 6.

   ____

   ____

   ____

   ____

Name ______________________ Date ____________

LESSON 13-5

Problem Solving
Use Logical Reasoning

There are 18 players on the Wildcats hockey team who have received penalties. Of those players, 15 players have served 2-minute penalties and 6 players have served 5-minute penalties. How many Wildcats players have served both 2-minute and 5-minute penalties?

To find how many players served both penalties, you can make a Venn diagram. A Venn diagram uses overlapping circles to organize data into three groups.

◆ Draw two circles that overlap.

- Label each circle.
- Label the overlapping part "Both."

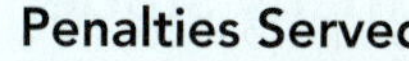

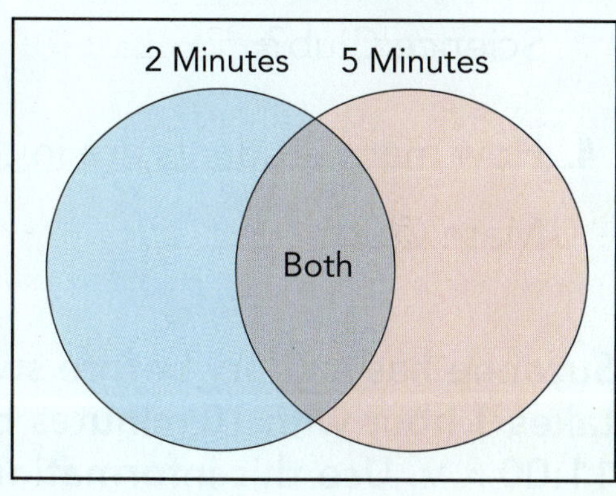

◆ List the data.

- 15 players have served 2-minute penalties.
- 6 players have served 5-minute penalties.

◆ Find the number of students for Both.

- Add the numbers of players who have served 2-minute penalties and 5-minute penalties: 15 + 6 = 21.
- There are only 18 players who have served penalties. To find the number of players who have served both types of penalties, subtract: 21 − 18 = 3.

There are 3 Wildcats players who have served 2-minute penalties and 5-minute penalties.

The final Venn diagram shows the actual numbers for each category. Three was subtracted from the 2-Minute and the 5-Minute circles. In the final Venn diagram, the sum of the numbers in the circles is equal to the number of players, 18, who have served penalties.

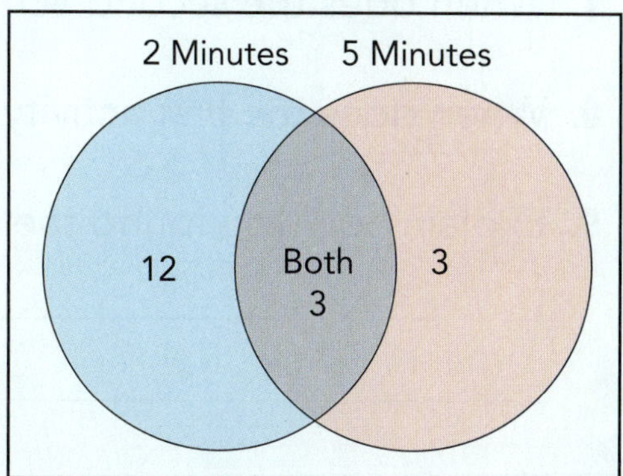

MORE PRACTICE

There are 26 students who belong to the Math Club, the Science Club, or both. The Math Club has 16 students and the Science Club has 18 students. Use this information and the Venn diagram for Exercises 1–4.

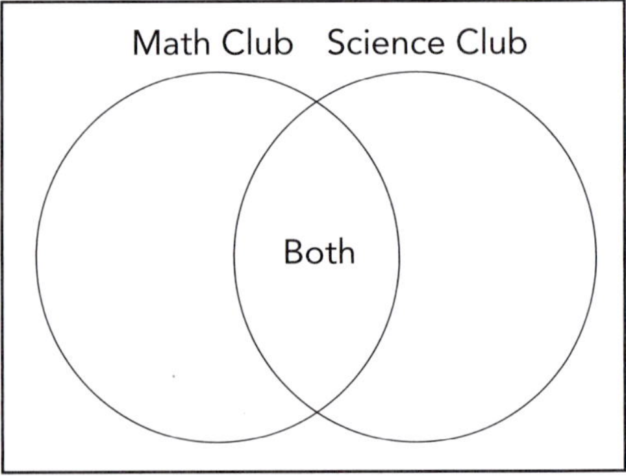

1. Complete the Venn diagram.

2. How many students belong to both clubs? ______

3. How many students are in the Math Club, but not the Science Club? ______

4. How many students are in the Science Club, but not the Math Club? ______

Suzanne has archery before swim and after soccer. Each activity takes 1 hour with 10 minutes between activities. Swim ends at 11:00 A.M. Use this information for Exercises 5–9.

5. Write Suzanne's activities in the correct order.
   1. ______
   2. ______
   3. ______

6. When does the third activity start? ______

7. When does the second activity start? ______

8. When does the first activity start? ______

9. Explain how you found the order of Suzanne's activities.

______

______

______

______

Name ______________________ Date ____________

Problem Solving
Use Logical Reasoning

HOMEWORK

Friends want to skate for 30 minutes at a rink, starting at 2:45 P.M. Once they buy tickets, it takes 20 minutes to get on the rink. It takes 10 minutes to wait in line for tickets. It takes 15 minutes to walk to the rink. Use this information for Exercises 1–2.

Event	Start	Finish
Skate		
Wait to Skate		
Wait for Tickets		
Walk to the Rink		

1. Complete the table.

2. What time should they leave for the rink? ____________

Use this information for Exercises 3–6.

Mr. Friend tutors 16 students each week.

- 9 students take 30-minute sessions.
- 12 students take 60-minute sessions.

Two students made Venn diagrams.

Blake's diagram

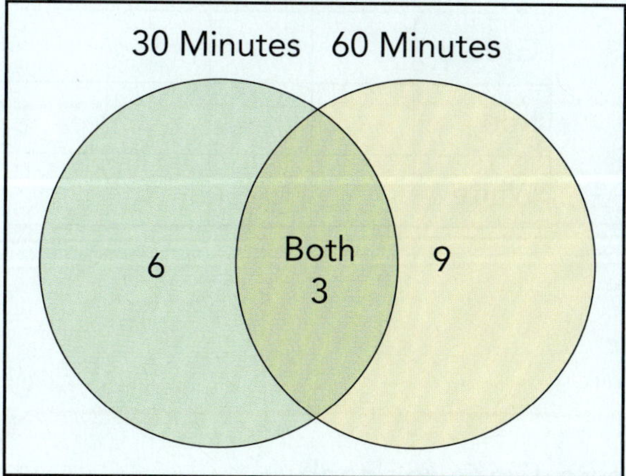

Trevor's diagram

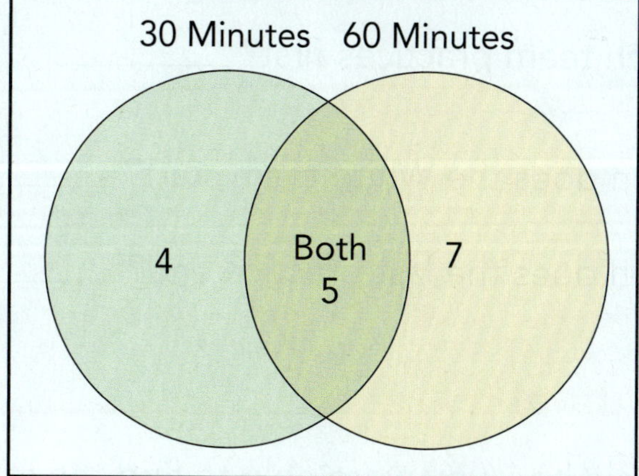

3. Whose diagram is correct? ____________

4. How many students only take 30-minute sessions? ____________

5. How many students only take 60-minute sessions? ____________

6. How many minutes does Mr. Friend tutor each week? ____________

HOMEWORK

Use this information and the table for Exercises 7–9.

Kyra, Lila, and Marta each ordered a different flavor smoothie.

- Kyra did not order papaya.
- Marta does not like honeydew.
- Kyra and Lila did not order guava.

	Guava	Honeydew	Papaya
Kyra			
Lila			
Marta			

7. Complete the table. Use Y for yes and N for no.

8. Who ordered guava? ________________

9. Who ordered honeydew? ________________

Each of four teams gets to practice for 45 minutes with 10 minutes between practice times. The Red team practices before the Blue team, but not right before. The Green team practices right after the Blue team. The White team does not go first nor last. Use this information for Exercises 10–13.

10. Complete the table.

	1st	2nd	3rd	4th
Blue				
Green				
Red				
White				

11. The first team starts practicing at 8:00 A.M.

Which team practices first? ________

12. When does the White team start? ________

13. When does the last practice end? ________

Write About It

14. Explain how you were able to find the starting times for each team's practice in Exercises 10–13.

____

____

____

____

Name ______________________ Date ______________

LESSON 14-1

Classify Polygons

A polygon is a closed, flat figure with straight sides. A side is a line segment.

A polygon is named by its number of sides and its number of angles. An angle of a polygon is formed by two sides that meet at one of the polygon's corners.

Here are the names of some common polygons.

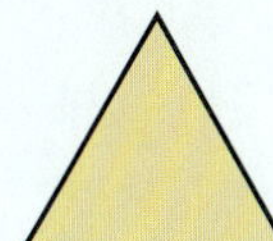
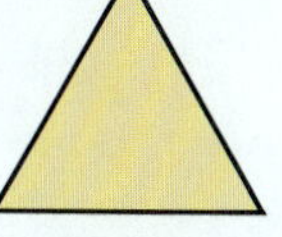

Triangle
3 sides
3 angles

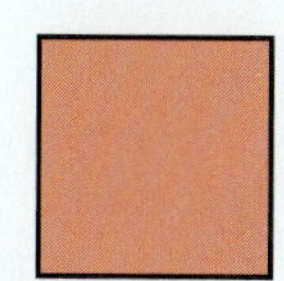

Quadrilateral
4 sides
4 angles

Pentagon
5 sides
5 angles

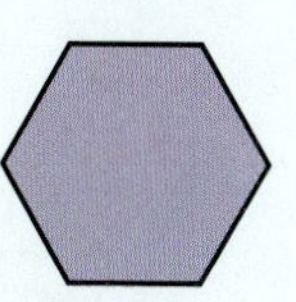

Hexagon
6 sides
6 angles

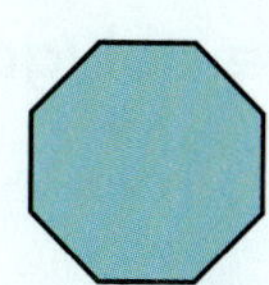

Octagon
8 sides
8 angles

A circle does not have straight sides. It is not a polygon.

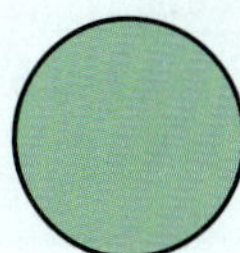

MORE PRACTICE

Circle the polygons. Cross out the shapes that are not polygons. If it is a polygon, write its name.

1.  ______________

2. 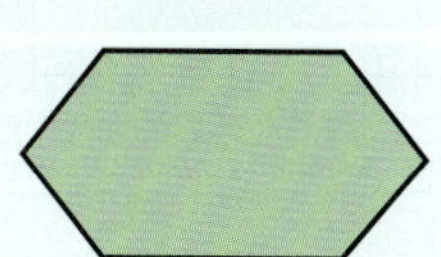 ______________

3.  ______________

4. 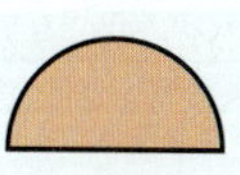 ______________

Complete the table.

	Shape	Number of Sides	Number of Angles
5.	Triangle		
6.			4
7.		6	

HOMEWORK

Circle the polygons. Cross out the shapes that are not polygons. If it is a polygon, write its name.

1. 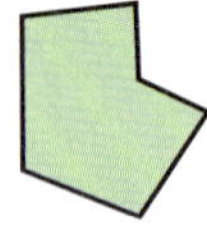 ____________

2. 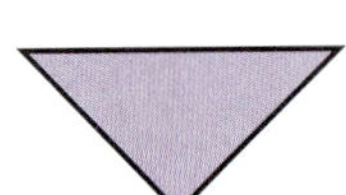 ____________

3.  ____________

4. 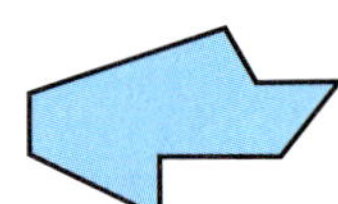 ____________

Describe the polygon.

5. 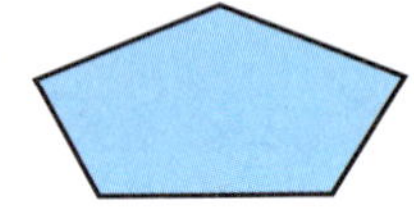

Name: ____________

Sides: ____________

Angles: ____________

6. 

Name: ____________

Sides: ____________

Angles: ____________

7. 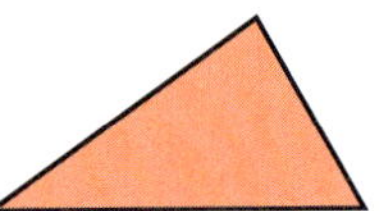

Name: ____________

Sides: ____________

Angles: ____________

Complete the table.

	Shape	Number of Sides	Number of Angles
8.	Quadrilateral		
9.			5
10.		8	

Problem Solving

11. A polygon has 6 sides. How many angles does this polygon have? ____________

12. The sum of the number of sides and angles of a polygon is 6. Which polygon is it? ____________

Write About It

13. Nina said this figure is a polygon. Kanisha said it is not a polygon. Who is correct? Explain your answer.

____

Name ______________________ Date ______________

LESSON 14-2

Classify Quadrilaterals

A quadrilateral is a polygon that has 4 sides and 4 angles.

Here are some special kinds of quadrilaterals.

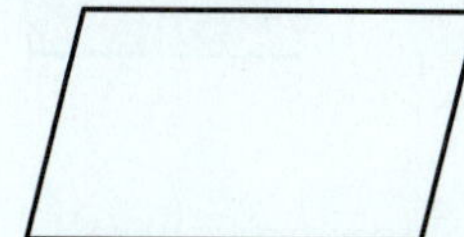

Parallelogram

- Opposite sides are the same length.
- Opposite angles have the same measure.

Rhombus

- 2 pairs of parallel sides
- 4 sides that are the same length
- Is a parallelogram

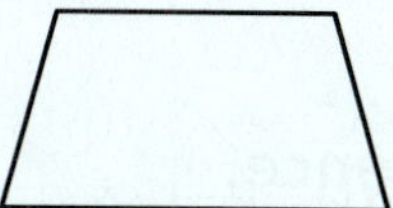

Trapezoid

- Exactly 1 pair of parallel sides
- Is *not* a parallelogram

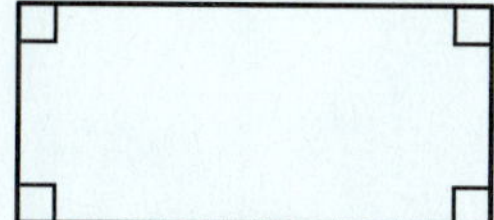

Rectangle

- 2 pairs of parallel sides
- 4 right angles
- Is a parallelogram

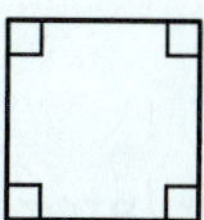

Square

- 2 pairs of parallel sides
- 4 sides that are the same length
- 4 right angles
- Is a parallelogram, rhombus, and rectangle

MORE PRACTICE

Classify the quadrilateral. Be as specific as possible.

1. 

____

2. 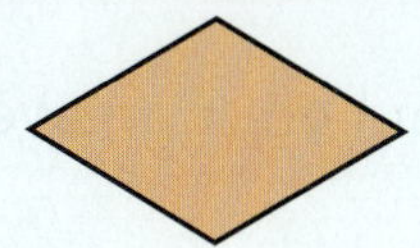

____

3. 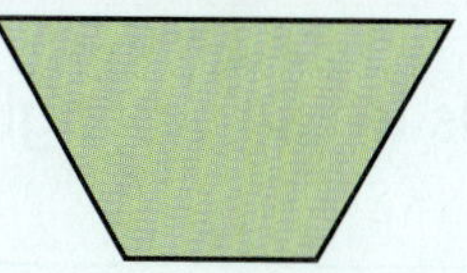

____

4. 

____

HOMEWORK

Circle the parallelograms. Cross out the shapes that are not parallelograms.

1. 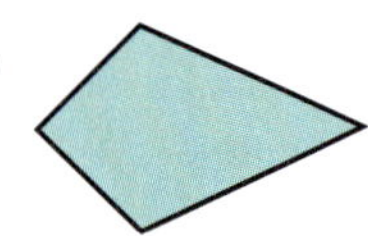

2. 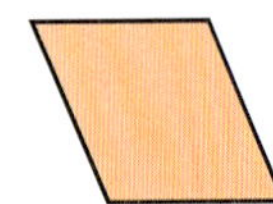

3. 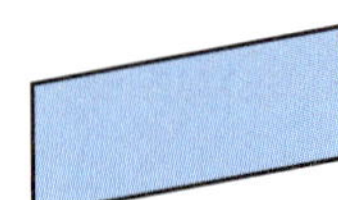

4. 

Complete the sentence.

5. A parallelogram has ______ pairs of parallel sides.

6. A rhombus has ______ sides that are the same length.

7. A square has ______ right angles.

8. A trapezoid has exactly ______ pair of parallel sides.

Problem Solving

9. Santiago says that a quadrilateral with 4 equal sides is a parallelogram. Hideki says that there is not enough information to determine that. Who is correct? Explain.

____

____

10. Irina says that a quadrilateral with 2 pairs of parallel sides is always a rhombus. June says that Irina means a parallelogram. Who is correct? Explain.

____

____

Write About It

11. How can a rhombus be a rectangle? Explain your answer.

____

____

____

Name ______________________ Date ______________

LESSON 14-3

Draw Quadrilaterals

Each player in a game is inside a shape drawn with red chalk that has 4 sides, 2 pairs of parallel sides, and 0 right angles. The sides of the shape do not all have the same length. Draw the shape.

Before drawing the shape, review the information you have been given.

- The shape has 4 sides, so it is a quadrilateral.
- The quadrilateral has 2 pairs of parallel sides, so it is a parallelogram.
- The parallelogram does not have any right angles. It is not a rectangle or square.
- The parallelogram does not have 4 sides that are the same length. It is not a rhombus.

The shape is a parallelogram that cannot be classified in any other way.

One possible drawing of the parallelogram is shown.

MORE PRACTICE

Draw a quadrilateral to match the description. Explain why your drawing is correct.

1. quadrilateral that has exactly 1 pair of parallel sides

____

____

____

2. parallelogram that is neither a rhombus nor a rectangle

____

____

____

HOMEWORK

Draw a quadrilateral to match the description.

1. parallelogram that is not a rectangle

2. quadrilateral that has exactly 2 right angles

3. quadrilateral that is neither a rhombus nor a trapezoid

4. quadrilateral that is neither a trapezoid nor a parallelogram

Problem Solving

5. Can a parallelogram have exactly 1 right angle? Explain your answer.

6. Nira wants to draw a quadrilateral with exactly 3 sides that have the same length. Can Nira draw this shape? Explain your answer.

Write About It

7. Can a quadrilateral have exactly 3 right angles? Explain your answer.

Name ______________________ Date ____________

LESSON 14-4

Compose and Decompose Shapes

The two trapezoids have the same size and shape. How can you compose a hexagon?

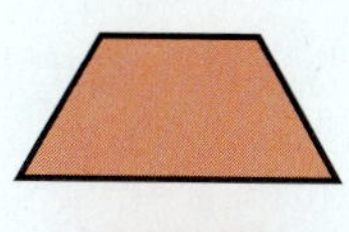

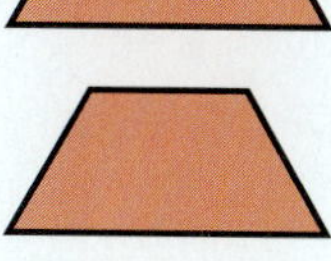

To compose means to combine shapes to form a new shape. To compose figures, move one or both of the figures. When you move a figure, the size and shape of the figure stay the same.

A hexagon has 6 sides. Each trapezoid has 4 sides.

Start with the two trapezoids.	Rotate the bottom trapezoid.	Move them together to form a hexagon.
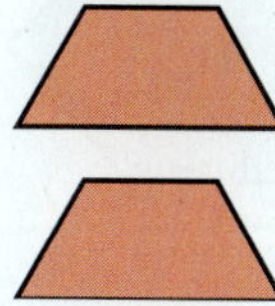	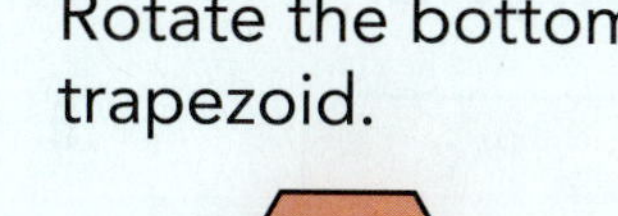 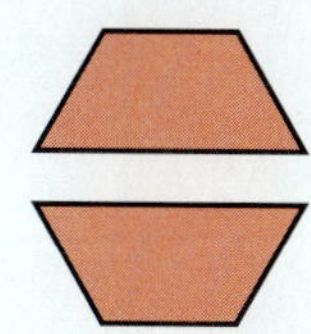	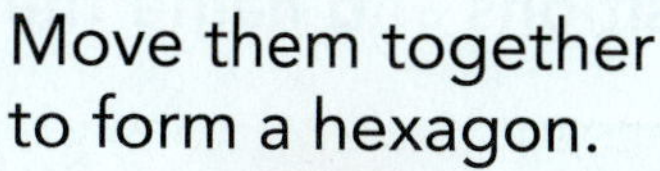 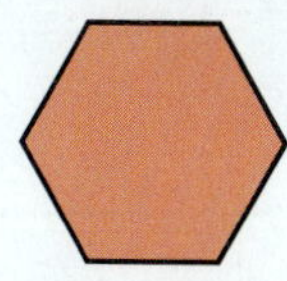

The hexagon shown is composed from the two trapezoids.

To decompose means to break into smaller parts. To decompose figures, draw a horizontal, vertical, or diagonal line.

Horizontal	Vertical	Diagonal
Two trapezoids with the same size and shape	Two pentagons with the same size and shape	Two trapezoids with the same size and shape
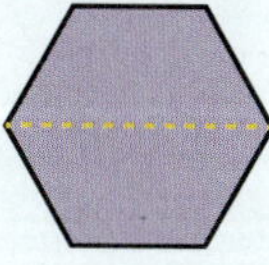	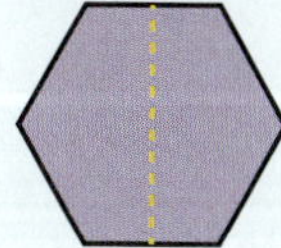	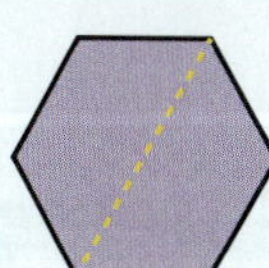

MORE PRACTICE

Decompose the polygon into two polygons. Show the decompositions and name the new polygons.

1. 

____

2. 

____

3. 

____

HOMEWORK

Draw a new polygon by composing the two polygons.

1. 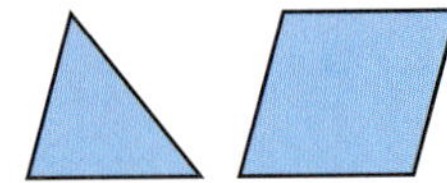

2. 

Decompose the polygon into two polygons. Show the decompositions and name the new polygons.

3. 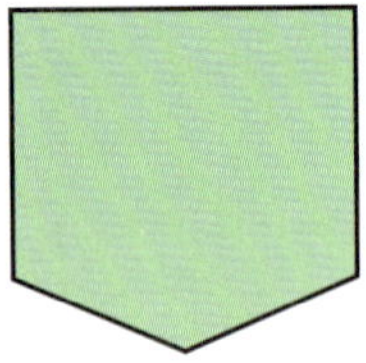

____

4. 

____

5. 

____

Decompose the polygon into three rectangles.

6. 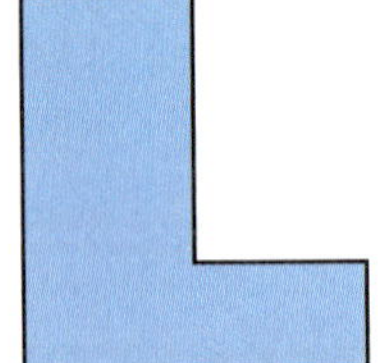

7. 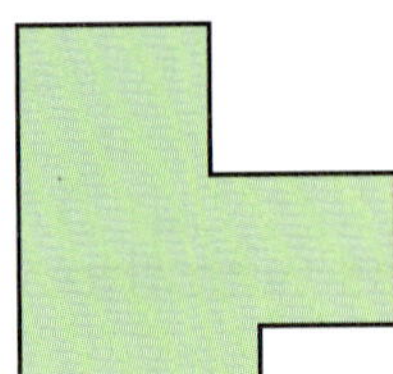

8. 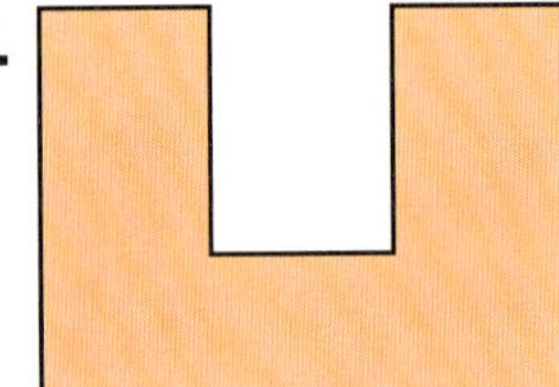

Problem Solving

9. A rectangle is composed by two triangles.
How many right angles does each triangle have?

Show your work. ________

Write About It

10. Can you compose a larger square out of two squares that have the same size? Explain your answer.

____

____

Name ______________________ Date ______________

LESSON 14-5

Problem Solving
Make a Table

If the pattern continues, how many stars are in Figure 5? Draw Figure 5.

Figure 1

Figure 2

Figure 3

Figure 4

One strategy that you can use is to make a table.

Figure	Stars in Bottom Row	Other Stars	Total Stars
1	2	1	2 + 1 = 3
2	3	3	3 + 3 = 6
3	4	6	4 + 6 = 10
4	5	10	5 + 10 = 15
5	?	?	?

- The number of stars in the bottom row increases by 1.
- After Figure 1, the total number of stars is found by adding the stars in the bottom row and the stars from the previous figure.
- In Figure 5, there will be 5 + 1 = 6 stars in the bottom row. There will be 15 other stars, because Figure 4 had 15 stars.
- Add: 6 + 15 = 21.

There are 21 stars in Figure 5 of the pattern. Figure 5 is shown.

Figure 5

MORE PRACTICE

Solve. Show your work. Tell which strategy you used.

Strategies

- Use Drawings to Solve Problems
- Look Back
- Make a Table
- Find a Pattern
- Work Backward
- Use a Picture
- Use a Model
- Make an Organized List
- Use Logical Reasoning
- Write an Equation
- Act It Out

1. Angela puts 40 cards into folders. She puts 10 cards in the first folder, 9 in the second folder, 8 in the third folder, and so on. If the pattern continues, how many folders will she use for the 40 cards?

____

2. Which quadrilaterals must have 4 right angles and 2 pairs of parallel sides?

____

3. Elias collected 15 more kilograms of recycling than Garrett. Garrett collected 18 fewer kilograms than John. John collected 40 kilograms of recycling. How many kilograms of recycling did Elias collect?

____

____

4. How many triangles can you make by drawing straight lines from one vertex of the orange hexagon to the other vertices?

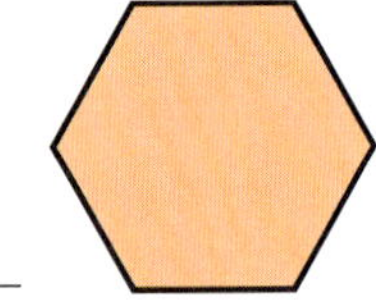

____

5. Raquel is going to choose an outfit from 3 tops and 2 pairs of pants. She has a blue top, a red top, and a green top. She has a pair of black jeans and a pair of khakis. How many different outfits can Raquel choose from using one top and one pair of pants?

____

____

6. There is a trapezoid, a triangle, and a square. Sharon did not pick a shape with 3 sides. Allie picked a shape with exactly one pair of parallel sides. Rose did not pick a shape with all equal sides. Each picked a different shape. Who picked what shape?

____

____

____

Name ______________________________ Date ______________

Problem Solving
Make a Table

HOMEWORK

Solve. Show your work. Tell which strategy you used.

Strategies
- Use Drawings to Solve Problems
- Look Back
- Make a Table
- Find a Pattern
- Work Backward
- Use a Picture
- Use a Model
- Make an Organized List
- Use Logical Reasoning
- Write an Equation
- Act It Out

1. Kavi bought 2 games that cost the same amount and a poster for $20. The poster cost $8. What was the cost of each game?

____

2. The kitchen floor has 8 rows of tiles. Each row contains 6 tiles. How many tiles does the kitchen floor have?

____

____

3. If the pattern continues, how many triangles will be in Figure 5?

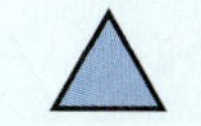
Figure 1

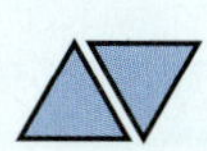
Figure 2

Figure 3

Figure 4

____

4. Paula wants to make a larger square using squares that are the same size. What is the least number of squares that Paula will need to compose the larger square?

____

____

5. Nathaniel studies for 25 fewer minutes than Randall. Randall studies for 30 more minutes than Alfonso. Alfonso studies for 40 minutes. How many minutes does Nathaniel study?

____

____

6. Decompose the green octagon by drawing line segments from one vertex to the other vertices. How many triangles are formed?

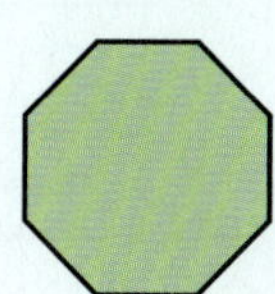

____

HOMEWORK

Solve. Tell which strategy you used.

7. Po has 6 toothpicks that are the same length. What is the greatest number of squares of the same size that Po can make from the toothpicks?

---

8. Keisha's first four classes are gym, math, reading, and science. Keisha has gym after math. She has math before reading. She has reading after science. Keisha does not have math first or reading last. What is the order of Keisha's first four classes?

---

9. There are 18 students that play on the tennis team. Twelve play singles and 10 play doubles. How many students play both singles and doubles?

---

10. If the pattern continues, how many sides and vertices will the next figure have?

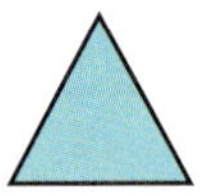 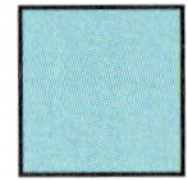 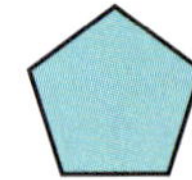 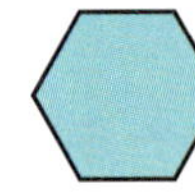

Write About It

11. If the pattern continues, explain how to find the number of stars in Figure 5.

Name ________________ Date ________________

LESSON 15-1

Understand Area

What is the area, in square units, of the triangle shown on the grid?

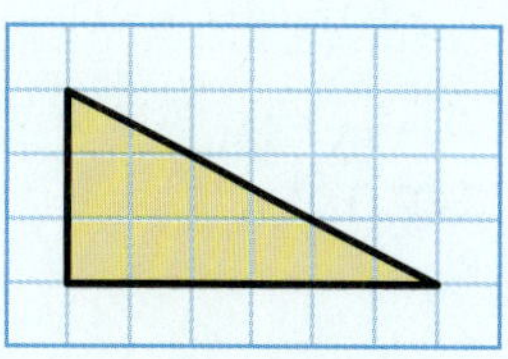

Area is the number of square units needed to cover a flat surface with no gaps or overlaps. A unit square is a square with side lengths of 1 unit.

The area of a unit square is 1 square unit. Area is measured in square units.

To find the area of the triangle, count the unit squares.

- Count the squares that are completely shaded.

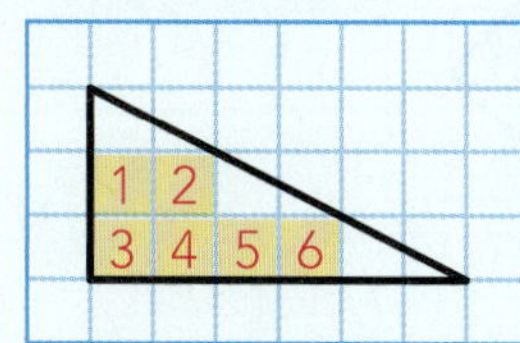

There are 6 completely shaded squares.

- Estimate the number of completely shaded squares that can be made from what is left.

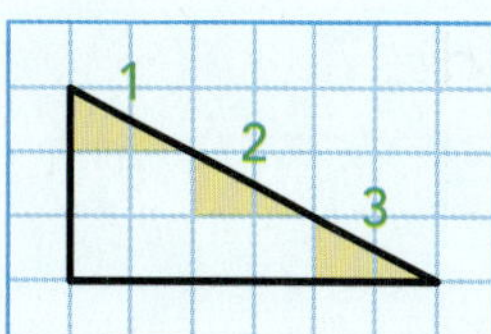

There are about 3 completely shaded squares that can be made.

- Add the estimate to the number of completely shaded squares: $6 + 3 = 9$.

It takes about 9 unit squares to cover the triangle, so the area of the triangle is about 9 square units.

MORE PRACTICE

Estimate the area of the shaded figure in square units.

1. 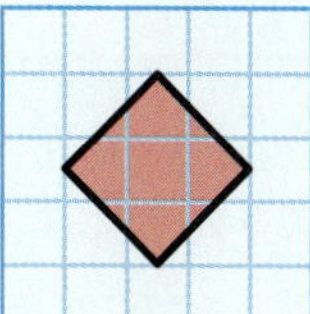

about ________________

2. 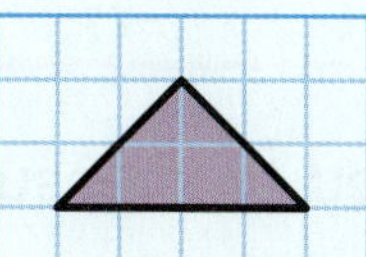

about ________________

3. 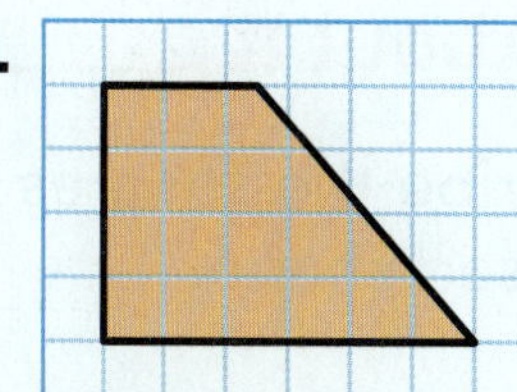

about ________________

HOMEWORK

Estimate the area of the shaded figure in square units.

1. 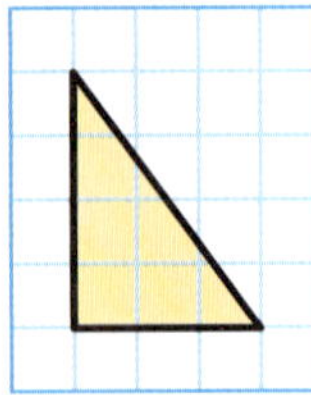

Full squares: ____________

Estimate of rest: about ____________

Estimate of area: about ____________

2.

Full squares: ____________

Estimate of rest: about ____________

Estimate of area: about ____________

3. 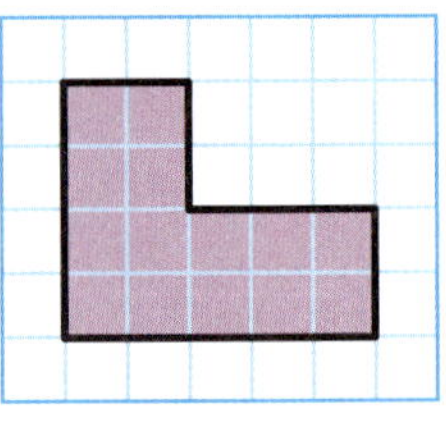

____

4. 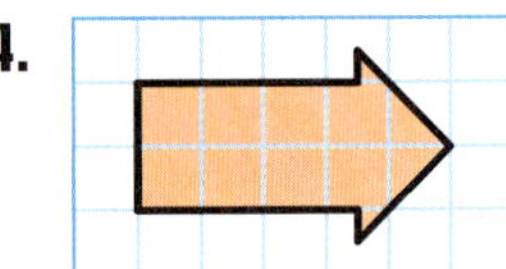

about ____________

Problem Solving

5. Kamal said that he can measure area using squares that are 2 units long and 1 unit wide. What mistake did Kamal make?

____

____

____

6. A shape on a grid covers 4 unit squares completely. Also, 6 unit squares are about half covered by the shape. What is the area of the shape?

____

Write About It

7. Describe the squares that are needed to measure the area of a closed shape.

____

____

Name ______________________ Date ______________

LESSON 15-2

Find Area Using Standard Units

The floor of Craig's closet is represented by the shaded part of the grid.

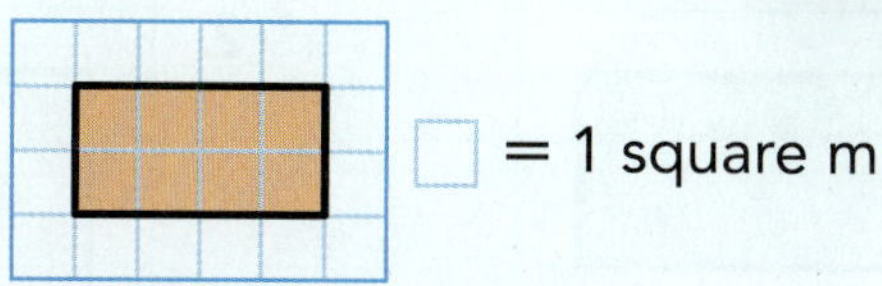

What is the area of Craig's closet floor?

You can measure area in square units. In the diagram, □ = 1 square m means that the unit square for this figure has an area of 1 square meter. This means that each side of the square is 1 meter.

A unit square is a square that has a side length of 1 unit.

Examples of square units include square inches, square feet, square centimeters, and square meters. For the area of a room, you would use square feet or square meters. For the area of the screen of a cell phone, you would use square inches or square centimeters.

You can find the area by counting the number of shaded unit squares.

- There are 8 shaded unit squares in the diagram of Craig's closet floor.
- Each unit square represents 1 square meter.

The area of Craig's bedroom floor is 8 square meters. Each unit square in the diagram represents $\frac{1}{8}$ of the total area.

MORE PRACTICE

Write the area of the shaded figure.

1.

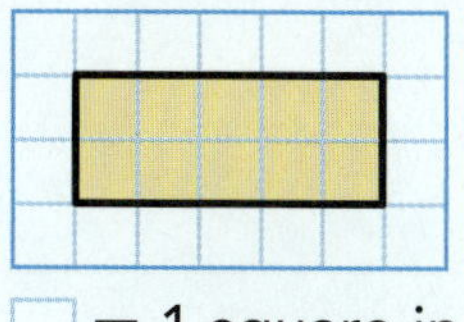

____

2.

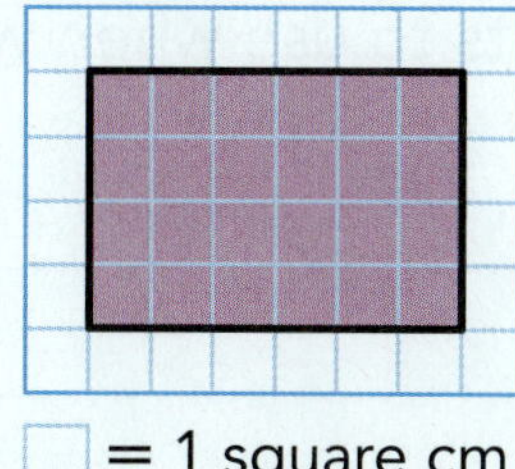

____

3.

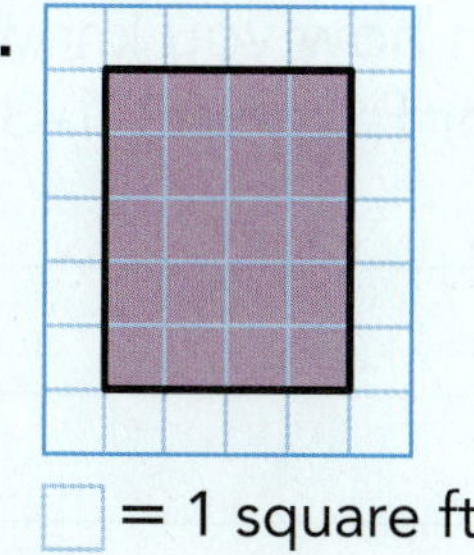

____

HOMEWORK

Write the area of the shaded figure.

1. 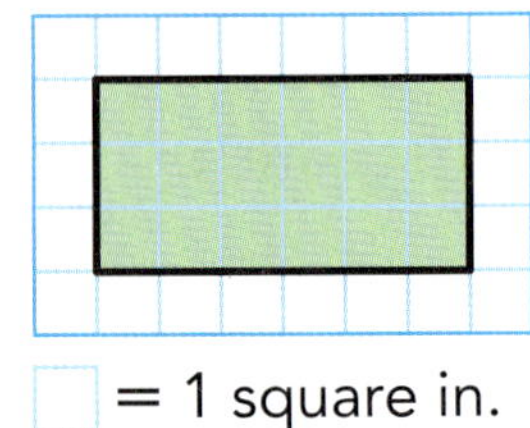

□ = 1 square in.

____

2. 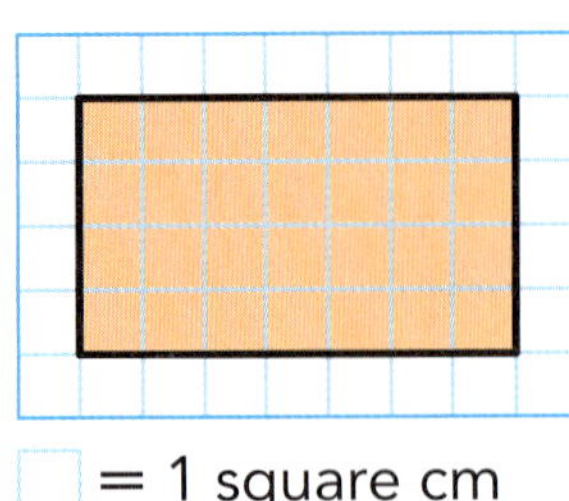

□ = 1 square cm

____

3. 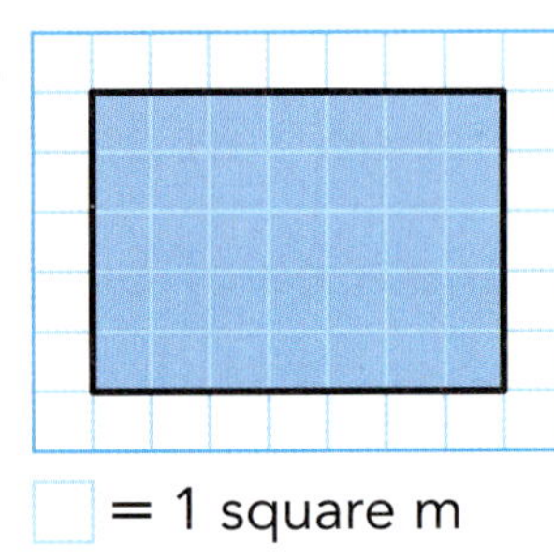

□ = 1 square m

____

Draw a shape with the given area. Each square on the grid is one square unit.

4. 15 square in.

5. 12 square ft

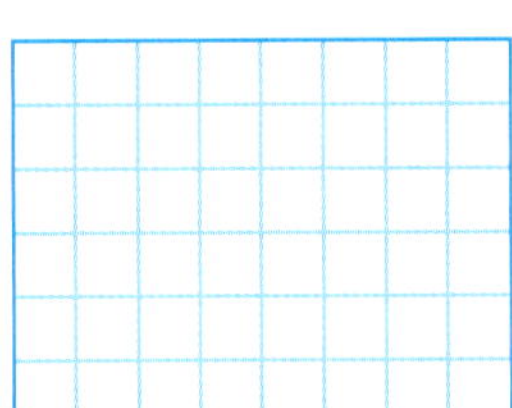

6. 16 square cm

Problem Solving

7. Raime's door is 7 feet long and 3 feet wide. What units are needed to measure the area of the door? ______________

8. A grid represents a rectangle that has an area of 6 square units. Each unit square is completely shaded. The grid has 3 columns. How many rows does the grid have? __________

Write About It

9. Explain how you knew which units to use when writing the area for Exercises 1–3.

____

____

____

Name ______________________________ Date ______________

LESSON 15-3

Find the Area of a Rectangle and a Square

Pedro's rug is shown.
What is the area of Pedro's rug?

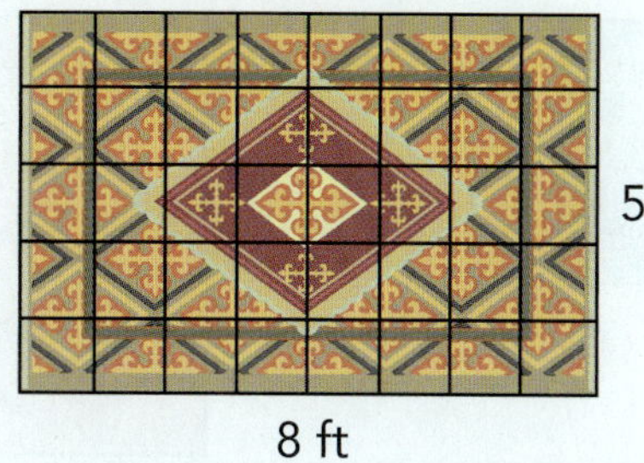

- You can find the area by counting the shaded unit squares. There are 40 unit squares, so the area is 40 square feet.

- You can also multiply to find the area.

  Multiply the length by the width.

  8 ft × 5 ft = 40 square ft

To find the area of a square, you can multiply one side by itself.

The area of Pedro's rug is 40 square feet.

MORE PRACTICE

Find the area.

1. 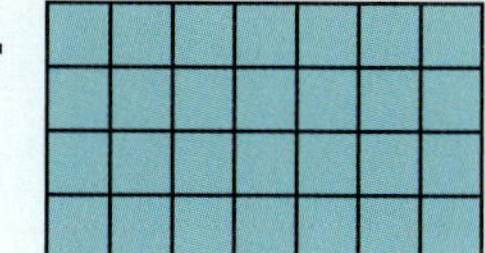

_____ × _____ = _____

_____ square units

2. 

_____ × _____ = _____

_____ square units

3. 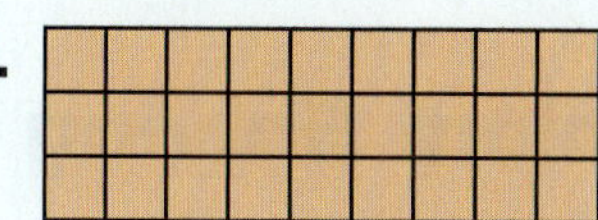

_____ × _____ = _____

_____ square units

Match the rectangle to its area.

4. 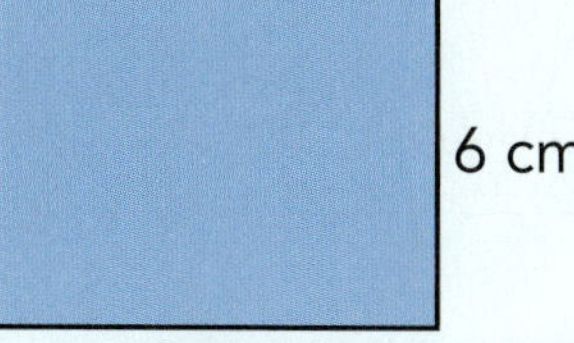

5. 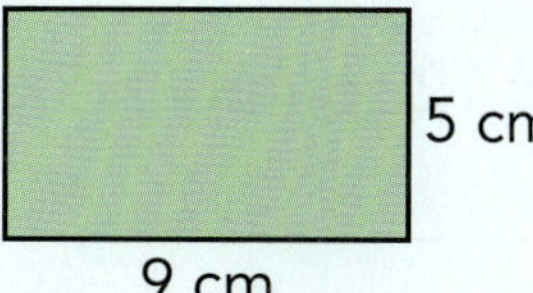

6. 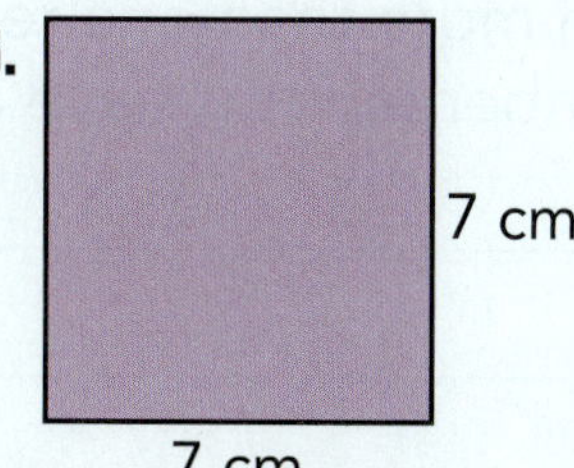

45 square cm

48 square cm

49 square cm

HOMEWORK

Find the area of the rectangle.

1. 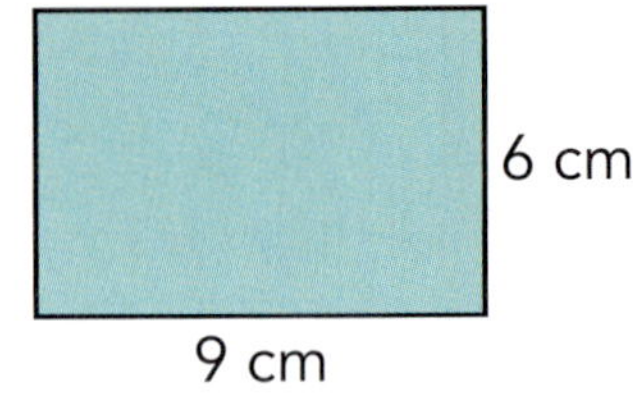

______

2. 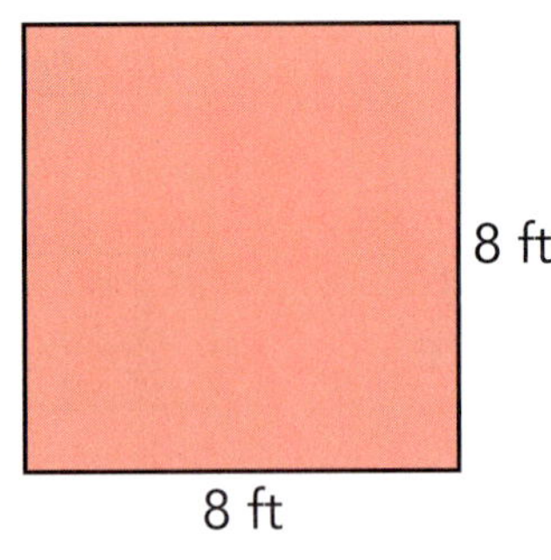

______

3. 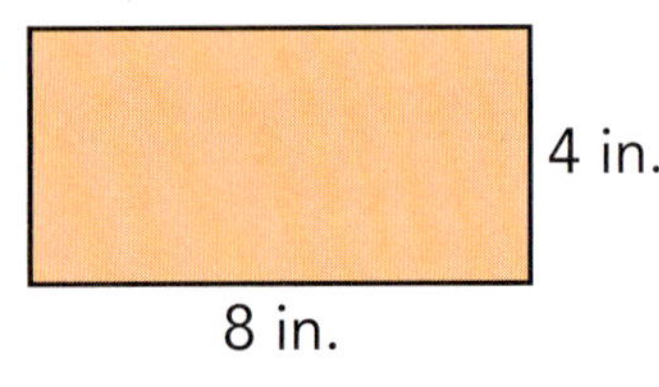

______

Draw a rectangle with the given area.

4. 24 square in.

5. 36 square cm

6. 30 square ft

Problem Solving

7. A square garden bed has sides of 3 feet. What is the area of the garden bed? ______

8. A rectangular index card has an area of 15 square in. The width is 3 in. What is the length of the index card? ______

Write About It

9. Can more than one rectangle with sides that are whole-number lengths have an area of 12 square in.? Explain.

______

______

______

Name ______________________ Date ____________

LESSON 15-4

Find Area Using the Distributive Property

The grid shown represents the area of Catherine's drawing. What is the area of the drawing?

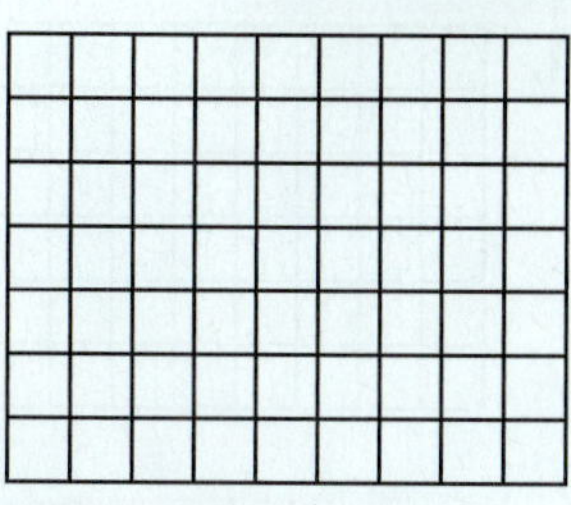

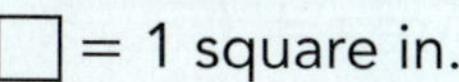

= 1 square in.

- You can break apart the figure into two rectangles. Then you can find the area by using the Distributive Property.
  - Find the length and the width of the drawing. The drawing is 9 inches long and 7 inches wide.
  - Break apart 9 into 5 + 4.

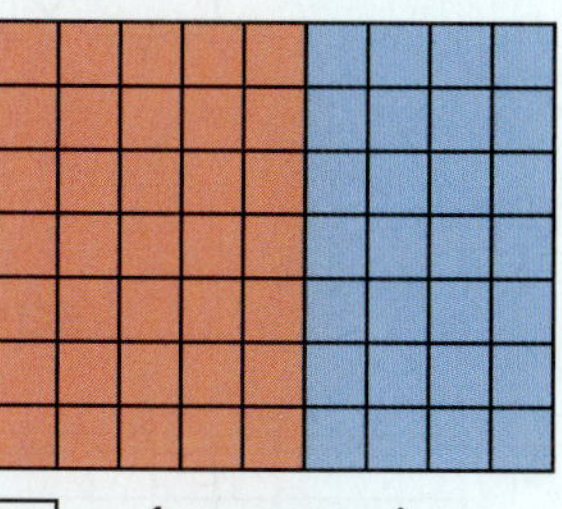

= 1 square in.

- Find the area of each section.
  - The red section is 5 inches long and 7 inches wide.
  - The blue section is 4 inches long and 7 inches wide.

Area $= (5 \times 7) + (4 \times 7)$
$= 35 + 28$
$= 63$

The area of Catherine's drawing is 63 square inches. You can check this by counting the number of unit squares in the entire rectangle.

MORE PRACTICE

Find the area, in square units, of the figure.

1. 

Area =

(3 × ____) + (3 × ____)

= ____ + ____ = ____

The area is

____ square units.

2. 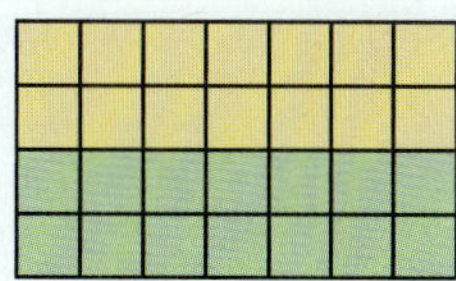 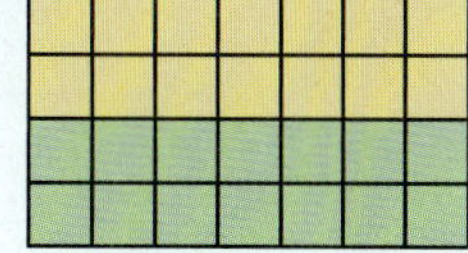

Area =

(____ × 2) + (____ × 2)

= ____ + ____ = ____

The area is

____ square units.

3. 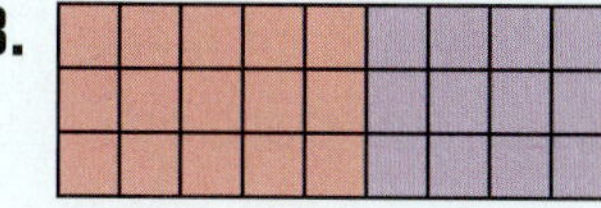

Area =

(5 × ____) + (4 × ____)

= ____ + ____ = ____

The area is

____ square units.

HOMEWORK

Find the area, in square units, by using the Distributive Property. Shade the grid to match your work.

1. 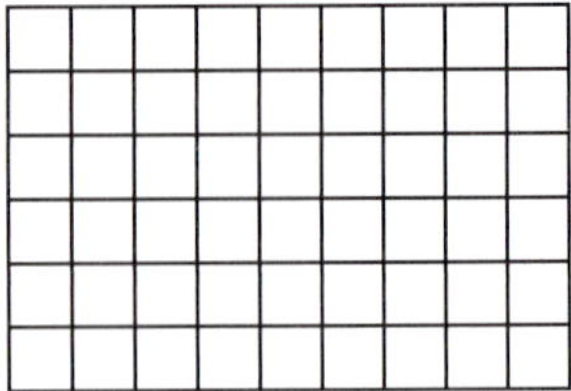

Area = (___ × ___) +
(___ × ___)
= ___ + ___
= ___ square units

2. 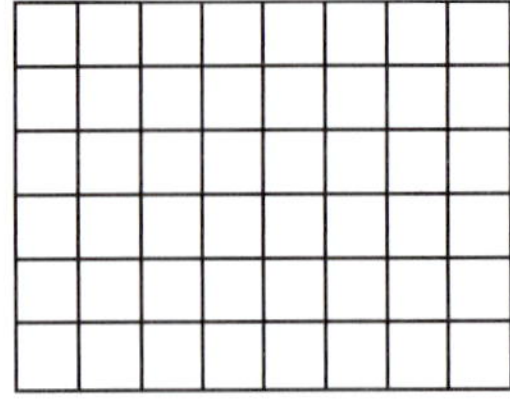

Area = (___ × ___) +
(___ × ___)
= ___ + ___
= ___ square units

3. 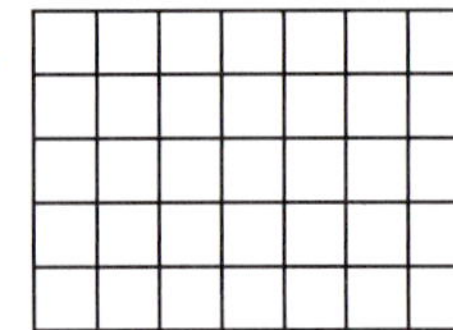

Area = (___ × ___) +
(___ × ___)
= ___ + ___
= ___ square units

4. 

____

____

5. 

____

____

6. 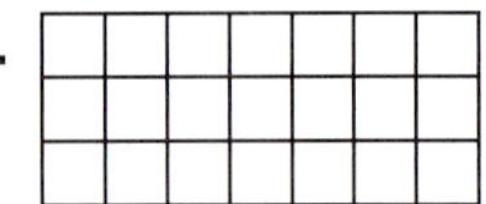

____

____

Problem Solving

7. A rectangular garden has berries and tomatoes. Its width is 6 feet. The area with berries has a length of 5 feet. The area with tomatoes has a length of 4 feet. What is the area of the garden?

____

8. A rectangle has sides of 9 inches and 15 inches. Explain how to use the Distributive Property to find its area.

____

____

____

Write About It

9. If a rectangle has an even length and an odd width, which number should be broken apart? Explain why.

____

____

Name ______________________ Date ______________

LESSON 15-5

Find Area of Composite Shapes

What is the area of the floor shown?

Decompose the composite shape into rectangles that do not overlap and that have no gaps. Find the area of each rectangle. Then find the sum of the areas.

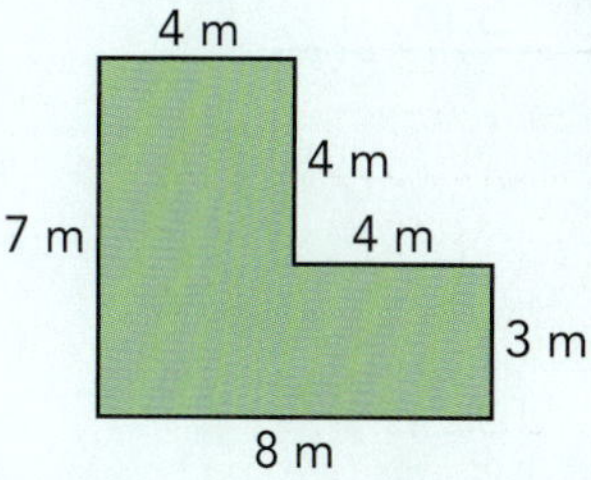

- Decompose the shape into two rectangles. Here are two ways:

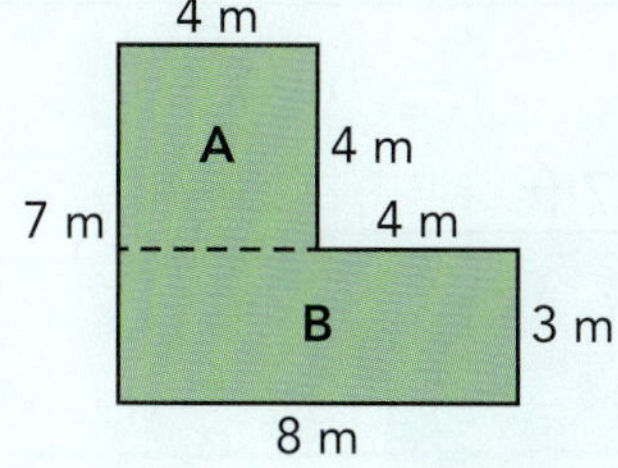

Rectangle A Area: 4 × 4 = 16

Rectangle B Area: 8 × 3 = 24

Total Area: 16 + 24 = 40

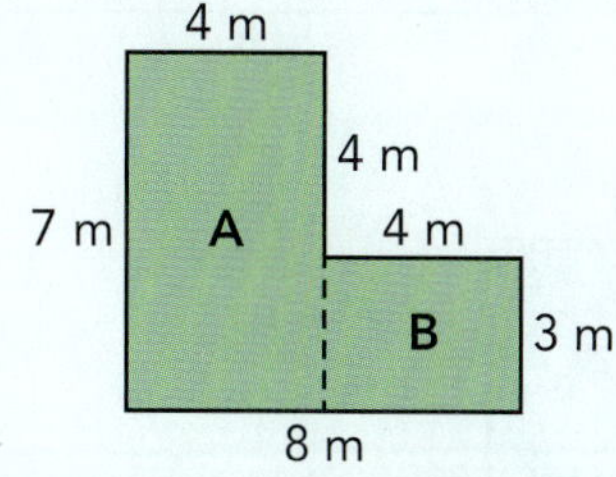

Rectangle A Area: 4 × 7 = 28

Rectangle B Area: 4 × 3 = 12

Total Area: 28 + 12 = 40

The area of the floor is 40 square meters.

MORE PRACTICE

Break each shape into two rectangles. Find the area of each. Then find the total area. Show your work.

1.

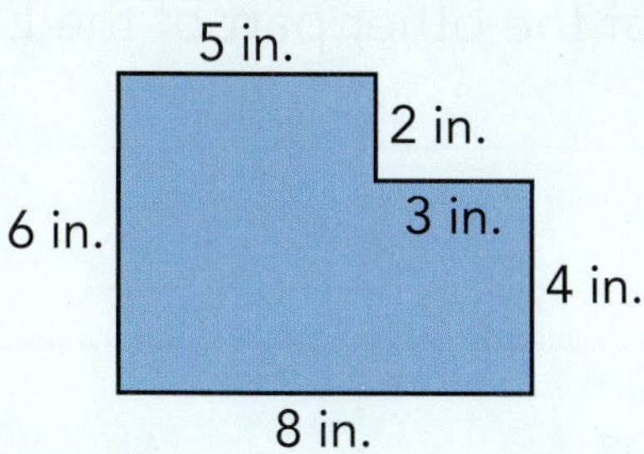

____ × ____ = ____

____ × ____ = ____

Area: ____ + ____ = ____________

2.

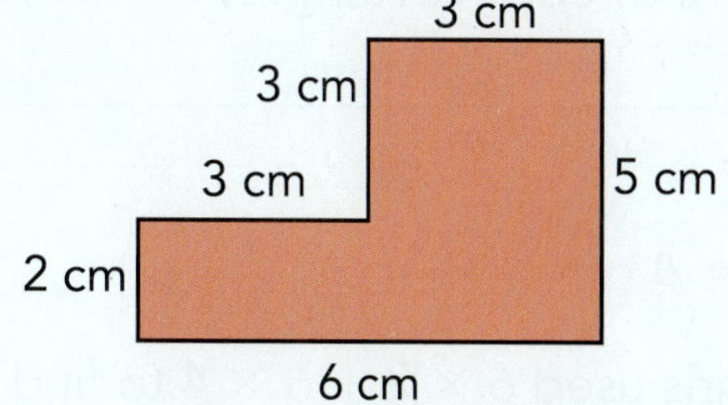

____ × ____ = ____

____ × ____ = ______

Area: ____ + ____ = ____________

HOMEWORK

Find the total area.

1.

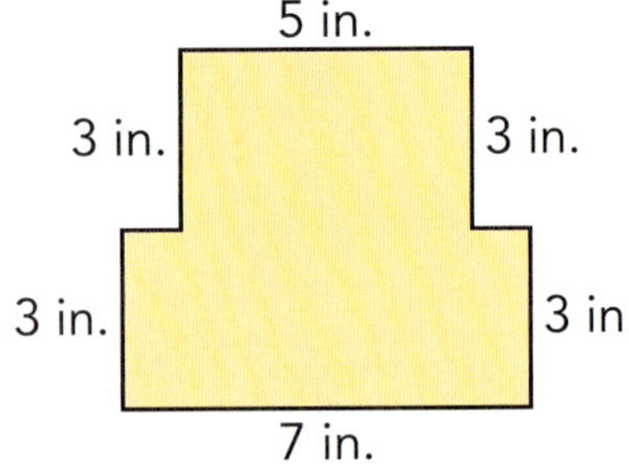

____

2.

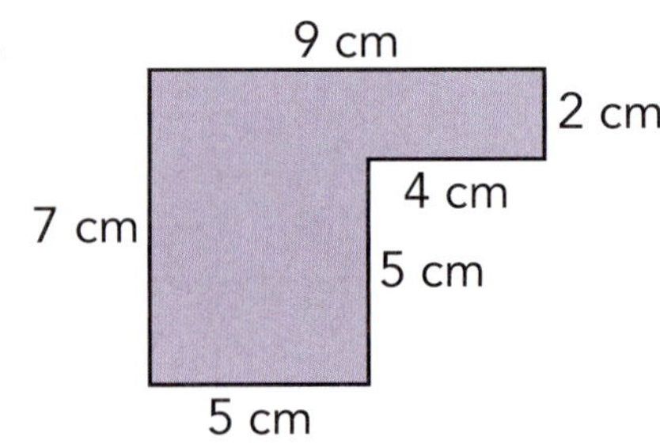

____

3.

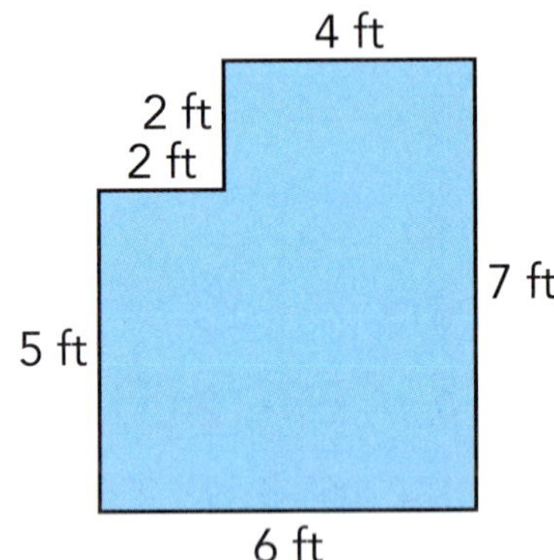

____

4.

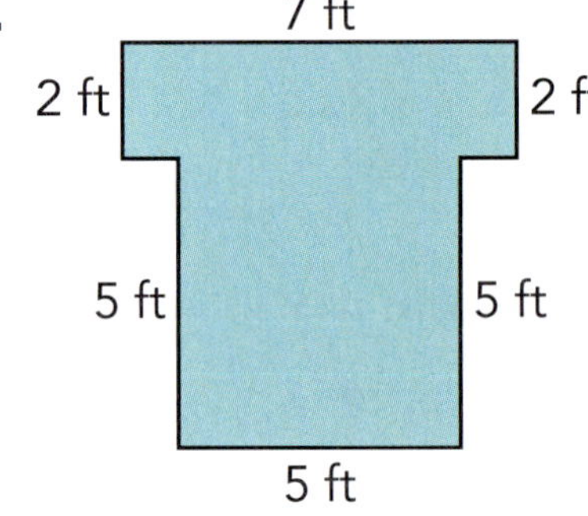

____

Problem Solving

5. A figure has an area of 24 square inches. It can be decomposed into three equal rectangles. What is the area of each rectangle?

____

6. An L-shaped floor has an area of 18 square meters. One part of the L is 6 square meters. What is the area of the other part of the L?

____

Write About It

7. Chris used $6 \times 2 + 6 \times 4$ to find the area of the shape shown. Patrick used $4 \times 3 + 6 \times 3$. Who is correct? Explain.

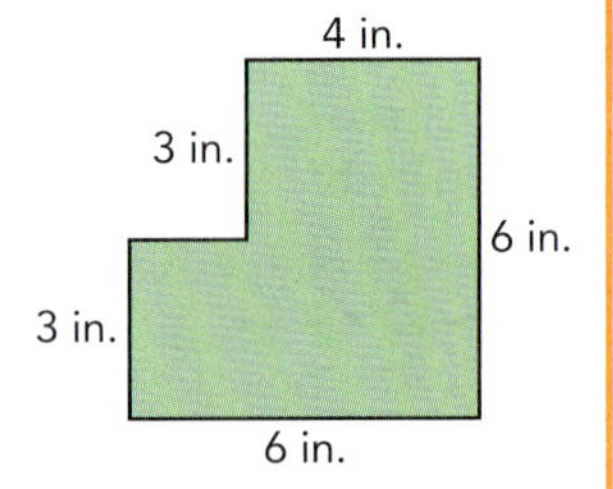

____

____

Name ______________________ Date ______________

LESSON 15-6

Problem Solving
Guess and Test

A photograph's area is 54 square inches. The length and width are whole numbers whose sum is 15 inches. The length is greater than the width. What are the length and width of the photograph?

Guess and test different sums of 15. Once you find the addends, you can multiply to see if the product is 54.

Try 10 and 5.

$10 + 5 = 15$

$10 \times 5 = 50$

The product is too low.

Try 9 and 6.

$9 + 6 = 15$

$9 \times 6 = 54$

That is correct.

The photograph has a length of 9 inches and a width of 6 inches.

Mila wants to design a garden that has an area of 30 square feet. The length and width will be whole numbers of feet. How many different ways can Mila design the garden?

Guess and test by dividing the area by the width to find the length.

- $30 \div 1 = 30$; the garden can be 30 feet by 1 foot.
- $30 \div 2 = 15$; the garden can be 15 feet by 2 feet.
- $30 \div 3 = 10$; the garden can be 10 feet by 3 feet.
- $30 \div 4 = 7$ with 2 left over; this cannot be one of the gardens.
- $30 \div 5 = 6$; the garden can be 6 feet by 5 feet.

Make a table to show the different sizes of the garden.

Area (in square feet)	Length (in feet)	Width (in feet)
30	30	1
30	15	2
30	10	3
30	6	5

There are 4 different gardens that Mila can design.

MORE PRACTICE

The area of a rectangular rug is 16 square feet. Each dimension of the rug is a whole number of feet. Use this information for Exercises 1–2.

1. How many different rugs can be made? ________

2. Write the possible dimensions of the rug.

____

A sticky note is in the shape of a square. The side length is a whole number of centimeters. The area is greater than 60 square centimeters and less than 90 square centimeters. Use this information for Exercises 3–4.

3. How many possible sticky notes can be made? ________

4. What could be the dimensions of the sticky notes?

____

5. Willie counts 8 vehicles in the parking lot. All of the vehicles have either 2 wheels or 4 wheels. Willie counted 26 wheels. How many of each vehicle did Willie count?

____

Write About It

6. In her basketball game, Adina made 9 shots and scored 21 points. All of the shots Adina made were either 2-point shots or 3-point shots. Explain how to find the number of each shot Adina made. Include the number of each shot that she made in your explanation.

____

____

____

____

____

Name ______________________________ Date ______________

HOMEWORK

The area of a rectangular print is 40 square inches. The length and width of the print are whole numbers of inches. Use this information for Exercises 1–2.

1. How many different sizes can the print have? ________

2. Write the possible dimensions of the print.

____

Ron will draw three polygons from the types shown below that have a total of 16 sides. He will choose two of one type of polygon and one of a different polygon. Use this information and the polygons for Exercises 3–4.

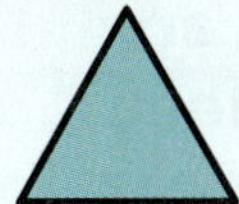   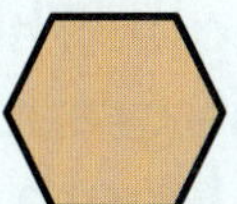 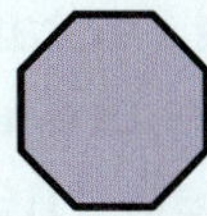

3. In how many ways can Ron draw the three polygons? ________

4. What are the ways that Ron can draw the polygons?

____

____

5. The sum of Jim's age and his grandfather's age is 64 years. Jim's grandfather is 54 years older than Jim. How many years old are each?

____

6. Hideki has 12 coins that are worth 40 cents in all. The coins are either nickels or pennies. Larry said that Hideki has more nickels. Travis said that Hideki has more pennies. Who is correct? Justify your choice.

____

____

____

____

HOMEWORK

The area of a rectangular stamp is 20 square centimeters. The dimensions of the stamp are each a whole number of centimeters. Use this information for Exercises 7–8.

7. How many different sizes can the stamp have? ________

8. Write the possible dimensions of the stamp.

____

9. There are 27 third-grade and fourth-grade boys in the school band. There are 5 more third-grade boys than fourth-grade boys in the school band. How many boys from each grade are in the school band?

____

A table is in the shape of a rectangle. The length and width are whole numbers of feet. The area is greater than 20 square feet and less than 50 square feet. The length of the table is 1 foot greater than its width. Use this information for Exercises 10–11.

10. How many possible tables can be made? ________

11. What could be the dimensions of the table?

____

____

Write About It

12. A game is played using the target shown. Yellow is worth 5 points, red 3 points, blue 2 points, and black 1 point. Each player will get 3 tosses. Derek scored a total of 10 points. If he scored at least 1 point on each toss, what targets did he hit during his 3 tosses? Explain.

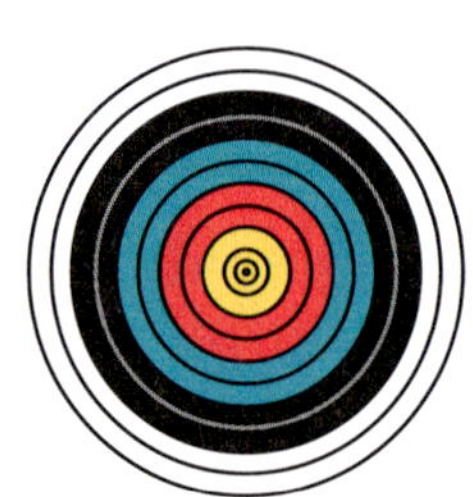

____

____

____

____

Name ______________________ Date ______________

LESSON 16-1

Understand Perimeter

Perimeter is the distance around a shape.
Perimeter is measured in units.

- You can find the perimeter of a shape by adding the lengths of its sides.
  - Find the length of each side.
  - Write an equation. Let P represent the perimeter.

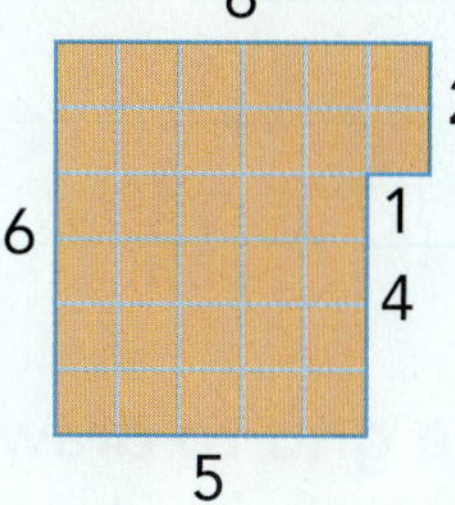

$P = 6 + 2 + 1 + 4 + 5 + 6$

  - Use the Associative Property of Addition to add. Group each pair of addends.

$P = (6 + 2) + (1 + 4) + (5 + 6)$

$P = 8 + 5 + 11$

$P = (8 + 5) + 11$

$P = 13 + 11$

$P = 24$

- You can also find the perimeter by counting along each side. Remember to count both sides of a corner.

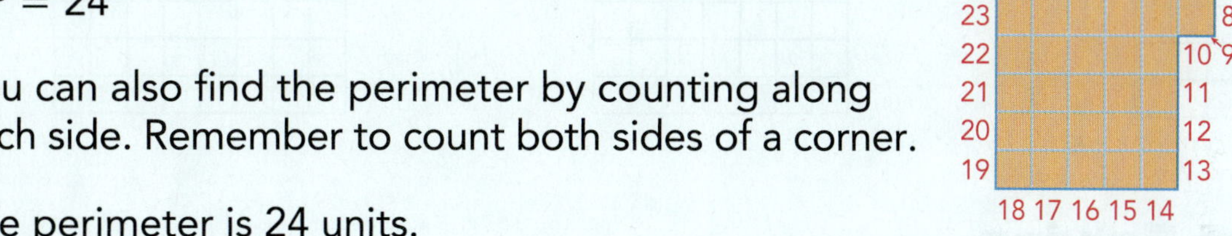

The perimeter is 24 units.

MORE PRACTICE

Find the perimeter of the shaded figure. Show your work.

1.

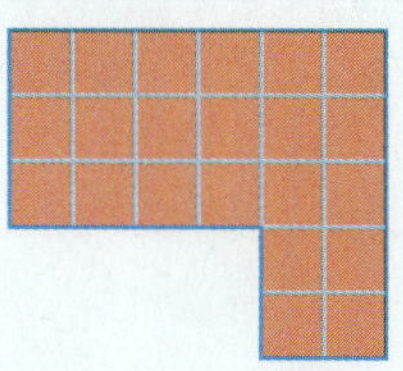

____

____

2.

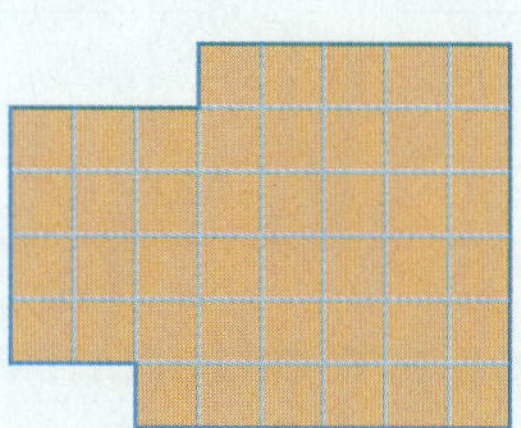

____

____

3.

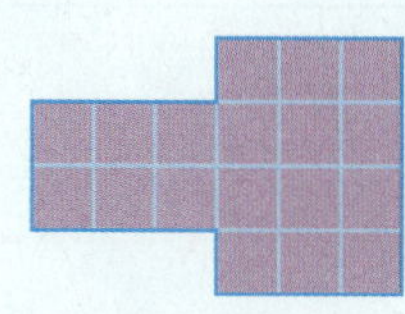

____

____

HOMEWORK

Find the perimeter of the shaded figure. Show your work. Label the side lengths on the figures.

1. 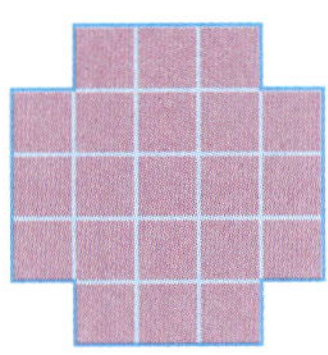

____
____
____

2. 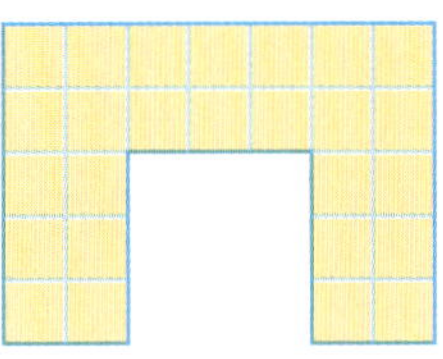

____
____
____

3. 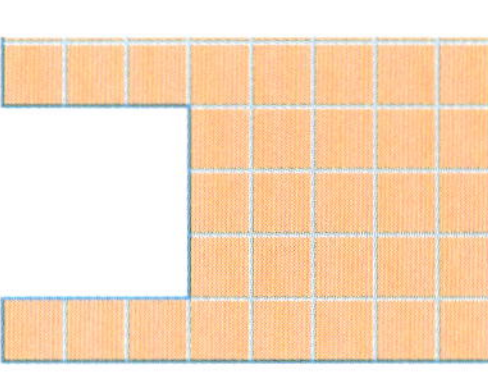

____
____
____

Shade in the grid to draw a shape with at least 6 sides that has the given perimeter.

4. 22 units

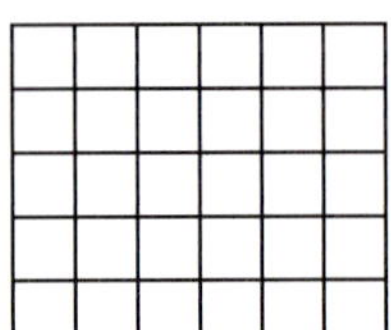

5. 26 units

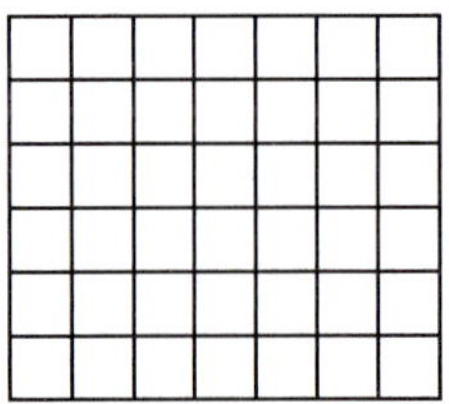

6. 36 units

Problem Solving

7. The sides of a shape are 6 units, 5 units, 3 units, 1 unit, 3 units, and 4 units. What is the perimeter of the shape?

____

8. A shape has 8 sides that are the same length. Each side of the shape is 3 units. What is the perimeter of the shape?

____

Write About It

9. Describe how perimeter and area are different measures.

____
____
____

Name ______________________ Date ______________

LESSON 16-2

Find Perimeter

What is the perimeter of the photograph?

- You can find the sum of the lengths of the four sides.

  4 in. + 3 in. + 4 in. + 3 in. = 14 in.

- There are two ways to use multiplication and addition.

  - Find the sum of the length and width and multiply by 2.

    $P = 2 \times (4 \text{ in.} + 3 \text{ in.})$

    $P = 2 \times 7 \text{ in.}$

    $P = 14 \text{ in.}$

  - Multiply the length by 2 and the width by 2, then add.

    $P = (2 \times 4 \text{ in.}) + (2 \times 3 \text{ in.})$

    $P = 8 \text{ in.} + 6 \text{ in.}$

    $P = 14 \text{ in.}$

The perimeter of the photograph is 14 inches.

A square is a rectangle with 4 equal sides.
You can find the perimeter of a square in two ways.

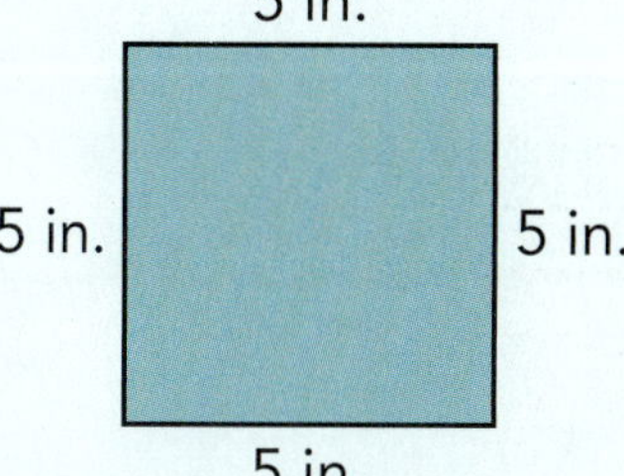

- Find the sum of the 4 side lengths.

  $P = 5 \text{ in.} + 5 \text{ in.} + 5 \text{ in.} + 5 \text{ in.}$

  $P = 20 \text{ in.}$

- Multiply one side by 4.

  $P = 4 \times 5 \text{ in.}$

  $P = 20 \text{ in.}$

The perimeter of the square is 20 inches.

MORE PRACTICE

Find the perimeter of the figure. Show your work.

1.

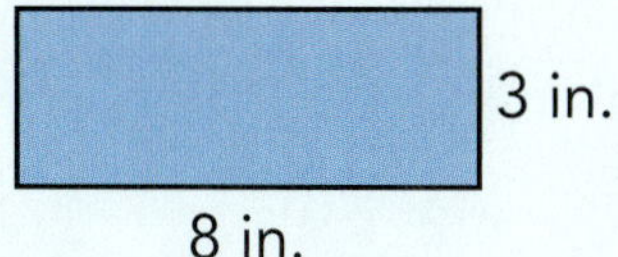

2.

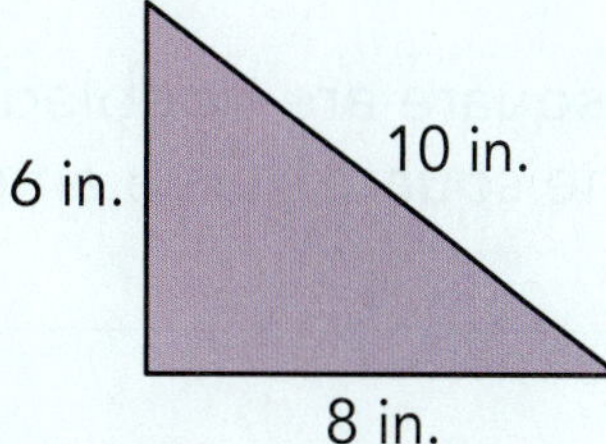

HOMEWORK

Find the perimeter of the polygon. Show your work.

1. 5 in.
4 in.

2. 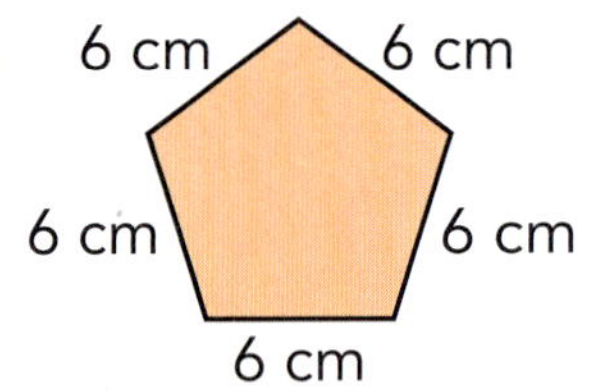

3. 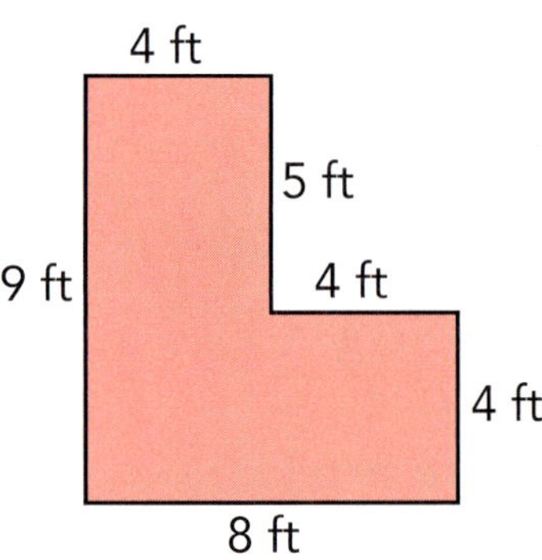

Draw and label a rectangle that has the given perimeter.

4. 20 inches

5. 28 centimeters

6. 32 inches

Problem Solving

7. A rectangular book cover has a length of 11 inches and a width of 9 inches. What is the perimeter of the book cover? ______

8. A square and a triangle each have sides of equal length. The triangle's perimeter is 12 feet. What is the perimeter of the square? ______

Write About It

9. The sides of a square are doubled. What happens to the perimeter of the square? Give an example.

______

______

______

Name ______________________ Date ______________

LESSON 16-3

Find Unknown Side Lengths

What is the length of the unknown side of this trapezoid that has a perimeter of 16 feet?

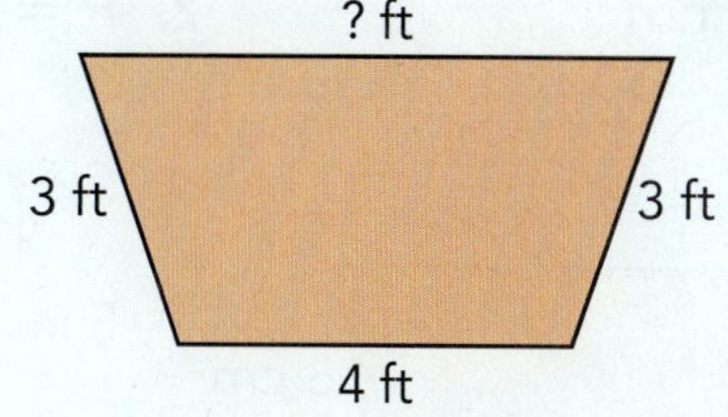

Use the given information to find the length of the unknown side.

- Add the known side lengths:
  3 ft + 4 ft + 3 ft = 10 ft
- Subtract the sum from the perimeter:
  16 ft − 10 ft = 6 ft

The length of the unknown side of the trapezoid is 6 feet.

What is the length of each side of a square that has a perimeter of 20 inches?

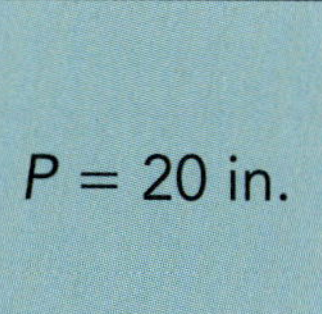

A regular polygon has sides of equal length and angles of equal measure. A square is a regular polygon.

When you know the perimeter of a regular polygon, you can divide the perimeter by the number of sides to find the length of one side: 20 in. ÷ 4 = 5 in.

Each side of the square is 5 inches long.

MORE PRACTICE

Find the length of the unknown side or sides.

1. regular triangle
P = 21 cm

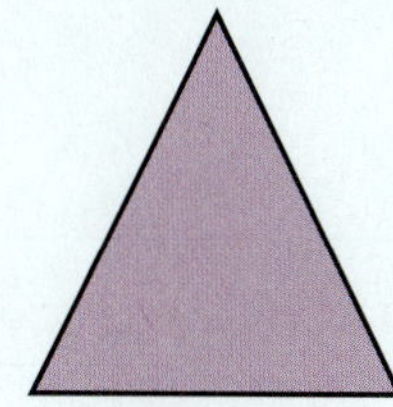

____

2. other sides are equal
P = 29 cm

8 cm
5 cm
8 cm

____

3. rectangle
P = 52 in.

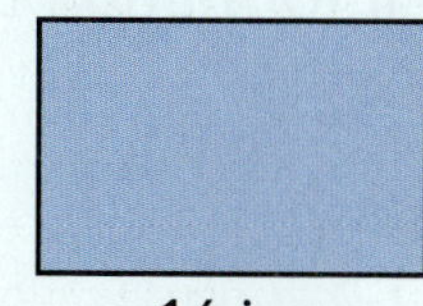

____

HOMEWORK

Find the length of the unknown side or sides.

1. $P = 49$ cm

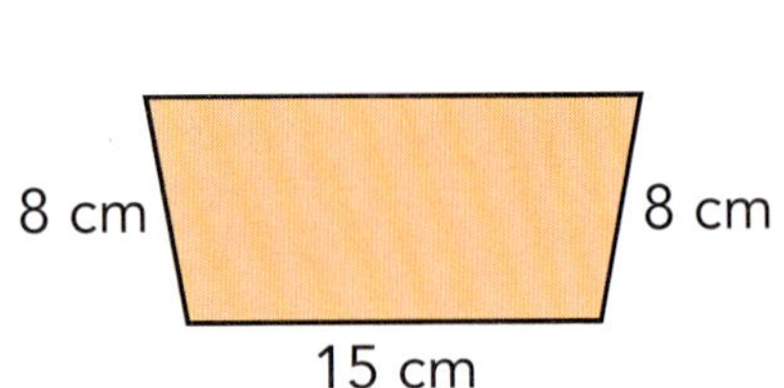

____

2. $P = 26$ in.

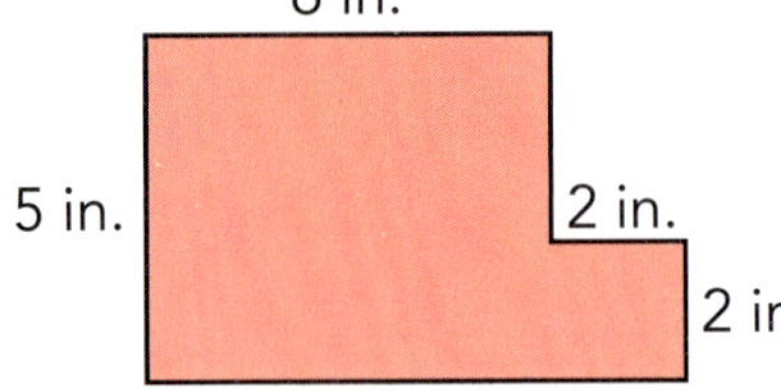

____

3. $P = 32$ cm

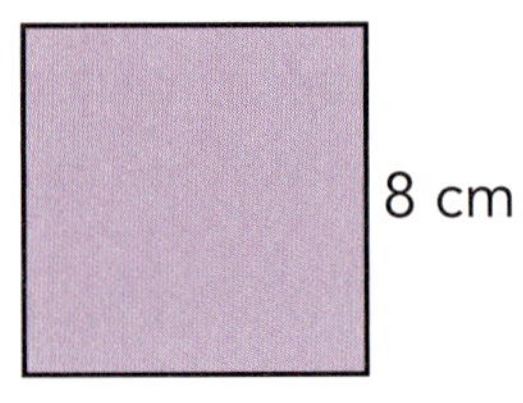

____

Find the lengths of the three unknown sides of the rectangle.

4. $P = 20$ in.

____

5. $P = 42$ cm

____

6. $P = 38$ in.

____

Problem Solving

7. The perimeter of a trapezoid is 24 ft. One side is 8 ft. Another side is 4 ft. The other two sides are equal in length. What is the length of an unknown side?

____

8. A rectangular picture frame has a length of 12 inches. The perimeter of the picture frame is 44 inches. What is the width of the picture frame?

____

Write About It

9. A rhombus has a perimeter of 28 inches. Do you have enough information to find the length of each side? Explain your answer.

____

____

Name ______________________ Date __________

Problem Solving
More Than One Way

Jessica's room is a square with side lengths of 5 yards. Kate and Natalia will use a different strategy to find the perimeter of the room.

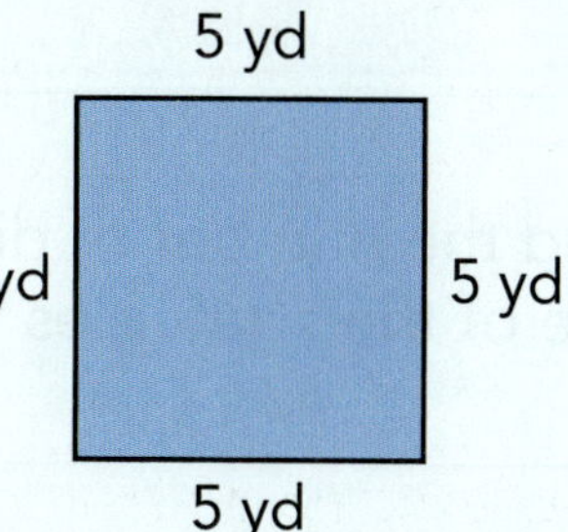

- Kate will draw a picture of a square. She will label each of the four sides.
  - All four sides are 5 yards.
  - Kate can multiply the length of a side by 4.

  4×5 yd $= 20$ yd

  Kate finds that the perimeter of the room is 20 yards.

- Natalia will write and solve an equation.
  - Multiply the length of a side by the number of sides.

  $P = 4 \times 5$ yd $= 20$ yd

  Natalia finds that the perimeter of the room is 20 yards.

The strategies Kate and Natalia use give the same answer. The perimeter of Jessica's room is 20 yards.

MORE PRACTICE

Use the information in the teaching box for Exercises 1–2.

1. Which strategy shown in the box do you think is better to find the perimeter of a square? Explain your answer.

____

____

2. Jessica said she could use the Find a Pattern strategy to find the perimeter of the square. How would she use that strategy?

____

____

MORE PRACTICE

Dean has two coins. Of his coins, none are worth more than a dime. Use this information for Exercises 3–6.

Strategies

- Use Drawings to Solve Problems
- Make a Table
- Find a Pattern
- Work Backward
- Use a Picture
- Use a Model
- Make an Organized List
- Use Logical Reasoning
- Write an Equation
- Act It Out
- Guess and Test

3. Name two strategies from the list that you can use to find how many different money amounts Dean can have.

____

____

4. Find the number of different money amounts using one of the strategies you chose.

____

____

____

____

5. How could you have found the number of different money amounts using the other strategy you chose?

____

____

____

____

6. Which strategy did you prefer? Explain your answer.

____

____

____

7. Which strategy would be best for finding the area of a square or rectangle? Explain your choice.

____

____

____

Name ______________________ Date ____________

Problem Solving
More Than One Way

HOMEWORK

A poster is in the shape of a regular hexagon. Each side of the poster has a length of 30 centimeters. Use this information for Exercises 1–3.

Strategies

- Use Drawings to Solve Problems
- Make a Table
- Find a Pattern
- Work Backward
- Use a Picture
- Use a Model
- Make an Organized List
- Use Logical Reasoning
- Write an Equation
- Act It Out
- Guess and Test

1. Name two strategies from the list that you can use to find the perimeter of the poster.

____

____

2. Find the perimeter using one of the strategies you chose. Show your work.

____

____

____

____

3. How could you have found the perimeter using the other strategy you chose?

____

____

____

____

4. Lee finished watching a 30-minute video at 4:25. He paused the video for 15 minutes and then later for 8 minutes. Find the starting time using the Work Backward strategy. Then explain how to find the starting time using Make a Table strategy.

____

____

____

____

____

HOMEWORK

Marcelo wants to build the frame for a bookcase. He wants the bookcase to be 6 feet long and 4 feet tall. Use this information for Exercises 5–8.

Strategies

- Use Drawings to Solve Problems
- Make a Table
- Find a Pattern
- Work Backward
- Use a Picture
- Use a Model
- Make an Organized List
- Use Logical Reasoning
- Write an Equation
- Act It Out
- Guess and Test

5. Name two strategies from the list that you can use to find the perimeter of the bookcase.

____

____

6. Find the perimeter using one of the strategies you chose. Show your work.

____

____

____

7. How could you find the perimeter using the other strategy that you chose?

____

____

____

8. Explain which strategy was better for finding the perimeter.

____

____

____

Write About It

9. Explain why knowing how to solve a problem in more than one way will be helpful when solving future problems.

____

____

____

Name ______________________ Date ______________

LESSON **16-5**

Same Perimeter, Different Areas

Artie has 20 feet of fencing to enclose a garden. Each piece of fence is 1 foot long. Artie wants to make the garden rectangular. What are the greatest and least areas that Artie can enclose with the fencing?

Rectangles can have the same perimeter and different areas.

- Draw the different rectangles that have a perimeter of 20 feet.

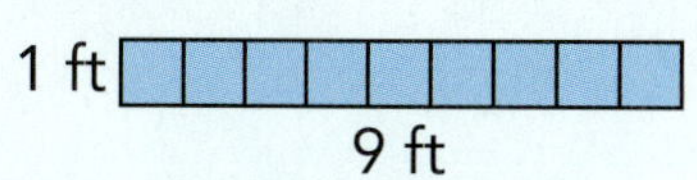

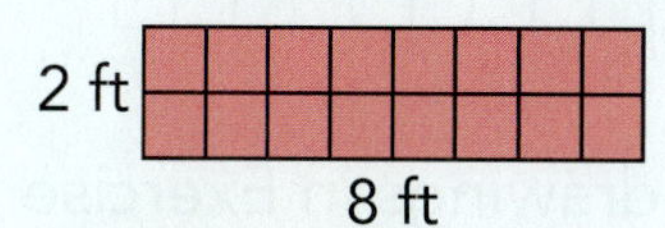

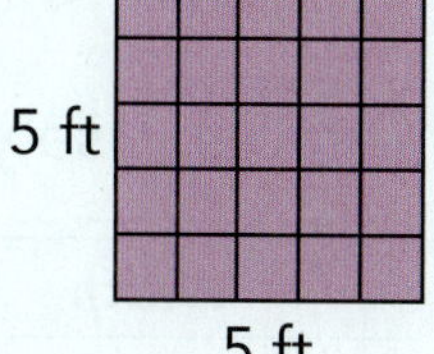

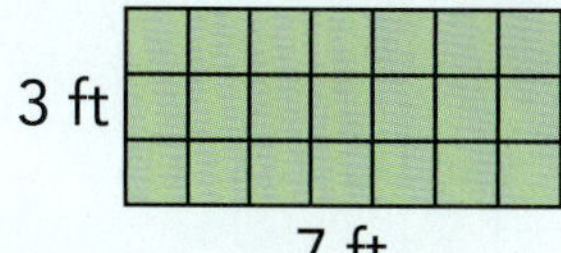

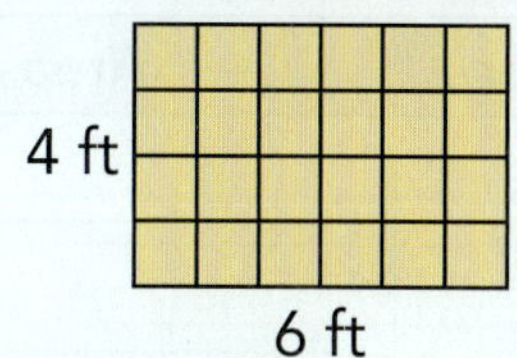

- Find the area of each rectangle.

Length	Width	Perimeter	Area
9 ft	1 ft	20 ft	9 square ft
8 ft	2 ft	20 ft	16 square ft
7 ft	3 ft	20 ft	21 square ft
6 ft	4 ft	20 ft	24 square ft
5 ft	5 ft	20 ft	25 square ft

The greatest area that Artie can enclose is 25 square feet. The least area he can enclose is 9 square feet. The purple square has the greatest area and the blue rectangle has the least area.

MORE PRACTICE

Use these rectangles for Exercises 1–2.

A. 1 ft × 4 ft

B. 2 ft × 2 ft

C. 1 ft × 3 ft

1. Which two rectangles have the same perimeter? ________

2. What is the difference of the areas of the two rectangles that have the same perimeter? ________

HOMEWORK

There are four different rectangles that have a length and width in a whole number of units and a perimeter of 18 units. Use this information for Exercises 1–3.

1. Draw the four rectangles that have a perimeter of 18 units.

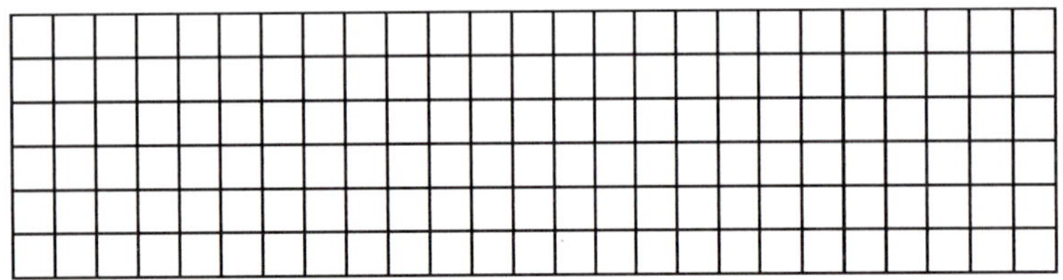

2. Complete the table. Use your drawings in Exercise 1.

Length	Width	Perimeter	Area
______ units	______ unit	18 units	______
______ units	______ units	18 units	______
______ units	______ units	18 units	______
______ units	______ units	18 units	______

3. The difference of the greatest and least areas is

______________________.

Problem Solving

4. A rectangle has a perimeter of 22 inches. Each side is a whole number of inches. What is the greatest and least the area can be?

____

5. A rectangle's perimeter is 32 in. Each side is a whole number of inches. What is the difference between the greatest and least areas possible? ______________

Write About It

6. Is it possible to draw a square with whole number side lengths that has a perimeter of 26 units? Explain.

____

____

Name ______________________ Date ______________

LESSON 16-6

Same Area, Different Perimeters

Cecilia is creating a rectangular flower bed with an area of 12 square feet. The length and width will be whole numbers. What are the greatest and least perimeters that Cecilia can use?

Rectangles can have the same area and different perimeters. Because the area of a rectangle is the product of the length and width, find the factors of 12. Factors are numbers that are multiplied to create a product.

- Draw rectangles to show multiplication facts for 12.

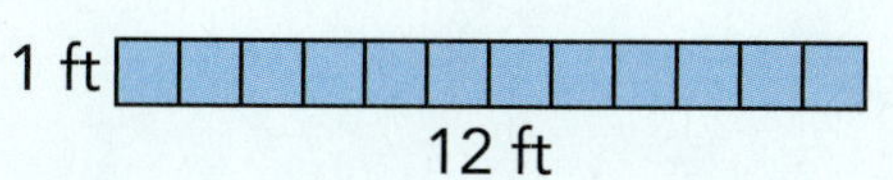

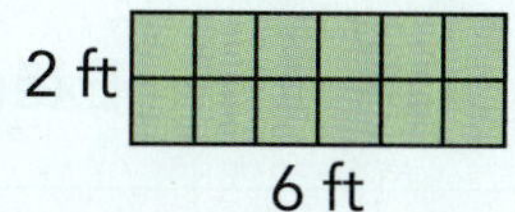

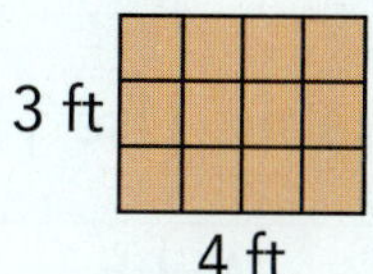

- Find the perimeter of each rectangle.

Length	Width	Area	Perimeter
12 ft	1 ft	12 square ft	26 ft
6 ft	2 ft	12 square ft	16 ft
4 ft	3 ft	12 square ft	14 ft

The greatest perimeter is 26 feet. The least perimeter is 14 feet.

MORE PRACTICE

Use these rectangles for Exercises 1–3.

A. 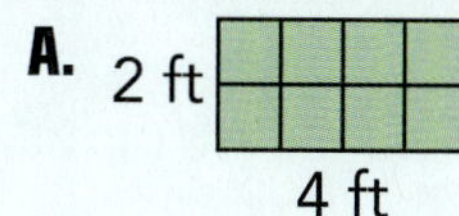

B. 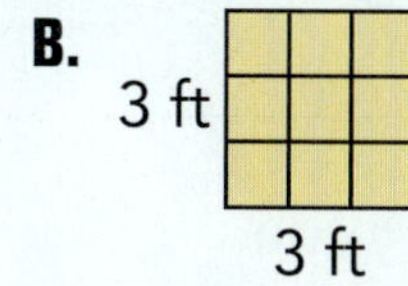

C. 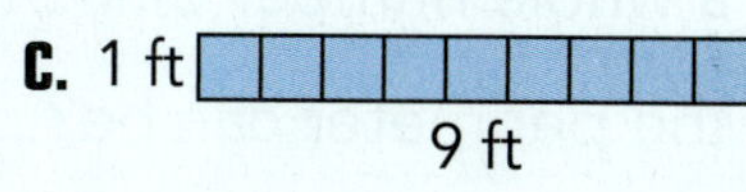

1. Which two rectangles have the same area? __________

2. Which two rectangles have the same perimeter? __________

3. What is the difference of the perimeters of the two rectangles that have the same area? __________

HOMEWORK

There are four different rectangles that have whole numbers for the length and width and an area of 24 square units. Use this information for Exercises 1–3.

1. Draw the four rectangles that have an area of 24 square units.

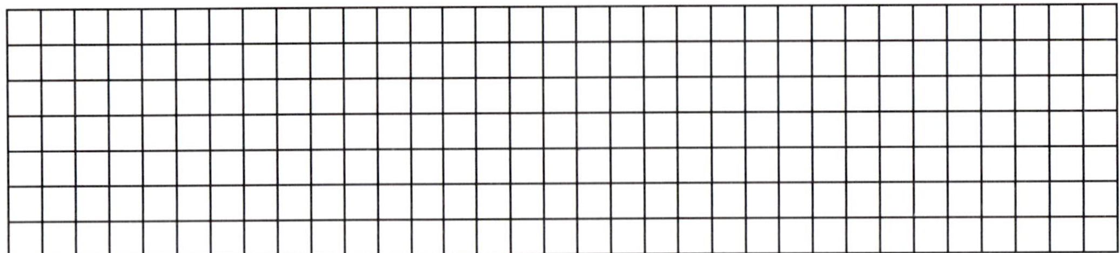

2. Complete the table. Use your drawings in Exercise 1.

Length	Width	Area	Perimeter
______	______	24 square units	______
______	______	24 square units	______
______	______	24 square units	______
______	______	24 square units	______

3. What is the difference between the greatest and least perimeters? ______________

Problem Solving

4. A rectangle has an area of 14 square inches. Each side is a whole number of inches. What is the greatest and least the perimeter can be? ______________

Write About It

5. Is it possible to draw a square with whole number side lengths that has an area of 20 square units? Explain.

____

____

1	2	3	4	5	6	7	8	9	10
11	12	13	14	15	16	17	18	19	20
21	22	23	24	25	26	27	28	29	30
31	32	33	34	35	36	37	38	39	40
41	42	43	44	45	46	47	48	49	50
51	52	53	54	55	56	57	58	59	60
61	62	63	64	65	66	67	68	69	70
71	72	73	74	75	76	77	78	79	80
81	82	83	84	85	86	87	88	89	90
91	92	93	94	95	96	97	98	99	100

tens	ones

tens	ones

tens	ones

tens	ones

tens	ones

tens	ones

tens	ones

tens	ones

tens	ones

tens	ones

tens	ones

tens	ones

tens	ones

tens	ones

tens	ones

dimes	pennies

dimes	pennies

h	t	o

h	t	o

dimes	pennies

dimes	pennies

h	t	o

h	t	o

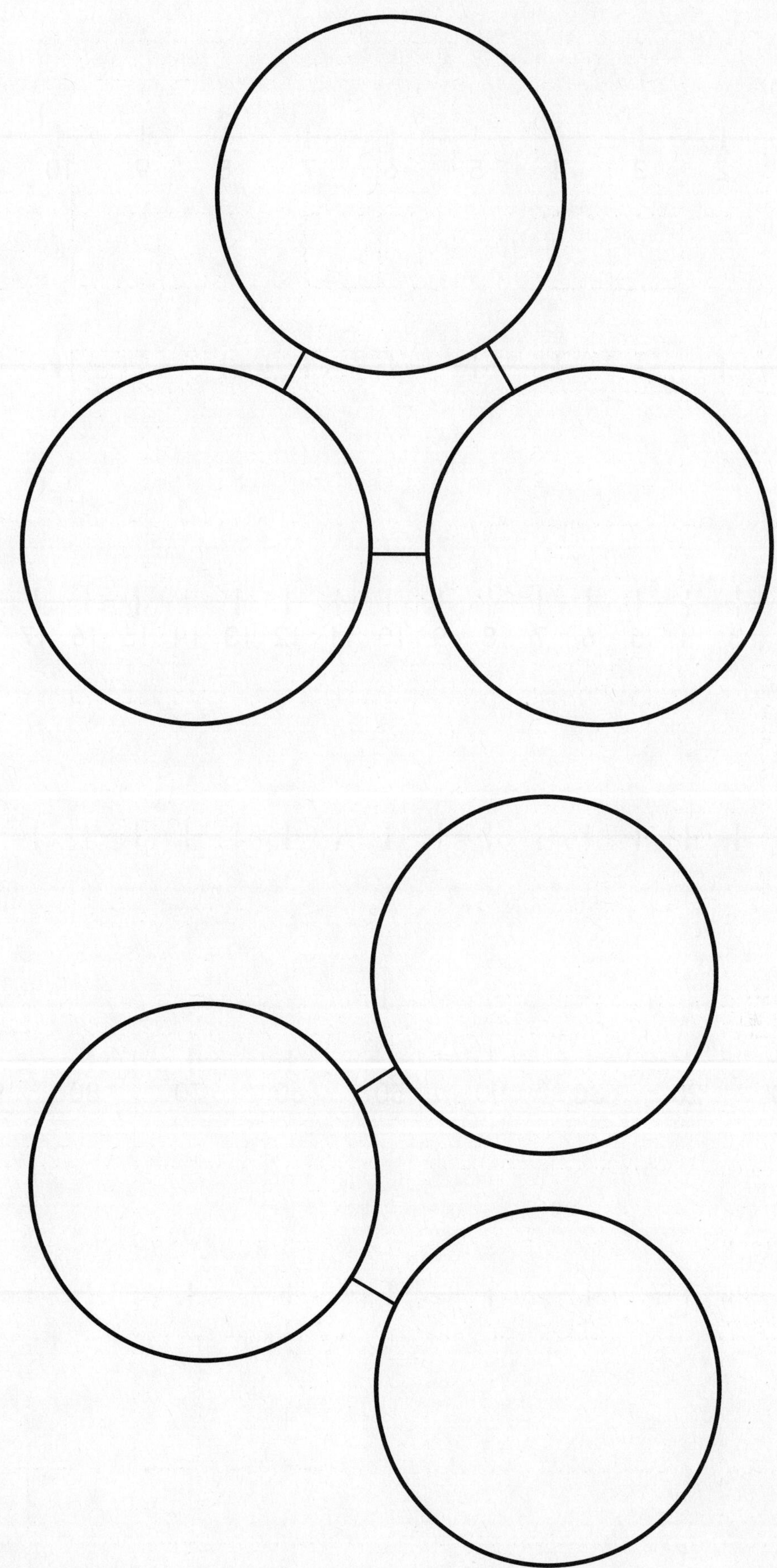

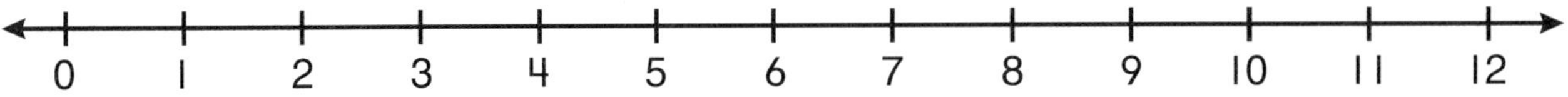

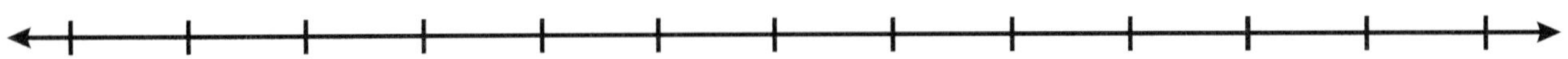

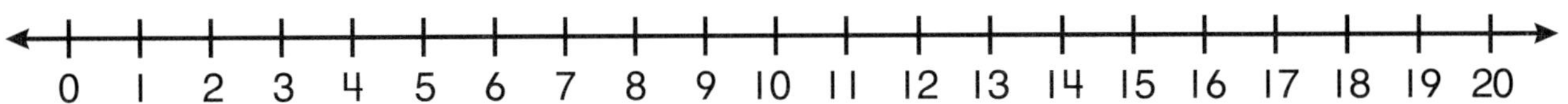

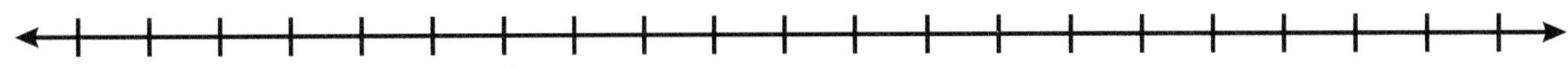

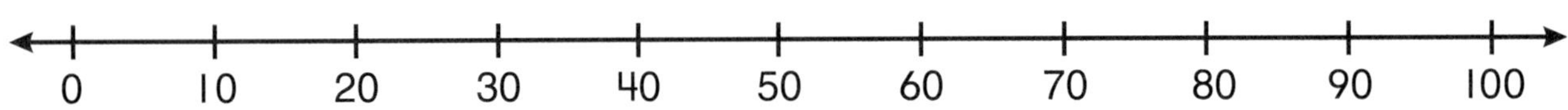

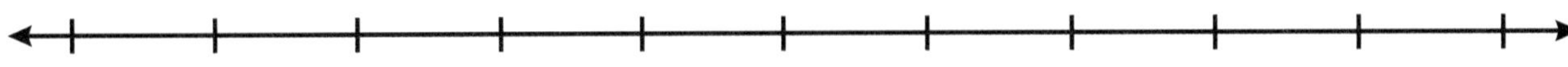

Number Lines

Fraction Circles & Spinners

1											
$\frac{1}{2}$											
$\frac{1}{3}$											
$\frac{1}{4}$											
$\frac{1}{5}$											
$\frac{1}{6}$											
$\frac{1}{7}$											
$\frac{1}{8}$											
$\frac{1}{9}$											
$\frac{1}{10}$											
$\frac{1}{12}$											

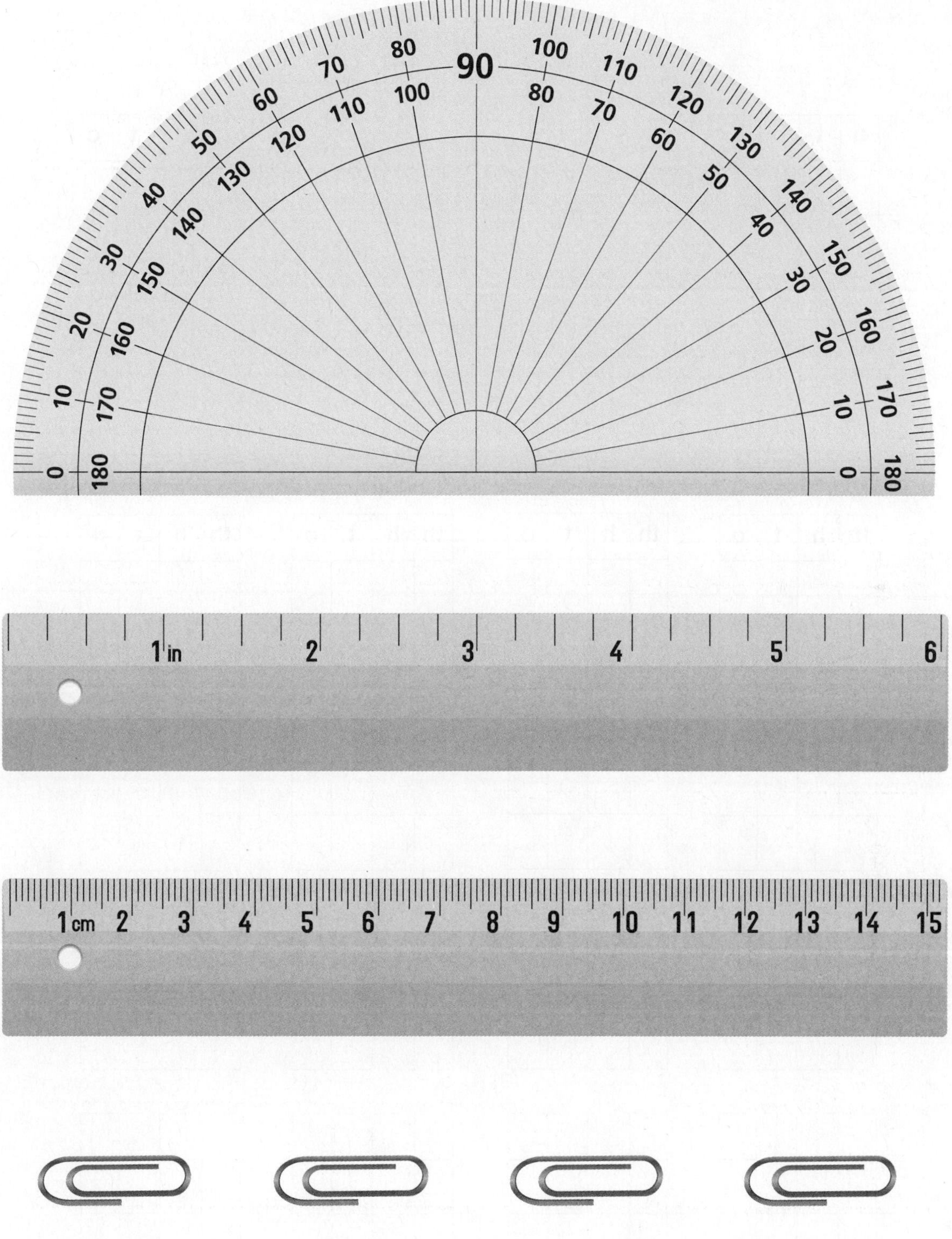

Measurement

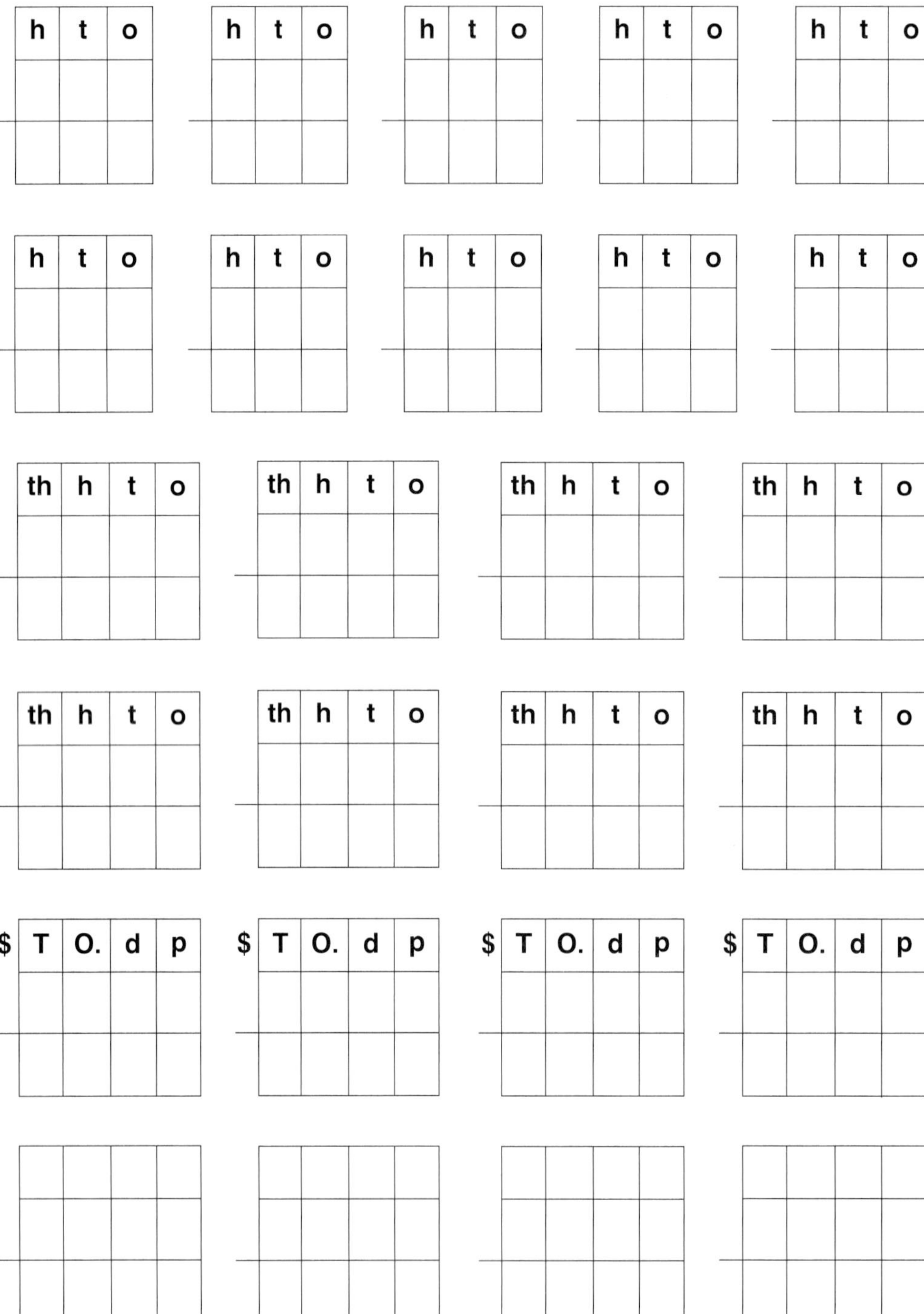

Place-Value Frames (Addition and Subtraction)

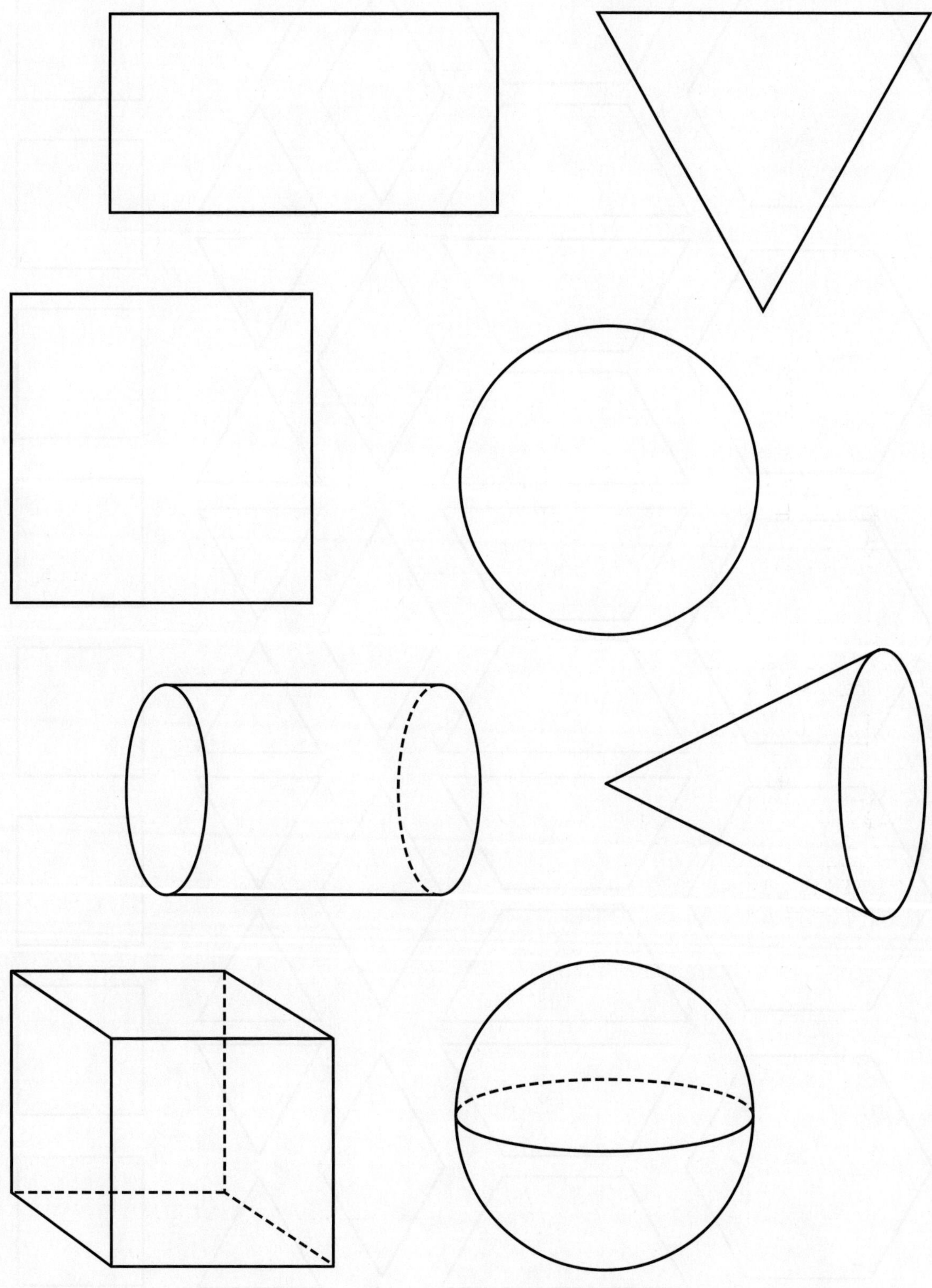

Plane and Solid Figures

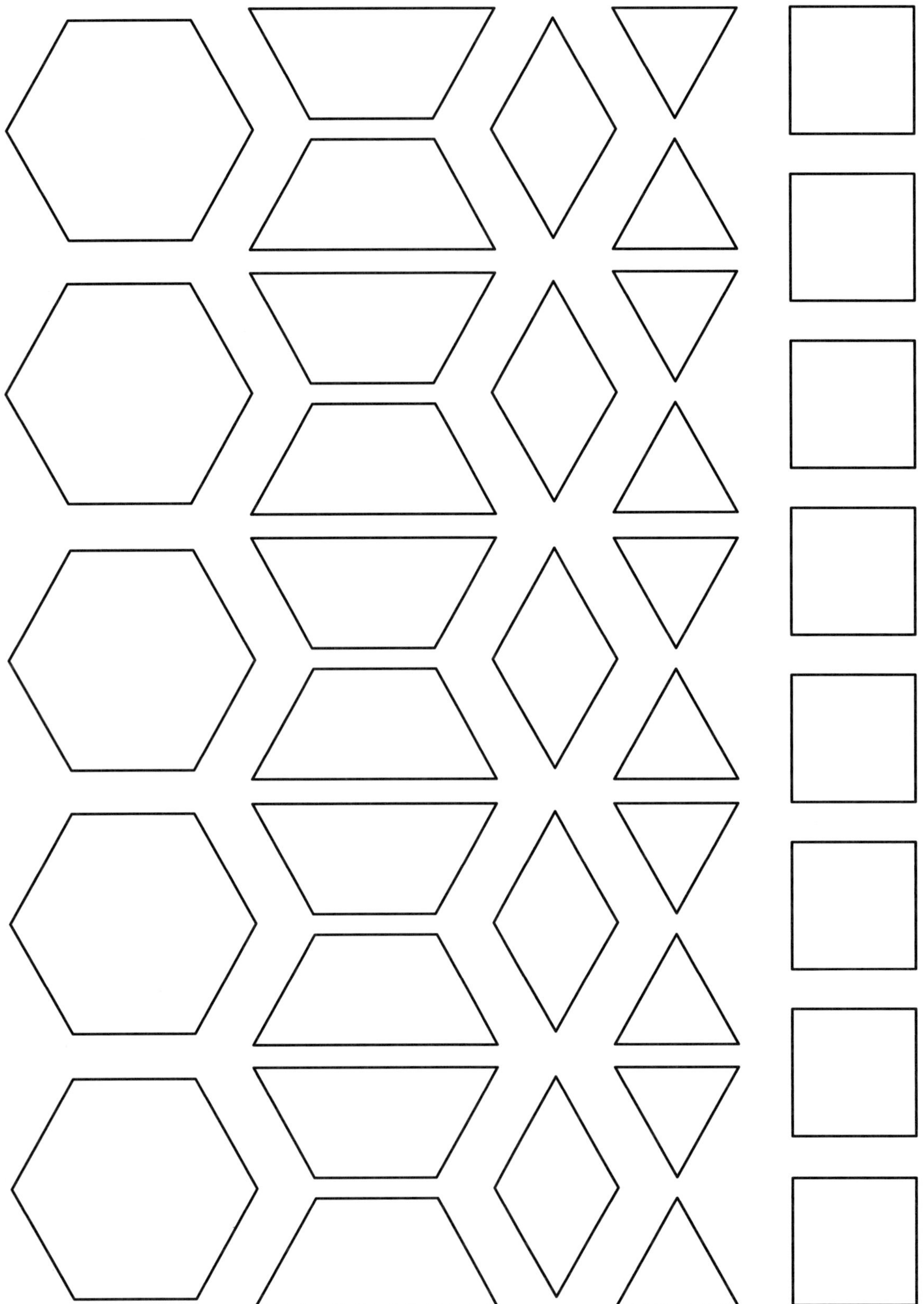

Pattern Blocks

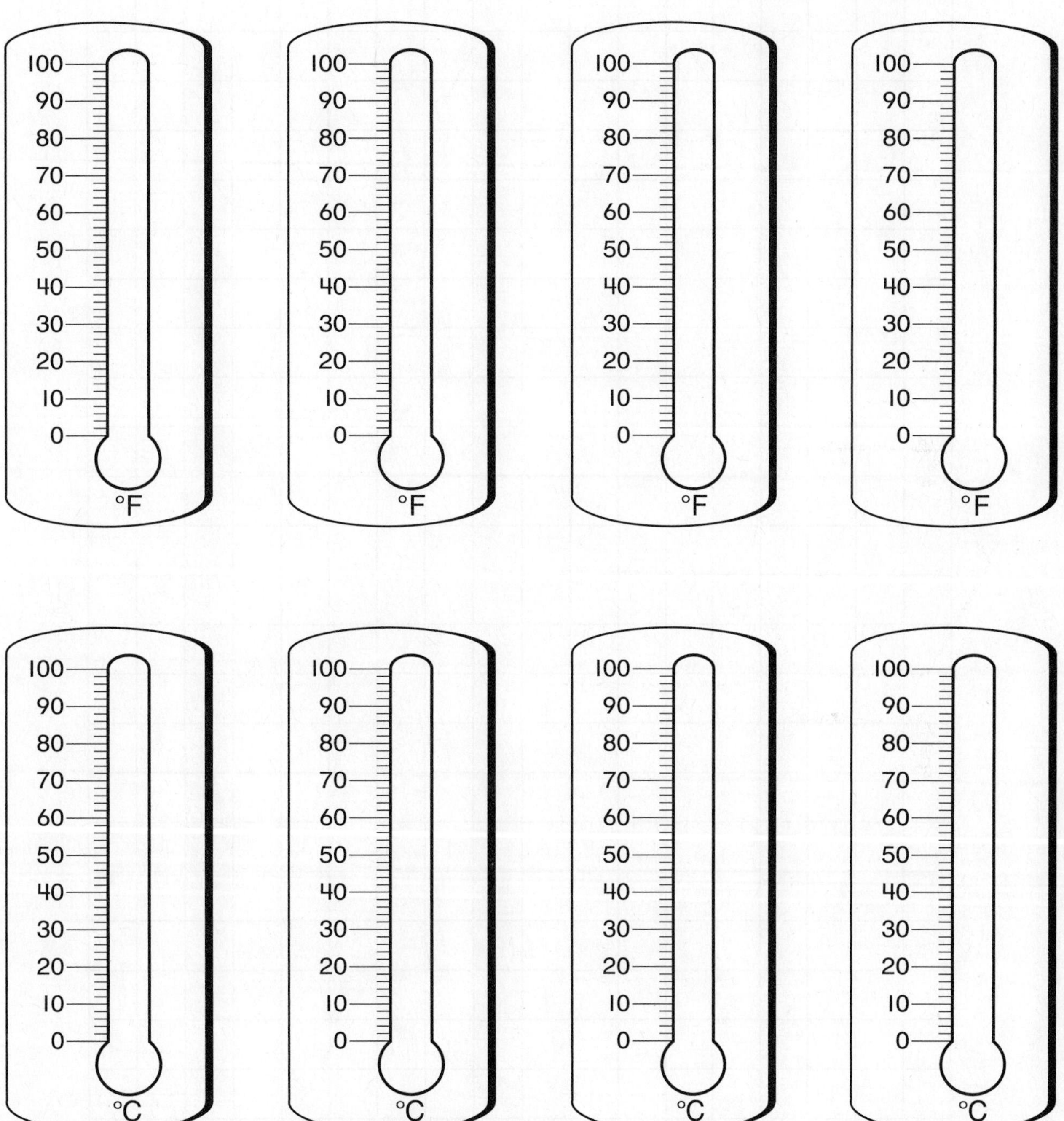

Thermometers

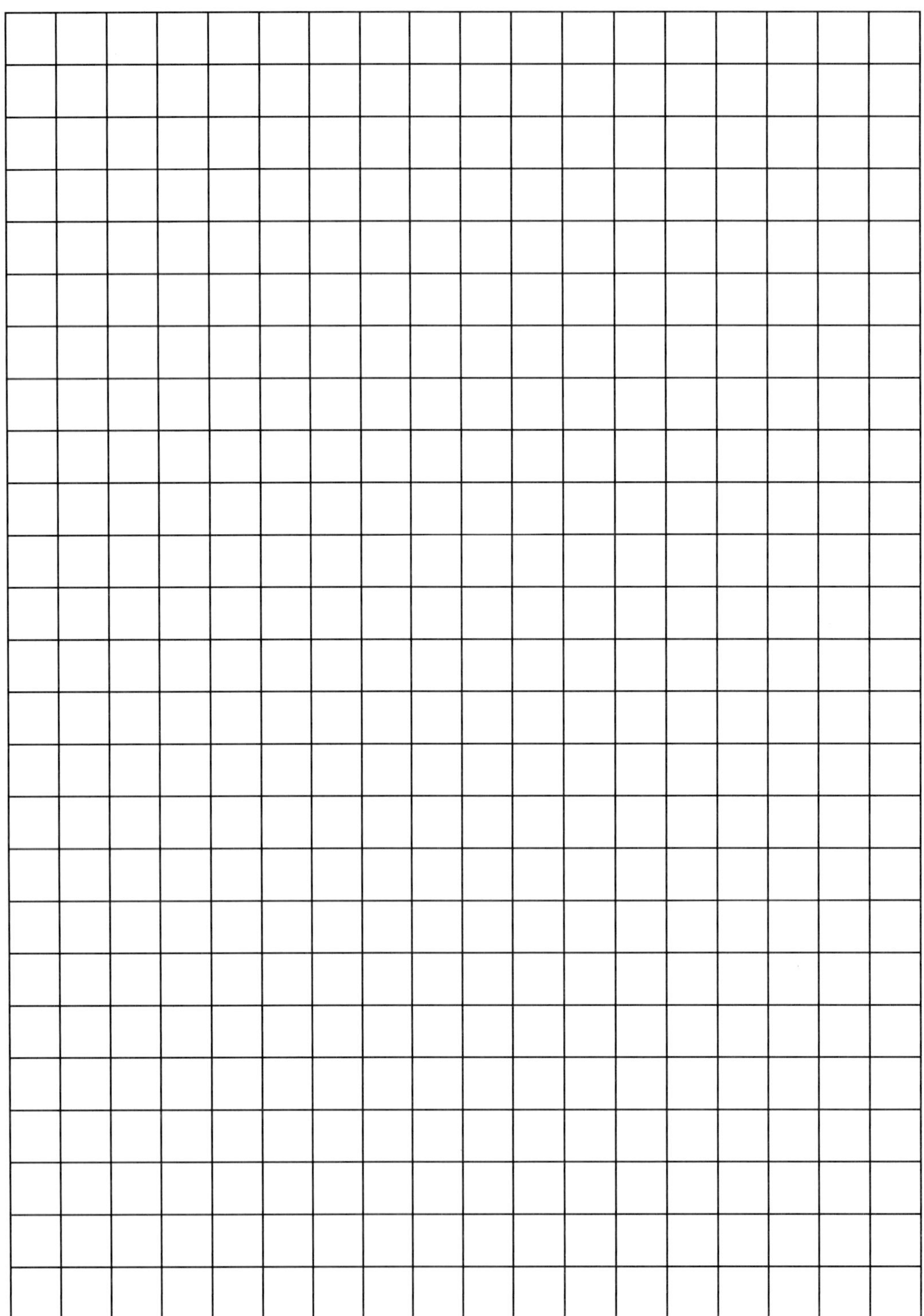

Centimeter Grid Paper

Dot Paper

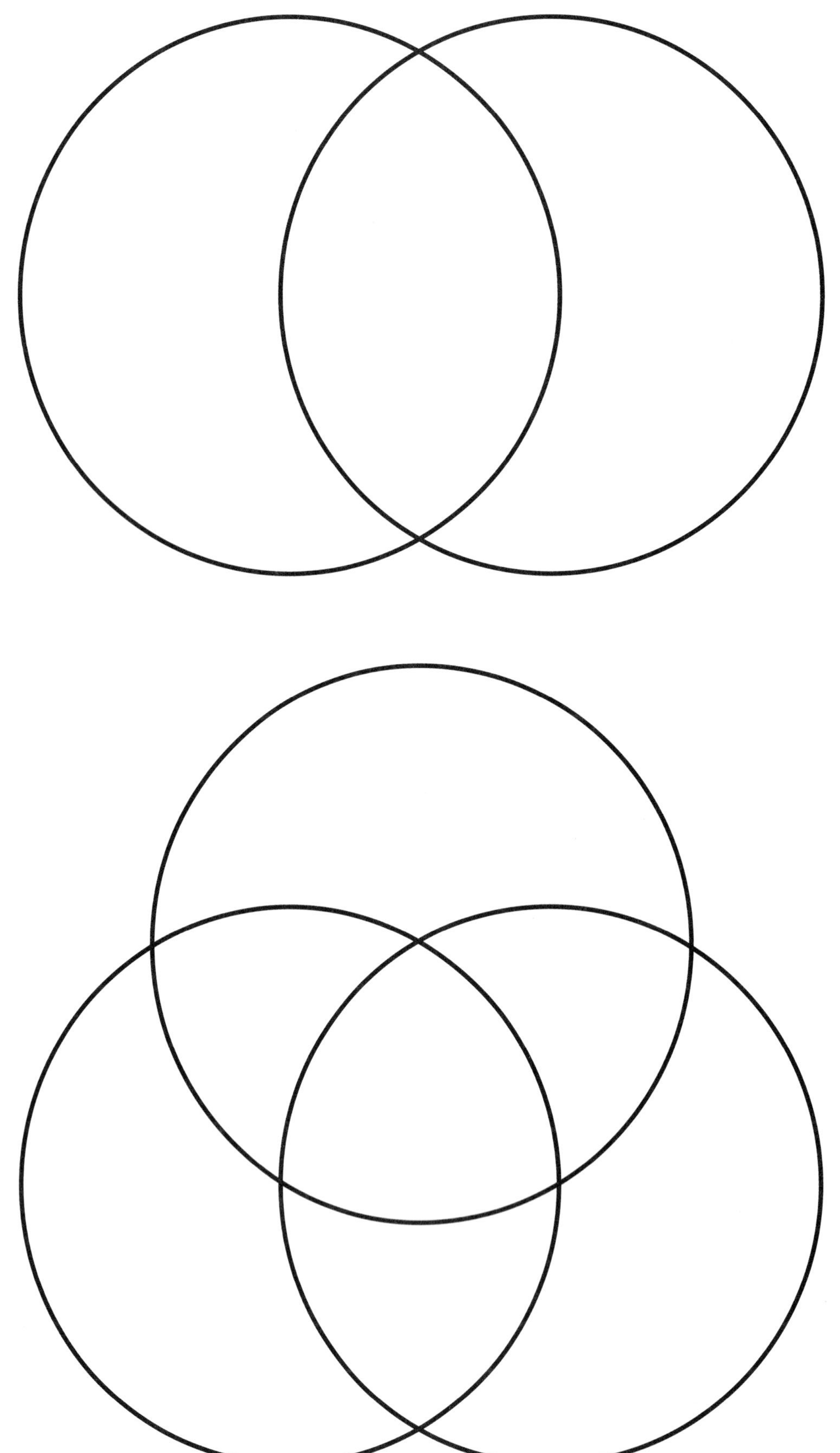

Venn Diagrams